MW00699599

The Other America

New World Studies

A. James Arnold, EDITOR

J. Michael Dash, David T. Haberly, and Roberto Márquez,
ASSOCIATE EDITORS

Antonio Benítez-Rojo, Joan Dayan, Dell H. Hymes,
Vera M. Kutzinski, Candace Slater, and Iris M. Zavala,
ADVISORY EDITORS

The Other America:
Caribbean Literature
in a New World Context

J. Michael Dash

New World Studies

A. James Arnold, editor

University Press of Virginia
Charlottesville and London

The University Press of Virginia
©1998 by the Rector and Visitors
of the University of Virginia
All rights reserved
Printed in the United States of America

First published 1998

∞The paper used in this publication meets the minimum requirements of the American National Standard for Information Sciences—Permanence of Paper for Printed Library Materials, ANSI Z39.48-1984.

Library of Congress Cataloging-in-Publication Data

Dash, J. Michael.
    The other America : Caribbean literature in a New World context /
J. Michael Dash.
        p.   cm. — (New World studies)
    Includes bibliographical references (p.   ) and index.
    ISBN 0-8139-1763-8 (cloth : alk. paper). — ISBN 0-8139-1764-6
(pbk. : alk. paper)
    1. Caribbean literature—History and criticism.   I. Title.
II. Series.
PN849.C3D36   1998
809′.89729—dc21   97-38884
                                                             CIP

For Cheryl, who now has one

Contents

Acknowledgments

I would like to express my gratitude to those who encouraged me in the writing of this study of Caribbean literature. I have a deep debt of gratitude to Edouard Glissant, whom I consider the single-most important theoretician to have emerged so far from the Caribbean and whose ideas are scattered throughout this book. I am equally indebted to Jim Arnold, who from the very beginning urged me to complete this work, which was started in 1990 during my attachment to the Library of Congress while on a Fulbright-Hays Fellowship. I am also grateful for the support of those who helped make my stay in Washington, D.C., a pleasant and fruitful one: Jan Byrd of the Council for the International Exchange of Scholars, Georgette Dorn of the Hispanic Division of the Library of Congress, and my very close friend John Olinger, who listened patiently as I fumbled with the ideas in this book. Equally, I would like to single out Herman Van Asbroeck and Herman McKenzie, who seemed particularly intrigued with what this project was attempting to achieve. I should also acknowledge those colleagues at the University of the West Indies (UWI), particularly G. R. Coulthard, Rex Nettleford, and David Nicholls, who encouraged me to see the anglophone Caribbean in terms of the history and culture of its French- and Spanish-speaking neighbors. I also wish to thank Cynthia Nangle for typing the first version and Julie Earle, who produced the final version of the manuscript. I am grateful to Dennis Marshall for his meticulous copyediting and to Cynthia Filer, at the University of Virginia, for bibliographic research.

The Other America marks a change from other books that I have written on Caribbean literature. My earlier books have been more conventionally centered on a single country, for example, Haiti, a single ideology, for example, nationalism, or on a single writer, for example, Edouard Glissant. However, the present work, while retaining my traditional interest in the literary imagination, attempts to deal with the region from a Pan-Caribbean perspective. This is as much in response to the changing nature of the Caribbean, marked today more by the consequences of massive, persistent migration and cultural globalization than in the past, as it is a reaction to the troubling contemporary critical tendency to view Caribbean literature in terms of a larger theoretical discourse, whether postcolonial, postmodernist, or primitivist, which is part of the current intellectual zeitgeist of the romance of otherness. My own feeling is that the more generalized, all-encompassing theories of Third World culture, which invariably turn on a fetishistic ideal of difference, tend to invest enormously in the unreadability of other cultures, as well as undervalue what is concrete and specific in Caribbean writing, and in so doing blur the particular ideological and historical circumstances that give rise to ideas, movements, and ideologies. *The Other America* tends, therefore, to leave out of account some of the more sweeping theories of postcolonial writing and concentrates on the work of regional intellectuals, for example, Martí, James, Fanon, and Glissant, who have compellingly extolled a Pan-Caribbean ethos and aesthetic.

No one at this time doubts the need for an encyclopedic, synthesizing account of Caribbean literature. The need to realize such a complex objective is made even more urgent by the generalized feeling that the Americas as a whole are being radically redefined in terms of race, culture, economy, and politics. Consequently, since *The Other America* argues that a hemispheric identity is an essential mediating context for understanding the Caribbean as a whole, its timeliness is not in question. In this regard, I am particularly indebted to Glissant for his emphasis on the importance of the concept of the region as a third possibility in the normally opposed categories of national and universal. In opposing the open frontier of the archipelago to the closed boundaries of the nation, Glissant proposes for the Caribbean a regional identity that assumes greater importance than that of any single territory within the archipelago. To a great extent, the present work is about the temptation to national self-invention and the impossibility of grounding Caribbean territories in terms of a single national entity.

I am very mindful of the fact that though the term *the other America* is drawn from Glissant's writings, the title of this book does stand in the shadow of Michael Harrington's 1962 study of urban poverty in the United States. However, Glissant's use of the term can be seen as part of the attempt to apply the word *America* to not just the United States but to the entire hemisphere. Also, his conception of otherness is not the dehumanizing process that Harrington analyzed in the economic underworld of U.S. cities but a process of self-definition that has been one of the more powerful catalysts in the Caribbean imagination.

What may be contested is whether this book does fill the need for an all-encompassing treatment of Caribbean literature. Scholars in this field of comparative Caribbean literature all suffer from the same handicap as that of the blind men in the joke trying to feel their way toward an understanding of an elephant. Like those blind men, we all know a little about certain parts of the animal called Caribbean literature and use this limited knowledge to guess at what the whole might look like. I would be the first to admit that my blindness to certain areas of the region's thought and writing distorts my vision of the whole. I also realize that there are gaps in this study. In this regard, I am particularly sensitive to the omission of the Dutch-speaking Caribbean, about which so little is yet known. My consolation lies in the fact that so far no one has attempted to write an all-inclusive, comparative literary study of the Caribbean. But it is merely a matter of time before such a work emerges. Already, Antonio Benítez Rojo's *Repeating Island* and Edouard Glissant's *Caribbean Discourse* point the way insightfully toward a conceptualization of the region as a whole.

Perhaps, if it accomplishes nothing else, this book will permit the eventual emergence of the ideal, comprehensive critical text on comparative Caribbean literature. The need for such a critical perspective goes back to early, transnational evocations of a Caribbean people that have been proposed by such diverse Caribbean thinkers as Antenor Firmin, Jose Martí, and C. L. R. James. A Pan-Caribbean critical approach is, arguably, becoming increasingly necessary, as Caribbean writers and artists are more aware than ever before of the shared heritage, parallel sensibilities, and commonality of interests that link them across the region, beyond nation, race, and language. It remains, however, distressingly easy to demonstrate that Caribbean regionalism does not exist in reality and to point to the various symptoms of divisiveness in the region. Derek Walcott's "abrupt fishermen cursing over canoes" are as likely as anything else to be swearing at their Martiniquan brothers for enchroaching on their St. Lucia fishing grounds. Nevertheless, it would be folly to deny the extent to which even the most isolated Caribbean community is marked by hemispheric and global changes. One of the region's major thinkers, Jacques Roumain, was deeply sensitive to this issue in the 1940s when he evoked in the totally closed world of the Haitian village of Fonds Rouge, a community that was mobilized to collective local action in order to achieve a regional and global consciousness.

The richly creative debate between national, regional, and global identities in the redefinition of Caribbean space is acutely apparent in the creative imagination of the region's writers and thinkers. Literary movements in the Caribbean, even when singlemindedly nationalistic or ethnocentric, have been invariably sensitive to the issue of multiple identities and a regional ethos. What is often not lived can be powerfully imagined. *The Other America* tries to feel its way around this elephantine subject and proposes a reading of Caribbean literature in terms of some defining moments in the region's literary experience. From the rise of the first nation-state in the Caribbean with Haitian independence to the present surge of interest in regionalism in the Caribbean's most dependent community, the French Department of Martinique, this book tries to encompass the dynamic relation between individual imagination, national communities, regional destiny, and global history through which new identities are envisioned in an archipelago itself so subject to mythification from the outside.

The Other America

Introduction

> The archipelago arched like the anxious desire to deny itself, as
> if it were a maternal anxiety to protect the delicate tenuity that
> separates one from the other America.
>
> —Aimé Césaire, *Notebook of a Return to the Native Land*

A Delicate Tenuity

One of the most urgent and complex issues left in the
wake of the quincentenary celebrations of Columbus's voyage to the New World—or the encounter between two
worlds, as it has been evasively called—is the definition of a new field
of research and scholarship termed *New World studies*. The very formulation of the term suggests some of the complexities and ambiguities inherent in mapping this new area of literary and cultural investigation. *New World,* because of its Eurocentric frame of reference, not
only retains the old polarization of inside versus outside, us versus
them, but the less-than-useful distinction of New World versus Old
World. By now the point has been made persuasively, and maybe exhaustingly, that to call this hemisphere *new* is to ignore centuries of
Amerindian civilization in the Americas. However, the use of the term
New World, as in New World Studies, has become an unavoidable
compromise. The only reasonable alternatives, American studies or
American literature, would not normally include South American or
Caribbean writing, or African-American for that matter. Conse-
quently, *New World* must now be understood as Pan-American in

scope, despite its inauspicious beginnings. Perhaps, this very study can help wrest the term free from its original connotations and allow for a new perspective on the Americas as a whole and the Caribbean in particular.

No discussion of the precarious nature of the term *New World* can leave out of account the increasing tendency to use the term *world literature* to denote a global, totalizing system of literary creation and influence. Naturally, literary traditions have never been self-contained. Whether bound by nation, region, class, or race, literary phenomena always involve complex relations with international ideologies or literary styles. This capacity of literary movements, even the most parochial or defensively inward-looking, to create new configurations out of a process of adapting, incorporating, and ultimately modifying other literary phenomena is particularly strong today. World literature derives its validity from its recognition of the fact that writing transcends boundaries, making new and surprising links between writers as diverse as Martinique's Patrick Chamoiseau and the Czech novelist Milan Kundera, between Dany Laferrière of Haiti and Henry Miller of the United States. The point is not a new one: George Steiner argued, in his book of essays *Extraterritorial*, that the modern age had created a "multilingual matrix" for the writer, who was now fated to be culturally unhoused and to become a wanderer across cultures.[1] Salman Rushdie, no stranger to exile and wandering, has argued strongly against the use of outmoded terms like *Commonwealth literature*, which he sees as a "phantom" category, largely encouraged by university teachers, that distracts us from the new, global interrelationships that exist in literature. He uses the example of the influence of South American magical realism on Indian-language writers in India to make a case for a concept of a global notion of imaginative affinities between writers that transcend linguistic, cultural, and political frontiers.[2]

Yet the question remains: Where would such an idea leave the hypothesis of a regional category for literature. Despite the obvious validity of Rushdie's claim, could there not be, as least as a tactical measure, a notion of a New World aesthetic particularly relevant to the exploration of those literatures like Caribbean literature that have been marginalized in the past and now risk being swamped in a postmodern flood of metanarratives that sweep away all boundaries? Using Octavio Paz's *The Labyrinth of Solitude*, George Lang has proposed a solution to this methodological problem. Paz proposes a dialectical relationship between self and the world, solitude and solidarity, diversity and sameness.[3] Lang concludes that "each point of cultural creativity constructs its own centre and projects its own truths. Since there is no single centre, we are all marginal."[4] This work proposes the idea of the New World as just such a provisional center and as a necessary context for grasping and exploring the idea of a regional imagination in the Caribbean. A New World perspective is not the product of a polarizing, exclusivist politics or an attempt to create a new cultural enclave, but rather concerns itself with establishing new connections, not only among the islands of the archipelago but also exploring the region in terms of the Césairean image of that frail, delicate umbilical cord that holds the Americas together.

A New World approach is also being proposed against the background of a still prevalent tendency to fragment the Caribbean into zones of linguistic influence or ideologically determined categories. For example, the literature of Cuba and sometimes Haiti is grouped with that of Latin America, and anglophone West Indian writers are grouped with their counterparts from other countries in the British Commonwealth. Aimé Césaire's importance to the negritude movement has caused many Guadeloupean and Martiniquan writers to be categorized as neo-African. Fragmentation is also evident on the inside, because histories of national literature in the larger Caribbean countries do exist; for instance, in Haiti. Given the wealth and abundance of literary activity in Haiti for almost two centuries, it has been inevitable that many national literary histories would be written. Also, it must be remembered that Haitian independence ushered in the first experiment in creating a nation-state in the region. However, national literatures, despite the temptations of insularity, have been harder to establish for other Caribbean territories. As Bruce King argues in *The New Literatures in English: Cultural Nationalism in a Changing World*, despite identifiable national features in West Indian writing, "unfortunately, no one country has yet produced a sufficient number of major writers to speak of its own literature."[5] To force a national model onto a literature that often identifies itself with larger regional and ideological entities would be a misleading simplification. Indeed, as Anne Walmsley points out in her richly documented study *The Caribbean Artists Movement,* the emergence of West Indian literature should not so much be tied to national contexts but rather be seen in a sequence of literary movements since World War I, from the New Negro Movement in Harlem in the 1920s through Afro-Cubanism, Haitian indigenism, and negritude in Paris. "CAM [the Caribbean Artists Movement] was in the mainstream tradition of such movements and shared many of their characteristics . . . it was also the first genuinely Caribbean-wide cultural movement: with its emphasis on the recognition and rehabilitation of Amerindian as well as African ancestry; its composition and its concept, in membership and activities, of the Caribbean as a region, one people among the continuing barriers of language."[6]

What the collaborators of the CAM movement sensed, as did many other of the majors writers in the region, was the tug of a loyalty greater than that of nation or territory. Perhaps this is due to what Edouard Glissant saw as the profoundly centrifugal impulse of creolization provoked by the determining presence of the Caribbean Sea, which is not reductive and monologic in character but is forever exploding outward. I shall elaborate on this idea later, but here we should note the centrality of the Caribbean to the experience of the New World. No one has put the case more clearly than Roberto González Echevarría. He has argued that it was in the Caribbean that the problematic of New World culture and history first manifested itself. It was also in the Caribbean that the most extreme features of the European imperial enterprise were witnessed. As he very persuasively concludes, "it was therefore in the Caribbean that Latin American literature 'began,' for it is in Columbus's diary that we first encounter what will become the most persistent theme of Latin American literature: how to write in a European language about realities never seen in Europe before."[7]

However, despite this growing sense of the need to establish a New World context for Caribbean writing, almost none of the critical and theoretical material produced recently to mark the quincentenary of Columbus's arrival in the New World makes any reference to the Caribbean. For instance, Earl Fitz's 1991 survey of writing in the Americas, *Rediscovering the New World: Inter-American Literature in a Comparative Context,* not only makes no mention of a single writer from the Caribbean but seems to have as its main purpose promoting the worthiness of writing from the Americas according to some vague ideal called world literature. In spite of his laudable efforts to make *American* apply to more than the United States and his informed treatment of the pre-Columbian era, Fitz conveys no impression of the complexities of the literature he is surveying. Indeed, he safely restricts himself to the well-known major authors from the United States, South America, and Canada and is apparently unwilling to take either theoretical or critical risks in his attempt at rediscovery. To a lesser extent, the Caribbean as a whole is also surprisingly absent from two very sophisticated and related treatments of writing in the hemisphere—*Do the Americas have a Common Literature?* (1990), edited by Gustave Pérez Firmat, and José Saldívar's *The Dialectics of Our America* (1991). Both works have much to recommend them from the methodological point of view, but both equally suffer from a reduction of the Caribbean to a few Cuban writers. The Pérez Firmat volume is particularly good at presenting the New World as a cultural crossroads, but one suspects that this idea is driven by a kind of nationalism that promotes Cuba as the quintessential American crossroads—the ultimate New World paradigm.[8]

Despite his predilection for things Cuban, Pérez Firmat is onto an important point; namely, the conception of the New World in terms of multiple identities and cultural indeterminacy, and, perhaps more importantly, the importance of the Caribbean to understanding this process. Including the Caribbean in any survey means ultimately more than than simply expanding the literary canon to include new minorities or the heretofore marginalized. It means dismantling those notions of nation, ground, authenticity, and history on which more conventional surveys have been based and exploring concepts of cultural diversity, syncretism, and instability that characterize the island cultures of the Caribbean. Indeed, because they are marked by an extermination of the original population, were subjected to repopulation, and became totally dependent on the metropole because of their plantation economies, the Caribbean archipelago witnessed the extremes of the New World experience, producing Pérez Firmat's cultural crossroads in a more intense way than is possible in a larger landmass or where the indigenous population manages to survive.

Because of the current interest in the issue of cultural diversity, there is increasing evidence of general recognition of the specific nature of the Caribbean in cultures within the Americas. For instance, in the relatively new field of postcolonial theory, the special contribution of Caribbean thought to the questions of cultural difference and hybridity is very highly regarded. Ashcroft, Griffiths, and Tiffin in their theoretical work *The Empire Writes Back* state clearly that the Caribbean has been "the most extensive and challenging" area for postcolonial literary theory.[9] Their interest stems from a growing acknowledgment of plurality and creolization as a global phenomenon. Even though their survey of a cross-cultural aesthetic in the Caribbean is restricted to the anglophone territories, with the one exception of the Haitian novelist Jacques Stephen Alexis's theory of "marvelous realism," they argue for the Caribbean as the vanguard in the process of cross-culturality that emerges as "the potential termination point of an apparently endless human history of conquest and annihilation, justified by the myth of group purity."[10] From this perspective, the Caribbean is seen as a metaphor for the human condition, characterized by unceasing change and creative discontinuity. This is precisely what James Clifford has in mind when, in his influential ethnographic study *The Predicament of Culture,* he praised Césairean negritude for being "syncretic, modernist, and parodic—Caribbean in its acceptance of fragments and in its appreciation of the mechanisms of collage in cultural life." He is so taken with the exemplary nature of Caribbean pluralism that he is moved to declare: "We are all Caribbeans now in our urban archipelagos."[11] It seems almost as though after not knowing what to do with the Caribbean, everyone now wants to be Caribbean.

The most useful recent attempts to reconceptualize the idea of the Americas and the Caribbean's place within it have been not only nonreductionist but have also benefited from the appeal of some aspects of postmodern theory. It is perhaps not too sweeping a generalization to state that the tendency to balkanize the Caribbean in terms of ideology, race, or language was invariably based on theories of political resistance, ethnic difference, or popular tradition. In this regard, the warning offered by Anthony Appiah against the illusions of the "alternative genealogizing" of nativist thought are well taken.[12] Postmodern approaches have both helped to dismantle these binary oppositions that traditionally fixed the Caribbean in terms of metropole against periphery, nationalist opacity against universalizing sameness, and so on. In championing a poetics of multiplicity and heterogeneity as opposed to exclusivity and opposition, postmodernism put the emphasis on liminality and indeterminacy, perhaps allowing for a proper theorizing of that "delicate tenuity" that Césaire saw as the Caribbean's defining characteristic. Consequently, the very heterogeneity of the region, which, as Michel Rolph Trouillot has suggested, is an obstacle to theorizing about it as a whole, has become the methodological ground that facilitates recent attempts to establish theoretical models of the Caribbean.[13]

Interlectal Space

> And this land . . . dead . . . in its essence, is reborn with another intention: a crossroads of space and time.
>
> —Edouard Glissant, *L'intention poetique*

One of the most important recent theoretical works to open new discursive possibilities for defining the Caribbean is Antonio Benítez-Rojo's *The Repeating Island: The Caribbean and the Postmodern Perspective,* the introductory essay from which had already appeared in Pérez-Firmat's collection of essays *Do the Americas Have a Common Literature?* Despite the fact that Benítez-Rojo's expertise on the Caribbean is restricted to Cuba (apart from the mention of Wilson Harris, no other nonhispanophone writer is discussed), his imaginative grasp of the region's complexity is impressive. *The Repeating Island* offers the conventional signals of its origins in postmodern theorizing; for instance, we are told from the outset that the Caribbean is a "meta-archipelago [that] has the virtue of having neither a boundary nor a center," and later Benítez-Rojo holds that "within postmodernity there cannot be any single truth but instead . . . momentary ones."[14] The text concludes with an essay on chaos theory that functions almost as the scientific equivalent of postmodernism. Had this theoretical work simply remained at this level of bland generalization, the author might have laid himself open to charges that he was merely applying the latest intellectual fad from Europe to the Caribbean. *The Empire Writes Back* warns us of the universalist pretensions of postmodernism and of the risk of reinforcing "the very European hegemony which these (Caribbean) works have been undermining or circumventing," were this model to be thoughtlessly applied to the region.[15]

However, Benítez-Rojo, in an uncanny and presumably unconscious reference to the Césairean image of the Caribbean as fragile link between the Americas, focuses on the archipelago as a "discontinuous conjunction," "an island bridge connecting in "another way"

North and South America" (*Repeating Island,* 2). Much of his theorizing is derived from his imaginative grasp of the possibilities of this image. He rejects the phantasm that there is some way of establishing an essence, a stable synthesis, or any fundamental unity from this broken chain of islands; rather, he uses his reading of the deconstructive impulse in postmodern theory to elaborate on the Caribbean as being always in motion, forever in a state of flux, not a fixed ground but an open field of signifiers. Indeed, he defines the region as a "meta Archipelago" with neither a boundary nor a center. It is this rereading of the Caribbean as open-ended that makes *The Repeating Island* so essential to a conception of the Caribbean in a New World context. Benítez-Rojo is particularly good at identifying the objective correlatives in Caribbean space that illustrate his syncretic approach. His analysis of the Cuban cult of the Virgen de la Caridad del Cobre as the epitome of a confluence of diverse, interacting cultural and religious influences assumes a paradigmatic role in his view of Caribbean culture.

He also usefully identifies other areas of the Caribbean experience that richly illustrate his point: the *carnaval,* the city, and the sea. Benítez-Rojo revives Octavio Paz's conception of the *fiesta* in order to explain the supersyncretic nature of the Caribbean *carnaval.* Not only in *performance* does he see the rhythms of chaos in the island; he sees them also, quite tellingly, in the *city.* It is in the city that the Caribbean's encounter with modernity is most evident, which explains why it is one of the most problematic spaces in the region. Benítez-Rojo theorizes that "every Caribbean city carries deep within it other cities, which live as fetal minuscule nodules of turbulence that proliferate—each different from the last—through marinas, plazas and alleys" (*Repeating Island,* 211). As opposed to pastoral zones of timeless seclusion, such as the hill or the garden, the city carries not only the convulsive beauty of bizarre juxtapositions but also layers of meaning. It is that zone of consent and opposition that is privileged by much contemporary writing from the region. Finally, the sea is proposed as the ultimate image of the Caribbean. In Benítez-Rojo's words, the Caribbean people are "aquatic," not "terrestrial." This image is as much tied to the author's sense of the precariousness of the ground in the Caribbean as well as the peculiar nature of the Caribbean Sea. The latter is the source of the images of waves, currents, folds, and fluidity that abound in the text. Perhaps, more importantly, Benítez-Rojo suggests that the Caribbean Sea explodes outward, constantly impelling the peoples of the region "toward travel, toward exploration, toward the search for fluvial and marine routes" (*Repeating Island*, 25), and naturally implying the links with the rest of the Americas that have been repressed in the past.

In his reading of the Caribbean as dynamic space, Benítez-Rojo avoids the temptation of seeing the cultural diversity of the region in terms of synthesis or the cliché of "the melting pot." In this regard, his critique of the official Cuban orthodoxy of *mestizaje* is illuminating. *The Repeating Island* is the best work so far by a Latin Americanist that explores the Caribbean as a zone of indeterminacy and metamorphosis. Other works by Latin Americanists have made preemptive strikes in favor of Caribbean cross-culturality. The earliest of these regionalist studies must have been G. R. Coulthard's *Race and Colour in Caribbean Literature* (1962), which was thematically organized. More recently, Vera Kutzinski's *Against the American Grain* (1987) and Richard Morse's *New World Soundings* (1988) use a more sophisticated methodology to view the Caribbean in terms of a comparative, Pan-American perspective. The former chooses the work of three New World authors to illustrate their capacity to "reinvent American history from a cross-cultural perspective."[16] Morse explores the Americas in terms of Mikhail Bakhtin's notion of the dialogic, thereby privileging the thresholds and borders that facilitate the heteroglossic nature of Caribbean culture. Both Kutzinski and Morse pay much attention to the Caribbean, but they are trained as Latin Americanists and tend, as a result, to be unfamiliar with the nonhispanophone Caribbean. This deficiency is not simply a question of academic specialization. Caribbean thought does present certain difficulties to the best-intentioned researcher. For instance, there is a lack of systematic theorizing in the region; the most original thought can be found in imaginative writing. Secondly, so much of Caribbean criticism, particularly West Indian criticism, is bedeviled by an obsessive nativism or nationalist self-affirmation that the project of relating individual movements or thinkers to a larger whole is daunting.

However, no survey of attempts to conceptualize the region as a whole would be complete without a consideration of the extent to which Caribbean thought has attempted over time to grapple with the issue of a regional ethos. The Cuban José Martí may not have been the first but he was the most influential of the early Caribbean intellectuals to extoll the idea of the Caribbean as part of the Americas. His audacious and pathbreaking notion of Nuestra America, developed in the late nineteenth century, not only directly challenged the United States' myth of Manifest Destiny but raised the revolutionary possibility of the rest of the Americas as a creole, heterogeneous entity, as distinct from the totalizing, hegemonic nature of colonizing cultures. Martí was as determined to denounce the expansionist impulses of North America as he was insistent on establishing a protective solidarity between the rest of the Americas that would make Cuba less vulnerable. His ideal, "Our America," was conceived in the shadow of North American imperialism, and Martí's reputation has survived as that of a romantic anticolonialist and the father of Cuban independence. What is at least as important for our purposes is the link between the political rhetoric of self-determination and the epistemological possibilities of the idea of Our America. Martí launched in the 1880s the possibility of a new self-consciousness, of collective self-discovery. As Iris Zavala rightly claims, Martí is a crucial antecedent to the project of an Other America not only because he situated himself within a modernist poetics of negation but especially because "his impulse was toward opening the future . . . and not toward unearthing mythical pasts or origins."[17]

It is no coincidence that Martí's ideas emerged at a particular crossroads in Caribbean history and from the perspective of a threatened area of the archipelago. The appeal of a collective identity is particularly strong among peoples faced with the urgent question of self-definition in the face of aggressive metropolitan interests. It is no coincidence, then, that the idea of a Caribbean or a hemispheric collectivity would originate from countries like Cuba, Puerto Rico, and Martinique that have experienced long periods of dependency or psuedodependency and that, certainly in the case of Martinique, continue to do so. Gordon Lewis points out in *Main Currents in Caribbean Thought* that it was the Spanish-speaking Caribbean that kept alive the idea of an Antillean nationalism from the turn of the century. "The leading spirits—de Hostos, Betances, Martí, Duarte, Luperon—dreamed of a united Antillean confederation that would bind them all together. . . . Whereas the British Caribbean Islands like Jamaica and Barbados lapsed into comparative obscurity after slavery emancipation—the Spanish-speaking islands, and especially Cuba, moved into the limelight and, more than any others kept alive the anticolonial ideology."[18] Indeed, one should therefore not be surprised that the idea of an Antillean identity should reemerge in the 1940s in the concept of a New World Mediterranean proposed by a Cuban the novelist Alejo Carpentier. This tendency, no doubt, has much to do with the elaboration of an Antillean aesthetic in a contemporary, postmodern context by Benítez-Rojo, who is Cuban. This ultimately brings us to the Martiniquan situation and Edouard Glissant's theorizing of "the Other America."

Glissant is the first Martiniquan writer to explore the possibility of a Caribbean identity in a thoroughgoing way. Despite the fact that Césaire sensed a repressed relationship between the continental mass of North and South America and the Caribbean archipelago, he never developed this image in his work. Indeed, as Glissant has pointed out, too often Caribbean intellectuals have difficulty turning toward the Caribbean and get caught up instead in *detours,* which are invariably characterized by a nostalgia for pure origins, whether metropolitan in the assimilationist *detour,* African in the *detour* of negritude, or national in the *detour* of the myth of *marronnage.* As with Jose Martí, to whom Glissant acknowledges a debt, the Martiniquan writer defines the Caribbean's creole identity in the face of the totalizing sameness of metropolitan assimilation. He sees the all-consuming force of universalizing sameness not only in colonialism but in every manifestation of Western values—Hegelian thought, Marx's "historical necessity," and all forms of reductive universalism. Martinique, because of its largely unbroken relationship with France, is particularly vulnerable to the destructive effects of "the universal." It is no coincidence that Martinique is a prolific producer of theories of difference. Envisioning opacity at all costs is the only form of resistance open to Martiniquans, and to this extent one is never in doubt as to the political implications of what Glissant is proposing.

Glissant wants to locate Martinique in its immediate hemispheric context and to end the nostalgia for prelapsarian origins. In so doing, Glissant is careful not to propose a creole, Caribbean identity as an alternative center. His contestation of a poetics and a politics of centering leads him to visualize a Caribbean discourse based on heterogeneity and interrelating. He uses the term *transversality* in *Caribbean Discourse* to refer to the synchronic system of converging forces that constitute Caribbean identity. Glissant's objective is to theorize an otherness that cannot be contained or appropriated. Consequently, his model is based on fluidity and movement—as he puts it, on "becoming" as opposed to "being." It should, therefore, come as no surprise that he derives his poetics from the centrifugal nature of all language, especially the creolizing impulse that is alive in Caribbean languages. The exemplary nature of the creole language in this concept of a Caribbean ethos is clearly expressed by Glissant's closest follower, Patrick Chamoiseau, in his novel *Solibo Magnifique* (Magnificient Solibo)—a better manifesto of the créolité movement than the polemical *Eloge de la Créolité* (In praise of creolity) by Bernabe, Chamoiseau, and Confiant. Chamoiseau praises the storyteller Solibo for his ability to use "the four facets of our diglossia: creole basilect and acrolect, French basilect and acrolect, spreading and rooting in an interlectal space which I thought was the most accurate representation of our sociolinguistic reality."[19] It is this image of "interlectal space" that is the key to understanding the créolité movement and also to grasping Glissant's idea of *antillanité,* a Caribbean opacity.

The idea of a creole Caribbean is conceived primarily in opposition to the reductive and homogenizing polarity of a transcendental sameness. As Glissant states in one of the key essays in *Caribbean Discourse:* "To assert that people are creolized, that creolization has value, is to deconstruct in this way the category of 'creolized' that is considered as halfway between two pure extremes. . . . Creolization as an idea means the negation of creolization as a category, by giving priority to the notion of natural creolization."[20] He illustrates the Martiniquan capacity to inhabit interlectal space creatively, even if at times unconsciously, with the example of the many variations he has observed of the bumper sticker "Pas Roulez Trop Près" ("Don't Tailgate"). He sees here the instinctive, subversive impulse to create a counterorder and counterpoetics. Consequently, creole opacity is neither an acquiescence to the status quo nor a kind of romantic otherness. Rather, it is characterized by an oppositional and inscrutable impulse that remains latent in the Caribbean imagination.

It is through the idea of repositioning Martiniquan opacity in terms of a mobile counterpoetics of diversity that Glissant makes the link with the Caribbean's hemispheric identity. If interlectal space opens up the possibility of disrupting a stable, secure plenitude of meaning and replacing it with errancy and dislocation—a going back and forth (reversion and diversion)—then no ultimate state can either be defined or fixed. Consequently, in *Caribbean Discourse* he reveals an uneasiness with terms like *creolization* and *metissage* because of their association with static states. Glissant uses the idea of cross-culturality to suggest the process of decomposing and recomposing, a new politics as much as a new poetics, born out of a need to demystify notions of power, resistance, and freedom. Diversity then becomes a vital characteristic of interlectal space, because it "is neither chaos nor sterility" but rather "the human spirit's striving for a cross-cultural relationship, without universalist transcendence" (*Caribbean Discourse*, 98). Glissant theorizes that it is this ethos and aesthetic that mark the peoples and the imagination of "the Other America." In this regard, his theories predate by about a decade a similar hypothesis developed by Benítez-Rojo, whose *Repeating Island* (1992) may have made Glissant's earlier *Caribbean Discourse* (1989; originally published 1981) more accessible.

Glissant from the outset has used the characteristics of interlectal space to define his concept of the Other America. The term is used as early as 1956 in a review of two novels by Alejo Carpentier. Glissant further develops this notion of an unregimented, relational space as a distinguishing feature of the novels of the Americas in *Caribbean Discourse*. He senses in the work of such New World novelists as Carpentier, García Márquez, and Faulkner a shared sense of space and time that is akin to his own. "And the language of my landscape is primarily that of the forest, which unceasingly bursts with life. I do not practice the economy of the meadow. I do not share the serenity of the spring" (*Caribbean Discourse*, 146). If cultural particularity in the New World is convulsive and incomplete, then the Caribbean archipelago is even moreso, in Glissant's view. Here he privileges the idea of an open insularity as opposed to the continental mass of North and South America. The Caribbean therefore is envisaged by Glissant as "the advancing front of America," precarious, but free of "its continental mass."

Glissant is acutely aware that one of the defining aspects of the Caribbean archipelago, as much as its location, is the combination of island space and the Caribbean Sea. Island space offers itself as easily mastered terrain that invites experiments in radical transformation. Radical modernization from the outside is the abiding feature of the Caribbean and initially produced one of the most salient features of the region—the extermination of the indigenous population and large-scale repopulation from diverse cultures. Therefore, the tropical island could have no essential meaning but, from the outset, to be a kind of tabula rasa on which various projects, experiments, and utopias could be conceived. Given its origins, Glissant sees it as pointless to conceive of the Caribbean as a diachronic model, it must rather be seen in terms of synchronic "transversality." Consequently, he focuses on the transformative power of the Caribbean Sea and its capacity to reveal a "subterranean convergence of histories" and not a single, linear history. The image of "submarine roots," which is repeated later in the rhizomatous rooting idealized in *Poetics of Relating*,[21] makes the Caribbean Sea—described in *Caribbean Discourse* as "the estuary of the Americas"—the fertile repository of a New World poetics. Glissant would later further emphasize the paradigmatic function of the Caribbean Sea by declaring, again in *Poetics of Relating*, that it should not be seen as a tropical Mediterranean. The Caribbean Sea is not an inland, centralizing body of water but one that explodes outward, thereby dissolving all systems of centering or totalizing thought.

In opposing both the temptation of a homogenizing universalism and a polarizing alterity, Glissant offers a new definition of the Caribbean that not only locates it squarely in its hemispheric context but also projects the truth of a culture marked by a creolizing incompleteness. Ultimately, the Caribbean functions as a site of intense cultural flux in a world where "there will no longer be culture without all cultures, no civilisation capable of being the metropole of others."[22] By implication, there can be no island entity without, to use the title of Glissant's early book of poems, "a field of islands," and no possibility of grasping the collective identity of the Caribbean without its insertion in the Americas.

A Lived Modernity

> In a scattered series of disparate islands the process consists of a series of unco-ordinated periods of drift, punctuated by spurts, leaps and catastrophes. But the inherent movement is clear and strong.
>
> —C. L. R. James, *The Black Jacobins*

When C. L. R. James wrote these words in the 1962 appendix to his famous study of the Haitian revolution, he, too, was attempting a survey of the Caribbean. From his particular Pan-Caribbean viewpoint, James set out to map the Caribbean in terms of a quest for national identity that began with the Haitian Revolution in 1804 and culminated in the Cuban Revolution of 1959.[23] James saw the Caribbean in terms of phases of resistance in a region characterized by a history of violent change, forced relocation, and prolonged colonial domination. Two important features of James's hypothesis are that he does not see the Caribbean as a collection of static, victimized cultures but in terms of a dynamic engagement with global history. In his view, the desire for emancipation was expressed in the form of the struggle to become modern states and to achieve technological power. By focusing on state formation as an alternative revolutionary strategy, James was already shifting attention from resistance as *marronnage* (that is, the creation of isolated communities, united by shared defiance of a dominant force) to the importance of the state— a state that would try to restructure relations shaped by the plantation or colonialism and produce a new self-consciousness through the creolizing power of the state. James's coining of the term *Black Jacobin* is telling here: the force of modern revolutionary impulses unleashed by the French Revolution are given a more radical and idealistic manifestation in the New World.

The impact of James's model for understanding the Caribbean's need to generate what Glissant would categorize as a New World opacity in the face of colonialism's refusal to accept the region's right to political and cultural difference has gone unappreciated for too long. For James, Caribbean opacity was conceived in the radical context of a global modernism. Here we are not simply using the definition of *modern* in terms of industrialization or technological progress; rather, it is the spirit of intellectual dissidence, imaginative restlessness, and dialectical struggle that informs the Jacobinism that James used to characterize the uncoordinated "spurts, leaps and catastrophes" of Caribbean thought. In this regard, it is important to shift one's focus from the first moment of modernity in the Caribbean to what James sees as the far more important second moment of a Caribbean appropriation of the modern.

One of the commonplaces of the history of the Americas is to see Columbus's "discovery" of the New World as the hemisphere's first contact with modernity. For example, Tzvetan Todorov in *The Conquest of America* asserts that no date is more suitable "to mark the beginning of the modern era than the year 1492, the year Columbus crosses the Atlantic Ocean. We are all the direct descendants of Columbus, it is with him that our genealogy begins."[24] The concept of Columbus as a founding father has been, with obvious justification, highly problematic for most of the Caribbean. As Simon Gikandi notes in his perceptive study *Writing in Limbo: Modernism and Caribbean Literature*, the modern is intimately associated with European expansion, and consequently modernism has been explicitly rejected and tradition and ancestry have been revalorized because "the modern has often demanded that the colonized peoples be denied their subjectivity, language and history."[25] As he goes on to show, this sense of the modern as an intrusive, Eurocentric force in the Americas has led to a fetishism of otherness that ultimately does not provide escape from the region's modernist heritage.

Unfortunately, Gikandi's study is restricted to the anglophone Caribbean, which is the least propitious ground for establishing a Caribbean modernism in the region.[26] C. L. R. James offered a different genealogy for Caribbean modernism by pointing to the experiment with the modern in Haitian independence. It is an experiment such as this that Glissant probably had in mind when he referred to the "lived modernity" of the Caribbean. In *Caribbean Discourse*, he often uses the term "our irruption into modernity" to describe the archipelago's experience of the modern and its essential link with the rest of the Americas. As he argues in the essay "The Novel of the Americas," "We do not have a literary tradition that has slowly matured: ours was a brutal emergence that I think is an advantage and not a failing. . . . The irruption into modernity, the violent departure from tradition, from literary 'continuity,' seems to me a specific feature of the American writer when he wishes to give meaning to the reality of his environment" (*Caribbean Discourse*, 146). What Glissant is proposing is a Caribbean-based modernism that is profoundly connected with resistance and a suspicion of any transcendent systems of centralization or totalization.

What Glissant raises in this conception of a Caribbean modernism is the basic hub around which the chapters in this book are organized. In the earliest Haitian poets, we shall see that the "lived modernity" of the Caribbean relentlessly informs the anxieties, contradictions, and skepticism of the Caribbean text. For instance, the extent to which Oswald Durand breaks from the pastoral myth of Haiti to launch a new spatial language in which Haiti emerges as an unrepresentable totality; the way in which the surrealist intuition of the relativity of culture is turned against European surrealism's desire for an essential resolution of contradictions; the emergence of the postmodern in the Caribbean as the latest assertion of the heterogeneous nature of all universals and the relational or dialogic nature of Caribbean cultures—all these are dramatic manifestations of the modernist impulse. However, it would be wrong to suggest that the impulse in this book is purely theoretical. *The Other America* is, perhaps, even more concerned with historicity and with attempting as full-blown a comparative study of Caribbean literature as is possible.

If the entire work has as its subtext the Caribbean's experience of the modern as a vital part of its New World context, it is only logical to begin this book with an examination of the creation of the notion of the Tropics within Europe's experience of the crisis of modernization. The Caribbean archipelago, conceived as an absolute "elsewhere," as irreducibly different, was from its very inception invented as a blank slate onto which an entire exoticist project could be inscribed. The repercussions of intensive industrialization in Europe and colonization's backlash of global cultural homogeneity created the need to see in the Tropics an antidote to Europe's sense of loss. The Tropics are then inscribed in terms of the primitivist project of a romantic otherness, a fetishistic opacity. In the desperate need to see the Tropics as utopian, alternative societies, the Caribbean emerges as the Crusoesque paradise of self-sufficiency, in contradiction to the dystopia of the plantation and dependency. Chapter 1 traces the evolution of a tropicalist discourse that generated stereotypes of pristine, premodern worlds; the idealization of landscape as the ultimate *fête champêtre;* the evocation of untamed fecundity and intense feeling in the face of the emotional atrophy and alienation of industrialized Europe.

Chapter 2 argues that, if the invention of the Tropics was a consequence of a pessimistic sense of the ills of European modernity, the Caribbean in 1804 asserted itself in terms of a paradoxical embrace of a modernist ideology. Revolutionary Jacobinism, with Haitian independence, ushered in the Caribbean's first experiment in the creation of the modern nation-state. The state as a totalizing and creolizing entity is the product of modernist politics since the contestation of the state was provoked by a modernist poetics. In the nineteenth-century Caribbean, the dual and contradictory nature of modernist thought is already apparent: there is the impulse to build systems and the attendant suspicion of all systems. In the fascination with an emancipatory discourse among the fathers of Haitian independence, not only is there evidence of reverberations of the revolutionary fervor of the 1790s in Europe but there also began a tradition of demystification of state ideology and a conception of the subject and identity as unfinalized—as always open-ended. As the state grew more totalitarian, modernism enabled writers to resist the temptations of nihilism in the periods of darkest oppression and draw on imaginative capacities for renewal and resistance.

Chapter 3 examines a particular phase in Caribbean modernism that was driven by nostalgia for a prelapsarian plenitude—the return to an ideal heterocosmic space. At this time, the discourse of ethnogenesis manifests itself in an anxiety for origins, the need for foundational myths, and the lure of the ideal of an organicist fantasy, outside of the contradictions of history. Fundamental to this reductive, polarizing poetics is the ideal of erasure or cancellation that created the possibility of conceiving of the artist as demiurgic authority and the text in terms of ideological closure. The movements of Caribbean negritude, Marxism, and indigenism were based on this fascination with a telluric wisdom outside of time and space that brings forth a new social and aesthetic order. This quest for the sublimation of all contradiction is charged with poetic as well as political significance and coexists at times with an equally powerful impulse to recognize the importance of the relativity and duality of all things.

Chapter 4 focuses on those writers who reject the delusion of conceiving the Caribbean in heterocosmic terms. The ideal of a New World Mediterranean is proposed as a model that accounts for cultural diversity and appeals to the longing for an alternative history. The image of the Mediterranean becomes the synthesizing matrix of values for grounding the archipelago in its hemispheric context. The appropriation of Greece as a New World idea represents a daring raid on the founding notion from which the imperialist project derived its authority. The Mediterranean offered powerful possibilities of renewal, of hallowing the everyday, of conceiving of the Caribbean as the magical crossroads of the Americas. Within this Mediterranean discourse the ideal of a fused identity evolves, producing ideals of creolization and *mestizaje*. Such an enabling context also unmasks the Mediterranean as an ideal synthesis. The flight into myth is disrupted by a fear that there can be no journey back through time, that the Mediterranean cannot assume the authority of a founding myth, and that all must yield to a sense of flux and mutation that characterizes the heteroglossic Caribbean.

Elements of the postmodern have been apparent from the earliest stages of the Caribbean's "lived modernity." Caribbean postmodernism transforms the Caribbean from prelapsarian Eden and Mediterranean center to a playground of deviant styles and carnivalesque mutations. In chapter 5, the radical critique of any systematizing ideology is driven by women writers whose explosive literary experiments dismantle the pretensions of the male-dominated avant-garde and set the stage for a literature based on the irreverent and the transgressive. If previous modernist phases focused on the ground or groundlessness of the Caribbean, it is the body—the carnal and the scatological—that mark this phase in which postmodern play predominates. Also given particular prominence is the street as the site of communal spectacle as opposed to the repression of enclosed space. In the street is enacted what some writers see as a perpetual orgy and others see as permanent revolution.

Chapter 6 returns directly to the issue of asserting a Caribbean otherness in that territory within the archipelago that has never been able to declare itself politically other: Martinique. Dismissed by some as little more than "mimic men" and by others as having an oedipal attachment to the *mère patrie*, Martiniquans are projected in the revisionist ideas of the créolité movement as capable of forms of opposition within the overwhelming context of adaption and acquiescence. This movement derives its theoretical underpinnings from Glissant's theory of the Caribbean as synchronic space marked by diversity and cross-culturality. Despite the fact that they both represent extremes of the Caribbean experience, independence and isolation on the one hand and dependency and assimilation on the other, Haiti and Martinique respectively mark the beginning and end of this book. Martinique at the end of the twentieth century revives issues that were raised by the Haitian experiment with the modern at the beginning of the nineteenth century. Durand's creole poem "Choucoune" initiates us into the complications of Haitian modernism. Similarly, Patrick Chamoiseau uses the aesthetics of a creole orality to suggest a new strategy of resistance that is used by the marginalized within a culture of consent. In so doing, Chamoiseau in his novels concentrates on what Glissant calls "the tiny infoldings" of Martiniquan space, as is seen in the setting of the market, the urban ghetto, or the Savane in Fort-de-France.

This book does not attempt to exhaust the comparative possibilities within Caribbean literature; instead, periods have been chosen and works grouped in such a way as to provide privileged stagings of the central issue being discussed—the Caribbean's modernist legacy within its New World context. As said at the outset, the New World as a context may be a crude and sometimes unsatisfactory one, but it does provide a sense of the whole that enables us to juxtapose works and ideologies beyond linguistic and national boundaries. Ultimately, the idea of a New World context allows me to make the point that the only useful approach to Caribbean literature is an intertextual one. As Glissant reminds us in *Caribbean Discourse,* the answer to the question, What is the Caribbean? is "a multiple series of relationships." Similarly, to the question, What is Caribbean literature? this book offers the answer: a multiple series of literary relationships.

1

Tropes and Tropicality

... let the historian go mad there
from thirst. Slowly the water rat takes up its reed pen
and scribbles. Leisurely, the egret
on the mud tablet stamps its hieroglyph.
The explorer stumbles out of the bush crying out for myth.

—Derek Walcott, *Another Life*

In *The Invention of America*, a remarkable, short study of the meaning of the New World, Edmundo O'Gorman observes that the Americas were not just discovered one fine day in 1492 but were "the result of an inspired invention of Western thought." In his inquiry, O'Gorman makes a devastating case against the notion of "discovery." In taking what he calls an "ontological perspective" on the idea of Columbus's discovery of the New World, he persuasively argues that there is a basic logical absurdity to anyone discovering what he or she came upon by chance. Such an idea of discovery would presume that "all things are something in themselves, *per se*, ... that all things are endowed for all time, for everyone and anywhere, with a set being, predetermined and unalterable."[1] O'Gorman's point is that reality does not come with preordained labels or innate meanings; that "this old substantialist way of conceiving reality is untenable," given the major "scientific and philosophical revolution of the present."[2]

What O'Gorman is alluding to, in this revolution in modern thought, is the idea that meanings are not preordained but provisionally assigned to things, and that these meanings are often culturally generated. Consequently, what Columbus did on encountering the

New World is "invent" it in terms of his geographical knowledge, the travel writing he had read, and, perhaps more importantly, his own fantasy, to which he tenaciously clung despite all evidence to the contrary. The importance of O'Gorman's approach is that it focuses on the New World as a fictive space—one that is ever subject to reinvention depending on the discoverer. As Robert González Echevarría observes "the discovery of America was the actualization of a fiction, the founding of a world that had its origins in books before it became a concrete and tangible *terra firma*."[3]

This view—that it is human beings who decide how to represent things; that objective truth is always subject to discursive practice—is at the basis of what has been called the "crisis of representation." If primordial presence, in the Derridean sense, is an illusion, the invention of the New World then becomes simply one of the most dramatic examples of how meaning is always latent, unstable, and shaped by prior interpretation. By extension, writing about reality is no longer an innocent activity. Indeed, writing is seen as constituting meaning rather than reflecting objective reality. This reconstructive power of narrative has had profound effects on such fields as history and anthropology. As Hayden White concludes, "a historical narrative is not only a reproduction of the events reported in it, but also a complex of symbols."[4] Similarly, Clifford Geertz refers to "a pervasive nervousness about the whole business of claiming to explain enigmatical others."[5] He goes on to list the spread of this "problem" to a diverse range of intellectual disciplines, "telling it like it is hardly a more adequate a slogan for ethnography than for philosophy since Wittgenstein (or Gadamer), history since Collingwood (or Ricoeur), literature since Auerbach (or Barthes), painting since Gombrich (or Goodman), politics since Foucault (or Skinner), or physics since Kuhn (or Hesse)."[6]

In this view of the world not as terra firma but as a series of intertextual sites, geographical space, landscape, and human communities are inscribed with the rhetoric and images of given discursive practices. Michel Foucault's work on the relation between knowledge and power is central to this area of investigation. His view of the capacity of a cultural order to constitute itself through binary categories, so persuasively argued in *The Order of Things*, can be readily extended to colonial situations in which a hegemonic discourse sharply defines otherness both politically and morally. Foucault's discursive categories (sane-insane, normal-deviant) produce in the colonial context a primitivist or exotic discourse that reduces other cultures to the realm of the id, the libidinal, and the savage. For instance, Edward Said's influential work *Orientalism* extends Foucault's ideas in a sometimes polemical way to criticize the concept of the Orient embedded in Western thought and culture.[7] Similarly, studies by Mudimbe and Miller have demonstrated the power of an Africanist discourse to reduce African cultures systematically to zones of darkness and irrationality.[8]

These Manichean categories of civilized and primitive are no less powerful in the construction of images of the New World in general and the Caribbean in particular. It is this belief that has provoked interest in the conquest of the Americas of a semiotician such as Tzvetan Todorov. His special insight into the success of the Spaniards into dominating the New World has to do with their "mastery of signs." Todorov concentrates on Columbus not as discoverer but as interpreter. As he puts it, "The first gesture Columbus makes upon contact with the newly discovered lands (hence the first contact between Europe and what will be America) is an act of extended nomination."[9]

For much recent scholarship, Columbus as inventor or interpreter is of much greater interest than Columbus as discoverer or hero. As Gordon Brotherston points out in *The Image of the New World,* "Once discovered, its terrain, climates, flora and fauna had to be reconciled with the known world. And above all the 'Indians' . . . had to be fitted in with the scheme of things."[10] Brotherston's "scheme of things" refers, of course, to the capacity of Western European thought to map the Americas in fictive terms, from images of alluring wilderness to metaphors of violence and savagery. The New World is then invented in terms of Europe's prevailing cultural order of the time. It is within this imaginative space that the Americas are essentialized and a pattern of cultural and moral dichotomies is established.

These early attempts to write the New World into existence must be central to any analysis of the literatures of the Americas. The binary categories of civilized and primitive haunt the representation of the Americas by not only European writers but the very inhabitants of these lands. As González Echevarría observes, in the context of Latin American literature, "the New World . . . occupies a doubly fictive space: the one furnished by European tradition and the one re-elaborated by Latin American writers."[11] The prevalence of a poetics of invention and reinvention may be central to a New World aesthetic. It is precisely this restlessness that makes the literature of the Americas, or at least that of the other America, the hemisphere's midportion, so modern—or, rather, modernistic—in its impulse toward self-invention. It is an acute sensitivity to the problem of representation that drives the other America's skepticism, which both decodes the sign systems that attempt to imprison it as it deploys its own opaque discourse to counter imposed meanings. Despite the stated concern with originality and rootedness, much New World writing is about repetition and remythification.

If this hegemonic, discursive practice that goes back to the arrival of the Spaniards in the fifteenth century fixed the New World in terms of otherness, the Caribbean is even more dramatically positioned within such a system of binary constructs. The special nature of the Caribbean archipelago, the fragility and openness of the broken chain of islands, makes this part of the Americas particularly vulnerable to domination and control. In this regard, the abiding feature of Caribbean society is, as Gordon Lewis points out, "the fact that the European colonial powers created Caribbean colonies *de novo*, practically virgin territories . . . peopled by means of the slave trade and, after slavery abolition, by means of various indenture schemes, by uprooted and decultured immigrant groups."[12] The absence of an essence, or essential meaning for Caribbean space, that Edouard Glissant sees as the main characteristic of the Caribbean, is tied to a lack of an indigenous base, of a cultured hinterland, and the creation of a society built on repopulation.[13]

The Caribbean became a fantasy theater for the imaginations of travelers, adventurers, and missionaries: communities whose relations with Europe had been longer and more complex than anywhere else; subject peoples who replaced the exterminated original inhabitants; societies shaped by the exploitative economy of plantation slavery and the racist beliefs that justified it. This susceptibility of the New World and the Caribbean in particular to mythmaking and the imposition of a primitivist discourse has been noted by Gordon Lewis:

> The American continent, and within it the Caribbean region, was a completely new, virgin, freshly discovered land. . . . Everything was new: the islands, the aboriginal peoples, the flora and fauna, the Indian customs and religions and, most especially, the tropical sensuality of the climate. This sense of utter wonder, indeed, is the very first

note struck in the history of Caribbean literature, and it lasted well into the nineteenth century.[14]

Much energy has been put into tracing how this "sense of utter wonder" has generated the idea of the New World as a narrative construct or historically textualized referent. For instance, Wayne Franklin in *Discoverers, Explorers, Settlers* makes the point quite clearly that "in 1492 America was, from the European standpoint, simply an event. But in 1493 it became a collection of words . . . one sees in his first act of expression, (and the thousands of similar reports which were to follow from other hands) the constitution of American in European minds as a verbal construct, an artifact."[15] What was important in this act of imaginative reconstruction is the fact that these images are derived not simply from observation and experience but from a psychological urge. As Franklin further points out in the main argument of his book, terms like *discoverer, explorer, pioneer,* and *frontier* constitute a rhetoric that is indebted to medieval chivalric romance.

Ultimately, this impulse toward mythmaking that is directed at other, non-Western societies tells us more about the West than it does about the societies written about. The need to harness, settle, and transform necessitates images of emptiness—disorder on which a design can be placed. Indeed, it has been demonstrated by such cultural commentators as Stanley Diamond and Marianna Torgovnick that the primitive belongs at once to an exotic world and a familiar one. Diamond writes: "The idea of the primitive is, then, as old as civilization, because civilization creates it in the search for human identity. This was already evident in the works of Herodotus, Tacitus, Ovid, Horace, Hesiod and other poets and scholars of Western classical antiquity; they tried to grasp the nature of their own ancestry and conceptualize the barbarian strangers who thronged the borders of their archaic states."[16] Torgovnick echoes Diamond in this regard, stating that "primitive discourse [is] a discourse fundamental to the Western sense of self and other."[17]

The structuring of this discourse, its grammar of images and metaphors and especially its application to the Caribbean, must be seen as the starting point for any critical treatment of the emergence of the Caribbean in imaginative literature. In this regard, Hayden White's *Tropics of Discourse* provides us with not only a basic methodology but raises some of the fundamental concerns that emerge within a New World and Caribbeanist discourse. White offers a clear and useful grasp of the importance of language as a mediative enterprise between perception and conceptualization:

> [T]ropics is the process by which all discourse *constitutes* the objects which it pretends only to describe realistically and to analyze objectively. . . . [T]ropic derives from *tropikos, tropos,* which in Classical Greek meant "turn" or "way." It comes into modern language via *ropus* which in Classical Latin meant "metaphor." All these meanings, sedimented in the early English word *trope,* capture the force of the concept that modern English intends by the word *style,* a concept especially apt for the consideration of that form of verbal composition we call discourse.[18]

Tropes, then, are the basic units of discourse and *tropics* is the vital process that renders the unfamiliar familiar or, to use the image of Michel Foucault, that tames a world of profusion. For our purposes, *tropics* leads to a special encoding of the New World Tropics. It provides insight into the way in which Europe, using White's metaphors of psychotherapy and the neurotic, reemploys its experience of the Americas in order to render it less threatening and traumatic.

White focuses in particular on two patterns of encoding: the trope of wildness and that of the noble savage. These two conceptual categories are arguably the basic alternating elements in a Caribbeanist or tropicalist discourse—the native as violent and libidinal as opposed to the native as mystical and free. The notion of wildness, White explains, is a self-serving fiction that allows the "civilized" imagination to project its anxieties about its own humanity onto unfamiliar places and peoples: "From biblical times to the present, the notion of the wild man was associated with the idea of wilderness—the desert, forest, jungle, mountains—those parts of the physical world that had not yet been domesticated or marked out for domestication in any significant way. As one after another of these wildernesses was brought under control, the idea of the wild man was progressively despatialized."[19] White's point is that the wild man is a dialectical partner to the extent that, when he could no longer be identified with "out there," he became interiorized. As Julia Kristeva notes, "with the Freudian concept of the unconscious, the involvement of the strange in the psyche loses its pathological quality and integrates within the supposed human whole an *alterity* which is at the same time biological *and* symbolic and which becomes an integrating part of the *same.*"[20]

This is a significant point, because the possibility has been created of a psychologically rehabilitative primitivism or a socially revolutionary wildness to which societies less restrained by civilization might have special access. The possibility of revolutionary change through liberating man's innocence may well be a basic component in the romanticizing of revolutionary ideals within a Caribbeanist discourse. To this extent, the championing of Caribbean radicalism by European intellectuals may itself be a compensatory fantasy.

The notion of a redemptive primitivism is, as White argues, also closely related to the other New World stereotype—the noble savage. White's treatment of this theme is particularly illuminating given the fact that this ideal is peculiar to Europe's perception of the Americas. It is not clear why this image is not associated with other areas of "wilderness," but inhabitants of the Americas came to be endowed, in the European imagination, with the attributes of purity, perfection, and a prelapsarian innocence. The New World, then, evolves imaginatively into a utopian site—a positive, idealized metamorphosis from earlier images of horror and disgust. This dramatic change in a system of classification does not come about by accident. White notes that "this idolization of the natives of the New World occurs only *after* the conflict between the Europeans and the natives had already been decided and when, therefore, it could no longer hamper the exploitation of the latter by the former."[21]

White also advances another, perhaps even more important, reason for this radical shift in metaphor. He argues that the idea of the noble savage "represents not so much the elevation of the idea of the native as a demotion of the idea of nobility."[22] The idea of the noble savage is meant to undermine the concept of nobility. It is no coincidence that it takes hold just at the time when the idea of the ignoble aristocrat was becoming widely held among the French *philosophes.* As White further explains, "Diderot and Rousseau both use the noble savage idea to attack the European system of privilege, inherited power, and political oppression. . . . The noble savage was a concept with which to belabour nobility, not to redeem the savage."[23] The revolutionary idea of demoting aristocracy then uses as its rationale the elevation of the wild man. What is significant here is narrowly related to essentially domestic issues in Europe: the European context

of the increasing critique of the nobility and the rise of the bourgeoisie claiming their own right to privilege explains the evolution of
the stereotypes of the inhabitants of the Americas. The idea of the
noble savage served the ideological needs of a rising bourgeoisie de-
manding revolutionary change "for it at once undermined the nobility's claim to a special human status and extended that status to the
whole of humanity."[24]

Interestingly, these idealized attributes were not extended to Europe's view of its own urban masses, who inherit the stereotypes of
wildness. It is beyond the scope of the present study to explore the relationship between the changing tropes of a New World discourse
and images of the idyllic countryside and the urban proletariat. A
change does, however, seem to have taken place in Europe that
shifted the imagery of pastoral tranquility away from the Rousseauesque ideal of unspoilt nature to a Zolaesque revulsion at the stench
of the poor. The masses in Europe are then "deodorized" with the ad-
vent of Marx's idealization of the worker as transforming superhu-
man force in a repressive capitalist system. The point here is that
these images are generated by massive social and political changes
taking place in Europe. Nineteenth-century modernism succumbs to
the idealization of the world "out there." As modern technology and
rapid urbanization took its toll on the capacity to have a profound,
authentic experience for the individual, an exoticist project emerged
that allowed for escape from the atrophied, industrialized world of
Europe in the realm of adventure outside of Europe. What White
makes abundantly clear is that a metaphorical characterization of the
New World is built around contending and alternating European currents of thought that are drawn from the negative stereotype of wildness and the new, democratic conception of nobility. This duality is
central to the eventual emergence of the New World in terms of exoticism. As Francis Affergan puts it in his *Exotisme et Altérité,* this
binary opposition is tied to repeated cycles of "l'effroi et l'attirance"
(revulsion and attraction).[25]

Inventing the Tropics

Whether the prevalent trope is savage wildness or pristine innocence,
the New World is overwhelmingly the realm of the natural. To even
the most benign commentators, there is no culture or civilization
worthy of mention. Europe, on the other hand, is the domain of cul-

ture, even if that culture is seen as decadent or repressive. This is an obvious but vital feature of the exotic discourse imposed on the Americas. It is destined to be an equally vital part of any attempt to create a counterdiscourse and assert the New World in general and the Caribbean in particular in terms of culture. Also, since the realm of nature within which the New World is inscribed is itself the product of representation, constituted in terms of Old World narrative, the natural will become a significant and problematic terrain within which a counterdiscursive practice will be situated. This may explain the fascination with Eden and the Adamic vision of man; it may also explain the amoral elusiveness of the sea in the American imagination. It may do so because these tropes are attempts to go back to a beginning before representation, to a world of nature—of objects freed from rhetoric and metaphor—or, in the case of the sea, to an unstable medium beyond the fixing power of any totalizing discourse.

Gordon Lewis discusses utopian thought in Europe and the ideal of "le bon sauvage" with special reference to the emergence of the Caribbean islands. The imaginary island where a natural order dominates and where there is no political absolutism, no class hierarchy, no religious intolerance "became the raw material for the construction of the European radical dream by the eighteenth century."[26] This is in stark contrast to the brutal realities of the genocidal beginnings of Caribbean history with its slave-based societies. The great European apostle of "nature," Jean-Jacques Rousseau, is the most important figure in the didactic naturism that is centered on the virtues of open air, forests, and mountains. Rousseau's imaginative geography was distinct from that of other contemporary *philosophes,* who put greater emphasis on scientific thought and technology. For Rousseau, nature was the route to the sublime, to a kind of transcendence of the here and now.

Rousseau's naturism would leave its mark on the literary imagination of writers in the following century. It is in the nineteenth century that an exoticist discourse truly emerges and it does so bearing the stamp of Rousseau's vision of the innate goodness of external nature. For instance, this cult of nature is directly linked to the imaginative rediscovery of the New World by Chateaubriand, who visited the United States in 1791 and later wrote his *Genie du Christianisme* (1802). In this work, the glorification of not only the metaphysical but of God, as the title implies, is experienced in the majestic beauty of the American landscape. "It is futile, in our cultivated fields, for the imagination to attempt to take flight; everywhere it comes up against the settlements of men; but in these savage regions the soul relishes its sinking into an ocean of forests, its soaring over the chasm of waterfalls, its capacity to meditate at the edge of lakes and rivers, and, as it were, to be alone in the face of God."[27] This evocation of a spectacular wilderness that ends with the human spirit soaring over the Niagara Falls is not only an early invocation of *le merveilleux* in the Americas but typical of this naturist phase of nineteenth-century exoticism. This ideal is extremely important to early European modernism. Its best-known resonance is perhaps in Charles Baudelaire's lines from *Les Fleurs du Mal* (1857), where nature is a place of worship, indeed a temple with living pillars, where the world's mystery could be contemplated.

Two sites in particular—the lure of imaginary New World space and the setting of the deserted island—have a special place in this tradition of utopian thought in Europe. However, the Rousseauesque immersion of the subject in a universe of unmediated presences is not the only image of the Americas that emerges from the realm of the natural. Two major texts that are relevant to Caribbean realities are variations of the paradisal tropes of Rousseau and project visions of nature that facilitate adventure and the dream of colonizing the unknown. These texts, *The Tempest* and *Robinson Crusoe,* are about the sovereign self—the domination of nature by a monarch or patriarch. What we have in these works is a manifestation of what Peter Hulme, in his insightful case study of colonial discourse *Colonial Encounters,* sees as an imaginative strategy for managing the encounter with otherness—"an ensemble of linguistically-based practices unified by their common deployment in the management of colonial relationships."[28]

Both *The Tempest* and *Robinson Crusoe* are about the destructive power of nature—tempests and shipwrecks—and do not project Rousseau's vision of the sublime in nature; rather, these phenomena suggest the potential for chaos in nature and therefore signal the need for conquest and transformation to establish some kind of order. This is what Hulme means when he calls Defoe's tale "the primary stuff of colonialist ideology—the European hero's lonely first steps into the void of savagery."[29] Nature, then, is not bountiful and majestic but a site that challenges civilized man to establish, on his own, a social order that generates development and progress. In this confrontation of man and nature, nature reveals its inadequacies: "Nature is posited as a poverty, an absence of goods."[30] None of the necessities of what was thought to be a civilized life are provided. Crusoe, in a touching yet ludicrous effort to cling to the trappings of a now vanished respectability, creates his leaf umbrella in defiance of the formless mystery of the world around him.

In both Shakespeare's play and Defoe's tale the island locale functions in a simplifying, ideological way. Hulme notes that utopian fiction favors the island setting, and Pierre Macherey concurs, observing that "the island is a way of showing, linking and ordering ideological objects . . . nature, industry, science, work, and even, to some extent, destiny."[31] Hulme, in his pairing of characters in these works, zeroes in on the relationship between colonizer and colonized in a stark setting that allows its paradigmatic nature to become evident. Consequently, both situations are enactments of self-formation, because a curious interdependence exists between the colonial adventurer and his "ghostly" partner," whether it be Caliban or Friday. The solitary subject needs the other, both to validate himself and to bring intelligibility to reality itself. The other's presence is a corrective and protection against a disintegrating self-doubt.[32]

It is not only nature that is impoverished; the look of the colonizer is, too. If the subject's certainty as to his existence is called into question, the other is required to provide a reassuring mirror. As Hulme reminds us, more than simply providing an insight into the questioning of the Cartesian notion of the sovereign self, which is pure mind divorced from nature, these fictions are a means of "negotiating the unspeakable—and eventually unclosable—gap between the evidence of slavery and the notion of a moral economy."[33] Defoe's tale, in particular, is an example of the colonial alibi of the benevolent sovereign alone on a desert island constructing a simple moral economy. Here even enslavement is voluntary and there is no sign of that colonialism that, in the form of plantation slavery, was built on violently extracted labor.

By the beginning of the nineteenth century, the Tropics, in particular, began to be seen in terms of a kind of pagan sensuality, very different from Rousseau's vision of the divine in nature or the impulse to establish a social and moral order in the face of nature's disorder. Interestingly, the sun plays a vital role in this vision of a hedonistic primitivism. The tendency, as nineteenth-century exoticism evolves, is to concentrate increasingly on nature as a pantheistic presence, an intensely physical experience from which a Rousseauesque transcendence is absent. Exoticism also becomes a shaping force in the definition of otherness. The other became the repository of that intense physicality that allowed certain writers to either escape from or rebel against the moral strictures of puritanical ideals. Ultimately, in the late nineteenth and early twentieth century, writers like André Gide in *Les Nourritures Terrestres* (1897) and D. H. Lawrence became fascinated with the South, with possibilities of sensual "defoulement," and gave a new primitivist and amoral dimension to the definition of otherness. The other would become the site for that liberating, guilt-free naturalness that had been stifled within European cultures.

An exoticist discourse emerged in Europe as the world began to shrink, as it were, because of increasing contact between North and South. Exoticism, then, to use Michel Foucault's formulation, became an enabling discourse that allowed Europe to make sense of the new, strange cultures it had encountered. It equally allowed an avant garde of writers and intellectuals to escape to strange places or to romanticize the liberating otherness of Europe's new colonial possessions. As has been pointed out, this new fascination with otherness had an explosive effect, on both intellectual and creative cultures, in nineteenth-century Europe.

Exotic art and literature flourished in the nineteenth century. This is a long way from the naturism of Rousseau or the utopianism of an earlier century. Fiercely primitivist, nineteenth-century exoticism in Europe was about the stereotyping of other cultures and peoples. In many ways, this exoticist discourse made the practices of colonial domination and the policy of assimilation in French colonies easier, because it was a worldview predicated on the native as embodiment of the natural. Exoticism may have existed, in an unbridled and fanciful way, in the arts, but its credentials were further enforced by the rise of scientific societies that made enormous intellectual investment in the notion of cultural otherness. By 1850, the Ethnological Society of London, La Société Ethnologique de Paris, and La Société d'Anthropologie de Paris had been formed. At this time, the new sciences—ethnology, philology, anthropology—all emerged in response to the new range of cultures, lands, and peoples that had come into view because of Europe's expansion into the world.[34]

From the benevolent, intellectual excursions of Rousseau, through the ideal of nature as private property, by the end of the nineteenth century nature began to be construed increasingly in demonic terms. The natural was viewed with a *frisson* of pleasure. It is this particular notion of cultural difference that is an essential ingredient in an exoticist discourse. It also means that the Tropics would have a privileged place within this new primitivist pantheism. That early apostle of cultural diversity Victor Segalen was aware of this tendency to see the Tropics as the quintessential exotic site: "Exoticism is given to 'tropicality.' Coconut trees and torrid climes."[35] Even though written in 1908, Segalen's attempt to theorize a new exotic practice in his *Essai sur l'exotisme* is already sensitive to the encroachment of modernization. He was painfully aware that European expansion was leading to a global monoculture. Exoticism was fast becoming an artificial and concocted aesthetic: "Diversity is waning. That is the greatest danger on the Earth. It is therefore against this waning we must struggle, fight."[36]

Segalen's sensitivity to the interrelatedness of modernity, modernization, and modernism offers an invaluable insight into the problematics of exoticism. For Segalen, the power of modern art is its capacity to defamiliarize—to estrange the reader of viewer; consequently, in a modernist aesthetic there would always be the temptation of exoticism. What Segalen rejected was the convention that defined other cultures in terms of strangeness. He saw this as a superficial and simulated solution to the modernist impulse to escape the world of bourgeois convention and the values of the marketplace. What for him was more important was the leap into the unknown that meant that the journey was essentially an interval—a subjective interval. For Segalen, external space was becoming more used up, more folkloristic, and ultimately monotonous. What we see in Segalen is a sensitivity to both the interrelation between subject and object and the realization that the spread of modernization was making the project of modernism increasingly impossible.

Perhaps always a symbolist at heart, Segalen put less emphasis on the physical journey. As a movement, symbolism valued the internal adventure over the reality of physical movement. Since the spread of imperialism was making exoticism less and less credible, Segalen insisted on the importance of diversity and the importance, not of colonizing, but of recognizing the other: "Let us not flatter ourselves with assimilating the customs, races, nations, the other; but on the contrary let us rejoice in never being able to do so; thereby assuring ourselves of the lasting pleasure of feeling the Diverse."[37]

It is this feature of Segalen's thought that Edouard Glissant refers to when he observes, "[H]e has not smothered the other under the weight of the Same, nor the other way round."[38] In Glissant's formulation, Segalen rejects "l'exotisme-accident" (accidental exoticism) for "L'Esthetique du Divers" (the aesthetic of the Diverse). Glissant naturally views Segalen as a precursor to the ideal of cultural interrelating and the sense of the world as irreducibly multiple. What is interesting, though is Segalen's sensitivity to the inadequacies of exoticism. This is important to tracing the durability of this discourse. Chris Bongie has written insightfully on this question in his *Exotic Memories: Literature, Colonialism, and the Fin de Siècle*. Bongie seems to identify three phases of exoticist discourse: Imperialistic exoticism, exoticizing exoticism, and exoticism in the pessimistic mode. As the title of Bongie's work suggests, exoticism is a project based on loss or absence. It is an impulse to recover lost values elsewhere, outside of the encroachment of modern culture. The irony is that exoticism is provoked by the very condition that makes its fulfillment impossible. As Bongie puts it, "if exoticism partakes of modernity and its promise, what the future promises . . . is a recovery of the past and all of that a triumphant modernity has effaced. Indeed, the very emergence of this project is unthinkable without such a triumph."[39] Therefore, it is the spread of the "same"—meaning the pervasiveness of modernization—that creates the yearning for alternative cultures as a refuge, a strategic zone of intense feeling. This dream of losing oneself in the realm of pure "difference" had, however, become impossible, since the world was a finite place and the possibility of discovering uncontaminated cultural wholes had become unrealistic. Exoticism in the imperialistic mode is less interesting because it is more naive, unproblematic; it simply disposes of the native as savage. It is the yearning for authenticity and disalienation of late modernism that reveals the nature of the imaginative mapping of space involved in exoticism. Bongie correctly defines the "exoticizing exotic" as an aporia—"a constitutional absence at the heart of what has been projected as a possible alternative to modernity."[40] The difference between Victor Segalen and others of his generation is that Segalen was acutely aware of this irony—of the fact that exoticism was an exhausted discourse, an ideology that could no longer be sustained by belief.

Segalen's realization does not so much undermine the exotic project as shift it into a different mode. Bongie's hypothesis is that the exotic is the inevitable product of the modern; it can be discredited, but it remains latent in modern culture and cannot be suppressed as a longing. Consequently, writers like Segalen conserve the exotic rhetorically as a "strategic dreaming." As Segalen argues in his *Essai sur l'exotisme,* exoticism must be removed from its exclusively physical, geographical context. The true value of exoticism is restored in the adventure within the uncharted space of the blank page. It is this almost Mallarmean aspect of Segalen's thought that Glissant celebrates: "After this, there is no longer the possibility of a touristy or literary exoticism, but only the writing of the poem which fixes the meaning of the struggle against the limits." Segalen might, in this way, banish the utilitarian and the material world from his renewed exotic project. However, this privileging of the purely literary does not completely shut out the reality of colonialism or solve the crisis of modernity: "stepping back from colonialism [Segalen] cannot step outside of it."[41]

What is important for our purposes is the nature of this "strategic dreaming." What are the fantasies that drive the imagination to seek cultural alternatives, to pursue, the dream of transgression? Bongie suggests that there is a dream of redemption associated with the non-European world that turns on the specific nature of the alienation felt in the modern world. If the exotic quest is a remedy for the ills of the modern world, it appears that the greatest single menace of modernization is seen as the loss of individuality. Here again Segalen proves perceptive in his emphasis—in *Essai sur l'exotisme*—or individualism: "Only those who possess a strong individuality can feel diversity."[42] Bongie directly addresses this question when he states: "As one of the privileged modes of recuperating this lost individuality, the exoticist project attempts to diffuse the supposed threat of homogenization that mass society poses." This "dynamic antagonism between the individual and a noxious plurality" is a fundamental aspect of literary modernism. The need for the individual to retrieve extreme and intense states of feeling in a distant "elsewhere" is, arguably, the driving force behind literary modernism. Whether this "elsewhere" is situated in space, time, or within consciousness itself, it is provoked by a sense of the devaluation of the individual self.

Ultimately, the exotic project has become deeply inscribed within the counterculture of modernism as an attempt to retrieve the sovereign self in the face of the encroachments of mass society. As Bongie again explains: "Hence the attraction of a project like exoticism, which appeared to offer the individual the possibility of self-realization: where better to escape the ills of mass society than in those "unenlightened" locales in which . . . the archaic model of subjectivity still persisted as a political system?"[43] Bongie, therefore, ties the privileging of the individual within romantic and modernist thought to colonialism and its preservation of the ideal of the individual that had been lost in the modern, democratic, postrevolutionary European state. The irony here is that his survey of some of the major literary practitioners of exoticism points to their celebration of the sovereign individual even to the extent that despotism is admired, since the superior individual was the incarnation of the *geist* of his society and culture. Charisma, organicism, the quest for a primordial wholeness—these then become fundamental to the exoticism and the imaginative mapping of the non-European world.

Perhaps this idea of the solitary individual has been ever present in the emergence of exoticism. From the figure of the solitary wanderer in the work of Jean-Jacques Rousseau, the founding father of naturism, to the idea of original sovereignty in Defoe's *Robinson Crusoe,* "elsewhere" is a place you can begin again. While contesting the values of the modern, industrialized state, modernism, in its innate exoticizing aspect, meant an aestheticizing of the ideal of mastery, even of the master-slave relationship. For our purposes, the problem is that the "elsewhere" has never been simply a theater where rehearsals for self-realization can be performed. It is not uninhabited space, As Hulme argues in his discussion of *The Tempest,* Prospero's claims to sovereignty are hollow since his totalizing authority is contested by Caliban's presence. As a result, "[a] space is opened, as it were, behind Prospero's narrative, a gap that allows us to see that Prospero's narrative is not simply history, not simply the way things were, but a particular *version.*"[44]

The Romance of Otherness

In his discussion of what he calls "the American existentialist—the hipster," Norman Mailer develops the apparent affinities between white-nonconformist and black countercultures. As he claims,

> it is no accident that the source of Hip is the Negro for he had been living on the margin between totalitarianism and democracy for two centuries. . . . And in the wedding of the white and the black it was

the Negro who brought the cultural dowry. So there was a new breed of adventurers, urban adventurers who drifted out at night looking for action with a black man's code to fit their facts. The hipster had absorbed the existentialist synopses of the Negro, and for practical purposes could be considered a white Negro.[45]

What we see here is the theorizing of radical chic as black culture provides the style for challenging the white establishment. Indeed, it was destined to be little more than a style, the word *hipster* itself having come to be exclusively associated with clothing.

What we have here in Mailer's claims is the familiar emotional investment in otherness by radical modern thought. As we have seen, this imaginative plundering of non-European cultures is a significant aspect of modernism. Chris Bongie, while concentrating on fin de siècle writing, is very aware that exoticism discourse is a powerful and persistent complicating factor in contemporary thinking. For instance, Bongie's suggestion that the lure of "elsewhere" may be related to the modernist longing for an organic state in which an enlightened despotism might allow for an individual's full self-realization is as pertinent to Loti's admiration of dynastic China in 1901 as Wade Davis's evocation of Duvalierist Haiti in 1988. In *Passage of Darkness,* Harvard ethnobotanist Davis revisits the dream of organicism in the mystical and magical world of rural Haiti. This is a society stalled in time, wonderfully unenlightened, in which Duvlierist dictatorship is organically related to the *vaudou* religion and its secret societies.[46]

"Elsewhere," or the Third World, in the twentieth century has become an exemplary site for transgressive fantasies. What Bongie calls the promise held out by the underdeveloped world continues to drive many avant-garde thinkers to see in the Third World alternatives to their own societies. Perhaps the most complex relationship between a radical European avant-garde and the Americas is the case of the surrealist movement. Surrealism, of course, as a movement, placed a very high value on otherness. Indeed, the surrealists seemed acutely aware that what appeared to be real and familiar often concealed the unreal and the bizarre. Also, by extension, that which seemed unacceptably "other" might well be more approachable than was first thought. This provocative and ironic interplay between familiar and unfamiliar is enough to make a Dogon mask assume the ordinariness of a domestic artifact or a humble teacup take on the threatening properties of a nightmare.

This is precisely why so many non-European artists were drawn to surrealism as a liberating ideology: it challenged the value system of European colonialism. Yet surrealism could not always conceal its roots as an essentially European disaffection. The lure of otherness took the surrealists to the East and to Africa and the Americas. In the New World, they seemed particularly drawn to the rites and myths of pre-Columbian America. Artaud in Mexico and Peret in Brazil are clear examples of this emphasis. The one important exception is that of the founding father of surrealism, André Breton, in the Caribbean.

The encounter between Breton and Césaire's collaborators in the magazine *Tropiques* in Martinique in 1941 is well known. Equally well-known is the explosive impact of Breton's visit to Haiti in 1945, where another group of activists involved in a magazine, *La Ruche,* proclaimed a revolution in his name. It is clear that outside of France, surrealism retained a revolutionary, political dimension it had lost at home. Yet in his evocation of the francophone Caribbean, Breton construed Haiti and Martinique in terms of nature and entrancing otherness. The essay *Martinique charmeuse de serpents,* inspired by a painting by Le Douanier Rousseau, consistently depicts Martinique as seductive and enchanting. In the section "Les Epingles Tremblantes," Breton evokes the statue of Josephine—"the Statue of Josephine de Beauharnais fixes the town under a tender, feminine sign."[47] This is followed by reference to the "little laughing chabines" and, notoriously, to the wife of Aimé Césaire, Suzanne Césaire, as "beautiful as a punch's flame."[48] In impoverished and unstable Haiti, Breton's stereotypes vary somewhat. Martiniquan *doudouisme* is replaced by the mysticism of *vaudou* and a heroic evocation of Haitian history. In his famous speech at the Rex Cinema, Port-au-Prince, on December 20, 1945, Breton praises the condition of "l'homme haitien," "considering this from the angle of the condition in those countries that pride themselves on being on the cutting edge of technical progress, I do not hesitate to think it is the latter that suffer spiritual privation and the most grinding distress."[49] Breton refers several times in this speech to Haiti's contact with natural forces and claims that the average American from a U.S. big city has much to learn from the Haitian peasant.

Despite his reference to the surrealists' denunciation of the colonialist war in Morocco, in an attempt to enhance his political credentials, Breton expresses ideas that are clearly shaped by the old binary oppositions of exoticism. It is, perhaps, worthy of note that gender polarization changes as Breton moves from Martinique to Haiti. The former is feminine and enchanting; the latter is mystical and explosive. Pierre Mabille, who invited Breton to Haiti, was himself deeply involved in studying the occult in Haiti's indigenous culture—in particular, *vaudou*. In writing about Haiti, Mabille confesses, "I cannot think of blacks without the image of the forest imposing itself on me like an obsession."[50] Haiti would emerge time and time again as that privileged space lost to modernity where the modernist sensibility could retrieve a sense of organic wholeness and purity.

Another member of that traveling intellectual avant-garde who came to Martinique at very much the same time as André Breton was Claude Lévi-Strauss. Driven to leaving Europe because of a sense of alienation in the modern, industrialized world and a personal sense of the immediate trauma of World War II, Lévi-Strauss, in his *Triste Tropiques,* sought a utopian "elsewhere"—an atavistic alternative to the congested, commodified world of Europe: "Our great Western civilisation, which has created the marvels we now enjoy, has only succeeded in producing them at the cost of corresponding ills. . . . The first thing we see when we travel round the world is our own filth, thrown in the face of mankind."[51] He goes on to express a fear of "monoculture" and "mass civilisation" sweeping the globe. *Tristes Tropiques* can be seen as a late and doomed project to recuperate a Rousseauesque utopianism.

The very title of Lévi-Strauss's travel book–cum–anthropological study suggests that the primitive alternative being sought is always elusive. The exoticist nature of Lévi-Strauss's work has been uncovered by Jacques Derrida in *Of Grammatology* and elaborated on by Mariana Torgovnick in *Gone Primitive.* Torgovnick, however, thoughtfully points out that Lévi-Strauss is well aware that primitive authenticity is a construct. Lévi-Strauss defiantly insists on the vital importance of this construct because it allows a perspective for a critique of Western civilization.[52] This level of intense self-consciousness and self-questioning is evident in his chapter revealingly entitled "Robinson Crusoe," where the anthropologist asks himself, "[w]as it not my mistake, and the mistake of my profession, to believe that men are not always men?"[53] Even though the alternative he seeks may be a mirage, the organicist dream remains alive in his tactical primitivism. If the exotic Tropics did not exist, as it were, radical modernism would have to invent it.

The need for a primitivist ideal as the point of contrast for the industrialized West is never as clear as in the Sartrean reading of the negritude movement in general and the poetry of Aimé Césaire in particular. In his influential essay *Orphée Noir* (1948), Sartre construes the poetry of negritude in terms of a redemptive anticapitalist fantasy. This view of Sartre's conception of negritude as revolutionary alterity is mentioned fleetingly by Bongie.[54] Yet Sartre's mythification of the black artist fits neatly into the construction of "Elsewhere" in terms of the transgressive and the natural. At one point in an essay that may have actually shaped the theoretical construction of negritude among black writers,[55] Sartre claims that the white industrialized proletariat has lost what the black peasant has preserved: "The black is first of all a peasant. . . . Techniques have contaminated the white worker, but the black remains the great male of the earth, the sperm of the world. . . . The sexual pantheism of these poets is without doubt that which will first strike the reader. To labor, to plant, to eat, is to make love with nature."[56]

In this romanticizing of black culture, Sartre is closer to the surrealists than he would care to admit. These sweeping generalizations again point to the power of the primitivist Tropics to mount a critique against the repressed, Christian West. Masculine, organicist, libidinal Sartre constructs black poetry in terms of an agricultural potency. This reductive and essentialist interpretation of Césaire's poetry is a critique of the puny, "retractile" imaginations of the white artist. Dionysian and explosive, Sartre's *Black Orpheus* is a provocative inversion of European culture and Michael Richardson is correct in pointing to Sartre's failings in his intuitive championing of negritude. Drawing heavily on Menil's critique, Richardson sees Sartrean negritude as a reified concept belonging more to Sartrean philosophy than to any actual, historical reality. "Sartre's unwitting role . . . emerged from his own relation to negritude which he was unable to see on its own terms, but which he wished to use as part of his own existentialist philosophy."[57]

As the intellectual fashions change so does the nature of the ideological appropriation of "Elsewhere." Surrealism and existentialism yield to postmodernism and the "other" is appropriated differently. For instance, we find Césaire represented by James Clifford, not as the incarnation of erect Sartrean potency but as a hybrid and heteroglot. In Clifford's estimation, Césaire's ideological coloration has acquired a distinctly postmodern line. Indeed, Clifford's embrace is all-encompassing as he follows Depestre's lead in seeing Alejo Carpentier, César Vallejo, and Gabriel García Márquez as "heirs of negritude," In his desire to proclaim a New World poetics of transgression built around marronage, Clifford pronounces that negritude "is no longer about roots but about present process in a polyphonous reality."[58] In identifying Césaire as a creolizing modernist and claiming Caribbean identity for himself, Clifford may well be no less guilty than Breton, Lévi-Strauss, or Sartre of succumbing to a romantic fantasy of liberation derived from an exotic notion of other cultures. Again the Tropics and, it seems, Césaire in particular, seem to feed on another's utopian dream.

We are warned by Ashcroft, Griffiths, and Tiffin in *The Empire Writes Back* of the dangers of "the tendency to reincorporate postcolonial culture into a new internationalist and universalist paradigm."[59] It is this incorporating practice that makes Clifford see himself as the polyphonous heir of negritude and leads Sartre to metamorphone into a revolutionary black peasant. What is most interesting about this repeated detour in modernist thought is not so much that it occurs as how it is absorbed and assimilated from that "Elsewhere" by the artist or intellectual who is drawn to modernism as a liberating practice. Tzvetan Tordorov in *Race, Writing and Culture* warns that far too much emphasis has been placed by critics on the manner in which a colonialist discourse engenders otherness. He sees the danger of a kind of Manicheanism in terms of its capacity to produce "subject matter . . . largely composed of stereotypes: racial Others are either noble savages or filthy curs, rarely anything in between. . . . The risk entailed is that this Manichean writing might elicit a similarly Manichean interpretation, with good and evil simply having switched places."[60]

Todorov is, with some justification, complaining about the simplifying effect of this emphasis on imperialist discourse and the attendant pessimistic view that either a full understanding of the other is impossible or that the other is forever a victim and can never emerge as a speaking or writing subject. Is this not also a reappearance of the romance of the other in terms of a postmodern primitivism? Is what has been termed the "epistemic violence" aimed at the other so destructive that the other is forever doomed to silence and can never emerge fully from the disfiguring representation? Surely, there is strong evidence that the imagination of the other, and in this case the other America, has been engaged in a sustained, creative struggle for self-definition within a modernist poetics. The nature of this interaction is our main concern. Perhaps the formulation of Paul Gilroy in his idiosyncratic work *The Black Atlantic: Modernity and Double Consciousness* is worth noting.

> The intellectual and cultural achievements of the black Atlantic opulations exist inside and not always against the grand narrative of Enlightenment. . . . Though African linguistic tropes are still visible for those who wish to see them, they have often been transformed and adapted by their New World locations to a new point where the dangerous issues of purified essences and simple origins lose all meaning. These modern black political formulations stand simultaneously inside and outside the western culture which has been their peculiar step-parent.[61]

Gilroy does overstate the case in his advocacy of modernism as the primary trope in the imaginative practice of his "black Atlantic." It would be difficult to accept his blanket defence of modernity given our survey of the perverse ambiguities present in a modernist poetics and in particular its fetishistic representation of otherness. Gilroy, however, does put his finger on the vital question of being both "inside and outside" of modernist modes of thought. This "double consciousness" is the crucial issue in the process of self-definition in the modern Caribbean. Even though he unfortunately draws few examples from Haiti's early experiment with modernity, Gilroy does assert that there is "a need for fresh thinking about the importance of Haiti and its revolution"[62] This is, in my view, precisely where Caribbean modernist practice begins, because it was in Haiti that Caribbean thought first emerged as a contestation of the reductive mystification of colonialism. Consequently, it is through Haiti that we can grasp the inescapable historical nature of the other America and the first Caribbean experiment with a foundational poetics and a collective self-invention in the face of the colonial refusal to grant opacity to the subjugated other.

2

Modernism, Modernity, and Otherness: Self-Fashioning in Nineteenth-Century Haiti

West Indians first became aware of themselves as a people in the Haitian revolution.

—C. L. R. James, *Black Jacobins*

Haiti was the second country in the New World to declare itself independent from colonial Europe. It was, however, the first state in the New World to declare itself "other." The United States, whose independence preceded that of Haiti, distanced itself from the rest of the Americas after 1776. In *The New Golden Land*, Hugh Honour argues that by the end of the eighteenth century the United States began to be seen as an extension and idealization of European culture, very distinct from the mysterious and untamed world of the "Other America." He argues that "in addition to liberating the United States from British rule, the Revolution decisively cut them off from the rest of the continent in the European mind."[1]

In contrast, the declaration of Haitian independence in 1804 was an attempt by a Caribbean state to establish a new beginning and to expunge the horrors of colonial St. Dominique. The nature of this act of revolutionary modernity has been subject to quite diverse interpretation. Certainly one strongly held view of the Haitian Revolution is that it was a dramatic, collective act of black *marronnage*. Perhaps the best known formulation of this point of view is Aimé Césaire's declaration in his *Cahier d'un retour au pays natal* that it was in the Haitian Revolution that "negritude stood up for the first time."[2]

Yet to conceive of a Haitian Revolution, engendered by the ideals of the Enlightenment and the French Revolution, as simply an early assertion of black marronnage is a distortion of historical reality. Eugene Genovese is perhaps closer to the truth when he argues that "the revolution under Toussaint, a leader of genius, did not aspire to restore some lost African world or build an isolated Afro-American enclave that could have played no autonomous role in world affairs. . . . Toussaint, and after his death, Dessalines and Henri Christophe, tried to forge a modern black state."[3] Genovese's view is that the fathers of Haitian independence were acutely sensitive to the question of modernization and the way in which modern ideologies and technology "pointed toward participation in the mainstream of world history rather than away from it."[4] At the very least, this means that the ideal of a Haitian opacity was a very complex one in 1804—a point especially important for the Caribbean since the Haitian Revolution signaled a new way of fashioning identity in the New World. In this regard, 1804 was as important to the other America as 1492 was to the New World as a whole.

It is this desire to be a functional part of a modern, global culture that may explain the enduring interest in postrevolutionary France and in modern Europe shown by Haitian leaders after the savage, twelve-year war of independence. This is especially noticeable because Haitians were either partly or wholly of African descent, unlike other elites in the Americas who could claim direct kinship with Europeans. This does not mean that racial pride did not feature prominently in the construction of a national identity in the wake of independence, but the fact is that for the fathers of Haitian independence Africa did not represent modernity. As David Nicholls observes, while Haitians "vehemently denied any notion of the inherent inferiority of Africans, they often assumed that Africa was a barbarous continent and that the only civilization worth considering in their own day was European."[5] This attitude to race and culture among intellectuals of the first black republic would later be dismissed as *bovarysme collectif* (collective self-denial), but it should be seen as a vital aspect of their attraction to modernity.

Haiti, then, in 1804 was conceived in terms of an ideology of unrealized possibilities. It would neither be relegated to the periphery of the world nor would it succumb to atavistic longings for a racial past.

The impulse was toward the future and not dwelling in mythical origins. If anything, Haiti was seen as the avant-garde that would rehabilitate the black race. For early Haitian essayists like Baron de Vastey, European imperialism had created a new breed of men and Haiti was at the forefront of this modern human phenomenon. Vastey, Henri Christophe's secretary and apologist, envisioned the unification of those oppressed and transformed by colonialism. He declares, in this remarkably early appeal to the power of the "wretched of the earth" to change an old world order, "Five million black, yellow, and dark skinned men, spread across the surface of the globe, lay claim to the rights and privileges that have been bestowed on them by natural right."[6]

The repositioning of race and culture that Vastey was articulating in 1816 is part of a larger, utopian vision of the way in which European imperialism had transformed the world for all time. Consequently, one would be hard put to find in early Haitian literature any references to the idea of maroonism as a founding myth for the new republic. Maroonism was viewed as premodern and, therefore, not progressive. Consequently, those themes of the retreat to the wild hinterland, heroic resistance to alienating modernity, and the poetics of negation are not evident in early Haitian attempts to conceive of a national identity. Neither Boukman nor Makandal are celebrated in nineteenth-century Haiti. As Ulrich Fleischman correctly notes, "Unlike Toussaint L'Ouverture, who represents the official resistance, Makandal hardly ever appears in the voluminous Haitian literature."[7] Perhaps this absence is tied to Glissant's hypothesis regarding the absence of founding myths in the Caribbean.[8] But the fact is that in Haiti the modern state was conceived as the alternative to the plantation. No such case was made for the isolated world of the maroon.

The longing for modernity did not simply mean that Haiti was expected to submerge without a trace in some universal culture; 1804 meant the revindication of opacity in the face of its denial. Haiti certainly declared itself "other," but this otherness seems to have been conceived in terms of a new composite culture. Founding the new republic and legitimizing a new culture for many early Haitian intellectuals meant exploring the issue of ethnic hybridity and cultural syncretism. An interesting comparison was made between the United States and Haiti by Emile Nau in 1836 in his newspaper *Le Républicain*. In Nau's view, Haitian society was profoundly creolized, whereas U.S. society was merely transplanted: "We quite like the

American are transplanted, stripped of traditions, but there is in the fusion of the European and African cultures, which constitutes our national character, something that makes us less French than the American is English. This advantage is a real one."[9] For Nau, Haiti and not the United States represented the exemplary emergence of the heterogeneous modern American nation.

It may be no coincidence that Nau demonstrated a deep interest in pre-Columbian Haiti. His *Histoire des Caciques* (1854) attempts to set the record straight for early Taino culture in Haiti. Without resorting to a pre-Columbian foundational myth, it suggests an awareness of Haitian space that precedes the arrival of the Spanish and in which the war of independence and the new black republic were a continuum of New World civilization. It was one thing for intellectuals to conceive of such an identity but another writer, in an unsigned article in 1839, expressed the fear that Haiti was "lost in the Archipelago of the Caribbean and snatched away from the ambitious purview of the old world by the two Americas."[10] The writer's fear was that the special nature of the Haitian experiment would be lost to the world. This again points to the fact that reciprocity and recognition played a crucial role in identitarian thought in the Caribbean's earliest experiment in heterogeneous ethnogenesis.

This particular problematic did not lead to simple or easy definitions of the nature of this new Haitian-American identity. Haiti's early theoreticians were constantly aware of the threat of a reductive sameness or a repulsive alterity posed by European colonization. Yet it was within this very context of universal civilization, or at least the sense that all men had the same rights and privileges, that the racist hierarchies of nineteenth-century thought were contested. This is surely what Antenor Firmin had in mind when, in his well-known refutation of Gobineau's *De l'inégalité des races humaines,* he wrote "an invisible chain joins all the members of the human race in a common circle."[11] Equally revealing is his preface to the book of poems *Feuilles de chêne* by Paul Lochard, where Firmin praises the poet for achieving a creative anonymity: "whether in the phrasing or the sensibility, there is nothing to distinguish him from a French poet, produced from the purest blood of the Gauls."[12] Writing was closely tied to national identity and was seen as a strategy for achieving recognition in a modern global culture.

If otherness would neither be an absolute, exclusive, or homogenous notion nor yield to some bland, global monoculture, it had to be conceived in terms of a new discourse that would both contest European hegemony and yet not succumb to the mirage of cultural or racial essentialism. It is perhaps within the elaboration of this alternative discourse that literary modernism plays a vital role. In a world that is the creation of books, it may well be that through books a new self-perception needed to be elaborated. For Haitians, imperialist discourse was deployed as a strategy of representational containment. This awareness made the countercultural potential of modernism relevant. It was through modernism that Haitian writers sought to elaborate a new self-awareness, despite the fact that, from what we have seen, modernist discourse was neither transparent not neutral. The place of the Caribbean writer within modernism has attracted a significant comment from Edouard Glissant as he distinguishes between a "lived modernity" of the Caribbean and a "mature modernity" of Europe: "I wish to speak of the question of lived modernity, which I will not simply add to, but which I will link directly to the notion of a matured modernity. By this I am opposing, not a kind of 'primitivism' to a kind of 'intellectualism,' but two ways of dealing with changes in contemporary reality. . . . 'American' literature is the product of a system of modernity that is sudden and not sustained or 'evolved.' "[13] Naturally, the exposure to a modernist poetics is not uniform nor simultaneous in the Caribbean. Whereas Haiti's literary modernism is already present in the early nineteenth century, the same is not true of the hispanic Caribbean until the 1880s. In the anglophone Caribbean, the characteristics of modernist thought are not apparent until the 1930s. The complications of early Haitian nationalism emerge from the fact of its involvement with a "lived" modernity.

The evolution of early Caribbean notions of identity in Haiti can be traced through the appropriation by nineteenth-century writers of modernist thought. For instance, much early Haitian poetry, in attempting to give expression to the issue of identity, is tied to the romantic movement's sense of the power of the individual imagination and a rhetoric derived from untamed nature. There is an obvious cartographic impulse in the poetic imagination at this time; the artists are preoccupied with mapping a new space, inventing a new speech and recovering their territory.[14] This triumphant inventory of Haitian space is the dominant feature of Oswald Durand, Haiti's national bard in the mid–nineteenth century. The problem is that the Haitian space being poetically mapped by Durand had already been fixed in the modernist imagination as a utopian, bountiful world.

A Modernist "Choucoune"

The legitimacy of the new, black, American nation that Haiti represented was literally grounded in the land. The image of the *terre mère* (literally, mother land) is a trope deeply embedded in the literary and political imagination from this time. Nature as rustic space would be promoted as the guarantee of authenticity, the source of a national ethos. The representational impulse is a direct parallel of the *novela de la tierra* that emerged almost a century later in Latin America. The irony of using nature in this way is immediately apparent. Nature is used poetically because in it are perceived the harmonies, the coherence, the organicism that provided a model for the state itself. The contradiction emerges from the fear that this idea of nature owes much, if not everything, to European romanticism. Romanticism, as an early manifestation of modernism, was attractive because its values contested the legitimacy of European rationality and, by extension, its cultural hegemony. The articulation of nature as the key to authenticity, self-possession, and mastery of the national terrain is a significant feature of early nationalist thought in the Caribbean. The ground, as it were, legitimized power and speech. A nationalist discourse could be inscribed on it.

However, modernist poetics makes the process of literary grounding very problematic. Literature both explicitly elaborates this early political rhetoric as well as points to the delusions harbored by such foundational myths. From the outset, what Glissant call the "lived modernity" of Caribbean literature pushes imaginative activity toward an interrogation of the rhetoric of control and reality's ability to be permanently mastered.

Jacques Stéphen Alexis astutely points to this deconstructive impulse in romanticism in his essay on "marvelous realism." Romanticism in Haiti is about new beginnings. "Romanticism is revolutionary in the sense that it understands that nothing is eternal, . . . that one can always transcend the grandiose acquisitions of the past by relocating man in his social milieu and in his experience of nature, by clarifying the contradictory character of human consciousness."[15]

To this extent, much Haitian literature, and ultimately Caribbean literature as a whole, functions as a critique of authoritarian discourse and systems of domination. If literature served the function of critical consciousness in nineteenth-century Haiti, an examination of what is seen as the greatest literary monument to Haitian nationalism in the nineteenth century, Oswald Durand's "Choucoune," might prove revealing. Celebrated by some as the first successful attempt to write poetry in Haitian creole, ignored by others because ultimately it survives as a popular song, "Choucoune" can be read as an early insight into the crisis of representation that would haunt postromantic modernist thought.

Much of Durand's poetry can be interpreted as an unproblematic literary extension of the political rhetoric of the early Haitian state. His poetic rhetoric owed much to Victor Hugo, who was the first of many French artists to be closely associated with Haitian literature. Durand repeatedly declared his pride in celebrating the beauty of the Haitian countryside. Perhaps one should say the *beauties* of the Haitian countryside, because this was an invariably feminized hinterland that yielded willingly to his poetic embrace. Durand's collection of poems, *Rires et pleurs* (1896), is filled with sensual odalisques—incarnations of a well-endowed, fertile motherland. In this regard, "Choucoune" seems unexceptional. As Fleischman points out in the only extended explication of the poem, it owes much to the tradition of the pastoral and to the related stereotypes of the idyllic countryside.[16] This is an important point because, paradoxically, conventions of the pastoral and chivalric romance would haunt Haitian indigenism into the twentieth century. The latter would see Durand as a precursor, partly because of his poetic exploration of the Haitian pastoral.

Read allegorically, "Choucoune" transcends the naive celebration of the burgeoning Haitian countryside evident in *Rires et pleurs*. It enacts Durand's most extreme effort to tame the Haitian muse as well as being a telling admission of poetic failure. In the internal drama played out in the poem, there emerges not only the problematic nature of the land itself but also a keen sense of the boundaries of poetic rhetoric. "Choucoune" is a poem of thwarted love: the male artist courts the peasant girl, but she resists his amorous attentions, which are expressed in what he takes to be her language, for a French-speaking foreigner. The dramatic, sexual tensions evident in this poem would later become a literary commonplace during the U.S. occupation; the plots of a number of texts turned on the relationship between a local militant, an embattled female, and an English-speaking intruder.

From the outset, the sexual characteristics of Choucoune (the girl) are highly visible.

Choucounce ce gnou marabout:
z'yeux li claire com'chandelle
Li gagnin tete doubout.

(Choucoune is a marabout:
her eyes shine like candles
She has firm breasts.)

Her sexuality is further emphasized as her mouth is compared to a purple star apple (*caimite*) and her shape is described as plump (*gressett*). The erotic dimension is accentuated by making her a marabout—in Haiti a woman with flowing hair and dark skin. Perhaps this also suggests a view of the Haitian hinterland as a synthesis of pre-Columbian and African ethnic types. The honest intentions of the poetic persona are signaled as the poet approaches Choucoune's mother and offers to marry her daughter. Yet the denouement of the poem is a sad one as Choucoune is seduced by a French-speaking white male, derisively called a "petit blanc." She becomes pregnant by him. At the end, the poet's love, however, remains constant, despite the idyll's having been destroyed.

The claims made for "Choucoune" as a successful literary use of creole notwithstanding, the evocation of language relations in the poem is not at all simple. A Freudian reading would certainly suggest the poet's oedipal need to return to the mother and a mothering tongue that is frustrated by the intrusive, male, fathering tongue of French. The detailed inventory of objects for the matrimonial home that houses the suitor and his beloved, the poet and language, does indicate the desire to restore some primal bond. Interestingly, all the poet is left with at the end is birdsong, a natural music that mocks both his emotional and linguistic failures. More than just a simple lament to thwarted love in rural Haiti, "Choucoune" betrays a deeper critical consciousness of the limitations of a prevalent nationalist script. It certainly alludes to the polyphonous quality of Caribbean reality as a seductive yet silent reality that is courted in creole speech, lyrical poetic discourse, and metropolitan French. Even though the indigenous world is mute, it is not passive or inert. Choucoune's choice, though a tragic one, since the product of the relationship is destined to be in chains, is one that reveals a kind of inscrutable independence. Perhaps the poet's incapacity to produce a happy synthesis reveals the problematic nature of the proprietary rights of poetic language, even in creole, to claim the landscape as a submissively homogeneous entity. Arguably, in the critical consciousness of the artist there emerged an interrogation of privilege and authority that were narrowly defined in political, economic, and sexual terms in nineteenth-century Haiti.

In suggesting the difficulty of a seamless fusion between reality and its expression, between the corporeal hinterland and male authority, Durand's poem reveals an early poetic intuition into the conflicts between a modernist literary practice and the authoritarian nation-state that would henceforth mark Haitian literature. This uneasy relationship between a transgressive poetics in imaginative activity and the political rhetoric of closure and control is deeply inscribed in the culture of the other America as a whole. Already we see in Durand the tentative beginnings of a demystifying process that, without providing an alternative, undermines the possibility of absolute possession of that telluric mother, the Haitian landscape. It is only within the modernist space of this fictive encounter between creole, French, and silence, urban, foreign, and rural, that this crucial skepticism would be raised. The dangers of posing this kind of question, outside of the fictive space, are evident in the fate of Durand's contemporary, the poet and military officer Massillon Coicou, who was executed in 1908.

If "Choucoune" hints at the drama of the reluctant referent, poets at the turn of the century would force this issue into the open. The severing of literary discourse from political rhetoric is dramatic in the generation of poets who followed Durand. The anxieties of "Choucoune" become a full-blown skepticism in the late nineteenth century. Both the foundational myth deriving legitimacy from the docile referent of nature and the conception of language as a tool of appropriation lose currency in the *La Ronde* movement, which contested the possibility between expression and reality, signs and things.

A Caribbean Fin de Siècle

In our discussion of Durand's "Choucoune," the poem is seen as a literary text that stages the conflicts provoked by the instability of metaphor. This role played by the artistic text becomes even more emphatic as literary modernism becomes more boldly experimental toward the end of the century. At this time, the imagination functions

as a radically subversive space where the representational bonds between referent and its expression are disrupted, where Haitian topography undergoes a cognitive remapping, where the self becomes a
very problematic terrain, and where an asphyxiatingly local, closed
discourse yields to more open possibilities.

Such a view of imaginative activity in the Caribbean at the turn of
the century has met with resistance from some literary critics and historians, who tend to dismiss much of this writing as gratuitously apolitical. The charge invariably leveled at turn-of-the-century writers is
that of cosmopolitanism, which was seen as neither an anticolonial
nor an emancipatory posture. Cosmopolitanism was frequently re-
viled as decadent and elitist, especially by the *noiriste* school of criticism that followed the U.S. occupation. One of the best known of
these critiques of *La Ronde* was by Henock Trouillot, who described
these writings as "littérature d'evasion" (escapist writing) in his *Les
origines sociales de la littérature haitienne.*[17]

This attitude is generally echoed in historical accounts of turn-of-
the-century Haiti and of the Caribbean in general. Haiti is treated as
debt-ridden and chronically unstable and this period tended to be
seen as a painful transition between emancipation from slavery and
the emergent nationalism after World War I. Little attempt is made to
investigate literary movements and intellectual concerns of the turn
of the century. Yet, in Haiti, a Caribbean-based modernism had
begun to react against a narrow parochialism in Haiti's intellectual
culture and to eschew the crude referentiality of early nationalistic
verse. Fresh ideas were sweeping the Americas at this time. Efforts to
redefine a new geographical space, to modernize literary activity, and
to establish a new hemispheric solidarity were apparent, in Haiti's
Antenor Firmin as in Cuba's José Martí or Latin America's Jose Enrique
Rodó and Rubén Dario. It is, perhaps, the very open-endedness of these
ideas that makes them suspicious to historians, some of whom describe *La Ronde* as the product of a betraying intellectual class who
were, in the words of Brenda Plummer, "prisoners of their cosmopolitan outlook."[18]

It is not that the turn of the century was not a period of great turbulence and economic uncertainty in Haiti. There was certainly a
major change in the imperialist presence in the Caribbean. France, its
naval power severely limited, steadily reduced its activities in the
Caribbean. In this void, Germany and the United States became more
brashly aggressive. The constant threat of U.S. imperialism in the

Caribbean in particular as well as that nation's remarkable economic development form an important backdrop to intellectual activity at the end of the century. The enviable material progress of the United States meant that Europe would fade as a symbol of modernity. American expansionism, however, would provoke among many a desire to cling to a European heritage. The Latin heritage of Latin America was used as a tactic to keep U.S. materialism at bay, at least intellectually. Rodó's "Arielism" fulfills this need as much as José Martí's concept of *nuestra America* (our America), which is an early articulation of what Glissant would later call *l'autre Amerique*. Martí's revival of the idea of America as a new, regenerative space is not unrelated to his friend Antenor Firmin's theorizing a Caribbean federation and a Pan-Americanism in his *Lettres de St. Thomas* (1910). These ideas of regional and hemispheric partnership are both a reaction against the U.S. hegemony as well as a departure from narrowly nationalistic ideals.

What is important here is the extent to which the new spatial theorizing of a Martí or Firmin becomes possible because of the transformation taking place in imaginative activity at the same time. Identity formation began to be shaped by a modernist suspicion of systems of totalizing and an exploration of a more unstable and interactive constitution of the subject. Plurality, indeterminacy, and heterogeneity now emerge as an enabling discourse that facilitates new, open-ended ideological formations. Iris Zavala affirms this view when she observes that "as a discursive entity, 'Our America' designates the production of the subject on the basis of the chain of its discourses, in the openness of the social and therefore by the unfixed or unfinalized nature of the national and identity construct."[19] If "dialogism," as Zavala claims, is symptomatic of Caribbean ideological discourse at the turn of the century, a similarly emancipatory impulse should be apparent in the contemporary creative imagination. Then what has been criticized as an apolitical formalism in *La Ronde* can be recuperated as a form of critical consciousness that both problematizes earlier pieties and reacts to freshly revealed contingencies of the time. Cosmopolitanism has its imaginative roots in the spirit of errancy and nomadism generated by a sense of groundlessness.

The period between the 1880s and the landing of U.S. marines in 1915 witnessed in Haiti the collapse of the dream of the progressive modern state of the early post independence years. The economic consequences of a fall in coffee earnings, the penetration of foreign capital, and the collapses of both the liberal and national parties open the way to brutal political rivalries and the emergence of a pattern of peasant insurrections and militarism in public life. The rebellions of landless peasants, called Cacos, and the machinations of commercial interests with political ambitions contributed to a state of chronic instability. This made for a state of anarchy by 1915 that presented an excuse for foreign intervention.

In both a literal and figurative way, Haitian space had become devalued. Nationalist discourse and the grounding of such a discourse in Haitian reality were now seriously contested. Haiti as political and social entity without common ground inevitably had a significant impact on imaginative activity that had traditionally grounded identity in the Haitian landscape. This governing trope in the literary imagination could no longer be sustained in depressing, unpredictable, fin de siècle Haiti. Indeed, the dominant feature in much writing at this time is an exploration of groundlessness, in that the Haitian ground could no longer guarantee an old referential validity for the Haitian writer.

The psychodrama that was glimpsed in Durand's poem became a fully developed skepticism in the movement of *La Ronde,* which fiercely advocated an eclecticism in the arts, as the name implies, and criticized earlier writers for succumbing to a referential fallacy in the use of nature for local color. Etzer Vilaire, one of the major voices of *La Ronde,* spoke of the need to eschew a crude referentiality. Nationalism, he felt, had blinded some Haitian writers to the fact that failure was inevitable for anyone who sought "a purely local, narrow and banal realism."[20] A few years later Seymour Pradel, writing in the *Haiti Littéraire et Scientifique,* also criticized writers for resorting to "an irritating, monotonous, unchanging ground."[21]

It is impossible to overlook the role of French symbolism in the poetics of *La Ronde.* The death of Victor Hugo in 1885 could be said to have ushered in a new era of symbolistic aesthetics. However, the aesthetics of absence as advocated by Stéphane Mallarmé and his contemporaries had a special resonance in Haiti, given the specific nature of the Haitian literary and political situation. This engagement with radical modernism would be repeated throughout Haitian literary history, whether the movement be surrealism, Marxism, existentialism, or postmodernism. At the turn of the century, symbolism opened up the possibility of an interrogation of space, nation, exile, and poetic language itself. These questions had been raised internally in

Haiti because of the experiences of the nineteenth century and the tradition of skepticism that had begun to manifest itself in the literary imagination.

The problematic nature of the Haitian ground is even apparent in the Haitian novelists of the time, who were normally opposed to the poets of *La Ronde*.[22] The novelists Frédéric Marcelin, Antoine Innocent, and Justin Lherisson are rightly credited with beginning a tradition of regionalism in the peasant novel. The reality of a landless peasantry and a heartland of political strife made nature a problematic terrain for these writers.

It was no longer the zone of local color fostered by the early poets. The erotics of Haitian landscape are not apparent in these novels because social conscience did not permit rural Haiti to be represented as a locale where an idyllic *amour courtois* could be practiced. Egalitarian and liberal in impulse, these novels both monitored the defects of the authoritarian state and unmasked the pastoral countryside, revealing stagnation and backwardness. Marcelin saw that the peasantry had become "cannon fodder for our appetites . . . playthings in our wretched quarrels."[23] This suggests, at the very least, a cognitive remapping of the hinterland and a view of the peasant not as an object of appropriation but as a subject worthy of recognition.

The same impulse provoked a deeper subversion of spatial representation in the contemporary poetry. The poets sought openness in their works that went beyond a mere revaluation of the mimetic impulse to see the text itself as a nonreferential space within which imaginative freedom could be guaranteed. The noncorporeal nature of this space is evident in poems that no longer celebrate female exoticism. For instance, the impossibility of creating a gendered space to facilitate the ideal of poetic mastery in Edmond Laforest's "Ombres dans l'ombre" (Shadows in the shadow):

Where then go these floating
slow female forms
like formless vapor
which are thick flakes
of shadow, dark mists.[24]

Reality had lost an earlier plenitude and was now represented as elusive and inscrutable.

An aesthetic that is not foundational and not grounded allows for outward spreading and a new range of interactive possibilities. The issue of exile as a creative poetic state is raised by *La Ronde,* perhaps for the first time in Caribbean literature. The old, romantic idea of the author housed within a community and language was now yielding to an aesthetic errancy indicated in the belief in eclecticism and cosmopolitanism. Words had been debased and stolen by political rhetoric. The writer's job was one of linguistic renovation, subversion, and translation. The crisis of representation at the turn of the century could allow for a new, interdiscursive, heteroglossic literary space. It is no coincidence that translation should be so important to one member of this generation, Georges Sylvain. Sylvain was both the author of a conventional collection of poems in French, *Confidences et Mélancolies,* and the translation into the creole of La Fontaine's *Fables,* both published in the same year, 1901. The possibility of a literary use of what is called this "maternal idiom" (*idiome maternel*) and the need for a body of works in creole are suggested in the preface to *Cric-Crac.*[25]

Whereas there was admittedly, a tendency in some of the turn-of-the-century poets to an etherealizing of poetic space, it is also true to say that the possibility of new, polyphonic possibilities was also beginning to be raised. The construction of a new collectivity is implied in Sylvain's shift from French to creole, from poems to fables. The poet as a translator seems crucial to this new transgeneric and translinguistic activity. Commentators on José Martí's ideas point to remarkably similar features. For instance, the ideal of an autochthonous creolization (*mestizaje autochtono*) is advanced by Martí in a style that Gordon Lewis describes as "combining Castilian Spanish with New World vocabulary" in a manner "uniquely American."[26] The same point is reinforced by Zavala, when she claims that "the force and originality of Martí's perception is that he suggests the incorporation of all cultural voices (each individual nature, each psyche) to embody the cultural polyphony of being at once plural with many ethnic roots."[27]

Not unpredictably, the self-certain subject is not evident in this verse. The representational crisis in *La Ronde* creates a poetic self that is absent or embattled. This is the unavoidable consequence of a general sense of the slipperiness of language and identity at this time. The poetic self has difficulty maintaining wholeness in a poetic space fissured by chasms (*abimes*) and gulfs (*gouffres*). This is a psychic world of hallucination and vertigo from which escape, temporary, if possible at all, is measured in terms of Vilaire's "Vastitudes," flight or the ultimate disappearance into *azure*. Perfidious ground, however, more often than not leaves the poet in a state of depressing perplexity. "My life is a funereal mirror and reflects / In a lugubrious space, a weeping phantom."[28] "Oh my god! What am I? / The land is so completely strange to me."[29]

The strange land, the phantom self, and a poetics of absence are the characteristics of *La Ronde* that make the movement so abhorrent to nativist ideologies. Efforts by the defenders of *La Ronde* to celebrate the artistic achievement of these poets in patriotic terms have also missed the special nature of the poetic adventure inaugurated at the turn of the century. Alain Ramire is perfectly correct when he declares, "Let us be perfectly clear: it is hardly important to know whether the poets of *La Ronde* were escapist or nationalist."[30] The true importance of this movement lies in its recognition of the problematic nature of literature and the inability to pursue a foundational poetics in Haitian literature. The silences, doubts, and hesitations of these poets open the possibility of a new creative space in the literary imagination. Unfortunately, as Ramire points out, these poets were men of their time; their aspirations were conventional. It is their sense of failure and their inability to fulfill the role of poet as privileged interlocutor that are instructive.

Modernism, by the end of the nineteenth century, had created in Haiti a creatively shattering crisis in the literary imagination. This meant that earlier strategies of representational containment manifested in the mapping of the Haitian countryside were seen as false. The consequences of this radically new intuition were neither merely formal nor apolitical. The possibility of any mastery or appropriation of the Haitian ground by either local elites or by foreign imperialists was raised as a major theoretical issue. To this extent, one should not be surprised at the later interest in *La Ronde* by the first generation of Haitian writers to contest Duvalierism. The group Haiti Littéraire saw Edmond Laforest and Etzer Vilaire as precursors largely because of their shared experience of the distortions of Haitian space created by a demagogic political discourse.[31] Similarly, no one should have difficulty understanding the role of Vilaire in anti–United States activities after 1915. The Occupation was predicated on a particular imperialist mapping of Haitian reality that drew on a fetischistic alterity.

The manifestation of Caribbean modernism has, in this regard, structural and formal differences from the practice of symbolism in

Europe. In fact, the real affinity with *La Ronde* can be found in the other America. It was difficult to replicate the intensity of the poetic and political crisis in Haiti in other parts of the Caribbean. The same sense of territoriality is not a major issue outside of Haiti since the need to assert a national origin, an authentic space, or a local pantheon of heroes is not yet the case elsewhere; therefore, the subversive force of *La Ronde*'s skepticism could not be provoked in the region by a poetics of national resistance. The only similar instance would be Cuba after the events of 1895. Nevertheless, in the early poetry of St. John Perse we find a similar rethinking of the cartographic impulse to conceive of nature as space to be mastered.

Glissant has done so much to alert us to the importance of St. John Perse as a vital presence in Caribbean literature. Perse's early poetry is a special echo of the concerns of *La Ronde* in its desire to unmask the text as final utterance and to evoke reality as an unknowable sea of possibility. Perse seems to have been equally sensitive to the poet's inability to synthesize space or turn nature into a poetic system. In *Caribbean Discourse,* Glissant notes the recurrence of "rotting vegetable matter."[32] The experience of space in Perse's work reveals a kind of salutary instability in Glissant's view, as he speaks of "the porous warmth of *Eloges,* the layered opacity of *Anabase,* the liquid space of *Exil.*[33] Derek Walcott, in praising Perse's early poetry, refers to the poet as unoriginally original in his openness to all discourse as opposed to a defiant rejection of intertextuality.[34]

Perse's sense of poetic space as interdiscursive has clear implications for the assertion of a coherent, stable poetic persona. The use of a nom de plume points to the importance of an interest in masking for the poet. The use of poetic personae such as Crusoe and the dialogue of voices in *Exil* point to the poem as a heteroglossic site allowing for an interplay of discourses. The pervasive site for poetic utterance is the sand—neither land nor sea but a mediating threshold. In such a space, writing itself is threatened constantly by erasure; hence, the notion of the *poème délébile* (erasable poem).

Ultimately, it is Perse's concept of the sea itself as a metaphor of human experience (*la commune mer*) that reveals the poet's fascination with the world as unstable, interdiscursive space. The sea represents the unstable referent, an ever-shifting space that refuses a totalizing or authoritarian discourse. Inscrutable, all-encompassing, the sea is introduced poetically in Caribbean poetry not simply in terms of formal innovation but as an interrogation of reality's ability to guarantee verisimilitude. We have in Perse an imaginative and epistemological rupture with the tradition of tropical exoticism in the French Caribbean. Perse's new experiments in representation, like the new, spatial language of his Haitian contemporaries, are of great importance in a Caribbean still mapped in terms of European colonization.

Turn-of-the-century Caribbean modernism meant a departure from the monologic, totalizing discourse of imperialism, whether expressed in terms of European colonialism or North American expansionism. The poetic imagination asserted a world that defied conventional representation and whose heterogeneity could not be domesticated and reduced to an undifferentiating sameness. Zavala notices the same pattern in turn-of-the-century modernists in the hispanic Caribbean.

> This emancipatory narrative is organized through diverse combinations in order to present a conjunctural unitary form based on geographical, ethnic and social diversity, in a truly heteroglossic construct. Within this multiple social formation, the past is questioned through both negations and affirmations, which in turn raise new questions about representation and reality. Sign and referent dissociate and distance themselves from the past, its norms and institutions, against the belief of a reliable, fixed, unproblematic reality.[35]

In conceptualizing the region as new, modern space, a new poetics of imaginative resistance was launched in the Caribbean. Not each manifestation of this imaginative configuration of the Caribbean was explicitly political. Yet it can be argued that the imaginative constructs of *La Ronde* that are echoed in Perse find political expression in the ideas of such thinkers as Puerto Rico's Betances, Haiti's Firmin, or Cuba's Martí. Zavala, in discussing turn-of-the-century modernism and Martí's idea of "our America," describes them as based on a "chain of discourses" and as an early discursive formulation of "the poetics of negation . . . directed against centered and centralizing histories and cultures."[36] Radical poetics and radical politics are, in Zavala's view, inextricably linked.

In an attempt to define a new space outside of the colonial system of relations, whether aesthetic or political, Caribbean intellectuals began to theorize new interdiscursive notions such as *criollismo, antillanismo,* or a new American identity. Hemispheric mappings of identity at this time were based on the belief in the uniquely mestizo nature of Caribbean society. This utopian impulse that projects a vision of collective modernity nourished by modernist poetics lost momentum in the twentieth century as the inequality of economic development and the expansion of North American capitalism undermined the sense of hemispheric patrimony. Also, *mestizaje* itself became frozen into a stable synthesis, so much so that Gordon Lewis would later argue that the ideal of Americanism became emptied "of any real, lasting content. It grew to be politically reactionary in its 'art for art's sake' bias, dreaming of democracy ruled by the artist, with his supposed superiority or feeling."[37]

The Pan-Caribbean and Pan-American cartographies of the fin de siècle that had begun to interest artists and intellectuals would yield to another sense of spatial representation—one that was not intertextual and open-ended but that theorized a Caribbean "heterocosm." An original presence outside the reach of both encroaching imperialism or any dialogic relationship was envisaged by a new generation of writers who were resorting to "the single most persistent and seductive of romantic tropes: the organicist ideas of art as a kind of second nature, a 'heterocosm' where all evil antinomies fall away and the imagination achieves a perfect union of subject and object, inner and outer worlds."[38] This Rousseauesque idealism would be at the heart of much of the nationalist, indigenist, Marxist, and *noiriste* politics of the next few decades. This subsequent phase in the mapping of the Caribbean was itself another manifestation of the crisis of representation that was deeply entrenched in the region's literary traditions from the preceding century.[39]

3

Orphic Explanations: Toward a Caribbean Heterocosm

Adamic, elemental man cannot be existential. His first impulse
was not self-indulgence but awe.

—Derek Walcott, "The Muse of History"

A Poetics of *Verrition*

Modernity first manifested itself in the Caribbean
with independent Haiti's utopian dream of technological progress. Modernity was an emancipatory discourse. It signaled the end of the oppressive hierarchies of the Old World and the
recognition of a New American spatiality. These demystifying and
cosmopolitan possibilities in both the ideology of modernity and the
poetics of modernism do not survive intact in the twentieth century.
The dialogic modernism of the turn of the century yields to a new
Caribbean theorizing of the modern, which is not future-oriented but
built around an unearthing of a mythical past or an Adamic self. This
new fantasy of emancipation was theorized outside of history and
disregarded the earlier ideal of an integrated yet diverse American
collectivity.

Radical poetics in the 1930s centered on an organicist dream of
the union between man and nature—an "existentialist" bonding, to
use Walcott's terminology, that was monologic, lyrical, and celebrated the primacy of the transcendental subject. Whereas in the
nineteenth century national identity was fashioned in terms of notions

of progress and participation in the mainstream of New World culture, nationalist movements in the early twentieth century were Rousseauesque in their reactions against what was seen as inhibiting and alienating materialism. Modern technology, in particular, and the spirit of rationality, in general, became so closely and negatively associated with the horrors of World War I and North American expansionism that Caribbean modernism invented a radical poetics based on an integration with a lost organic totality.

Caribbean negritude, indigenism, and even Marxism all shared an ideal of communion with a natural primordial world that was opposed to what was seen as the degenerate Western modernity. The theoretical work that most clearly articulates this phase of Caribbean modernism is a somewhat overlooked essay by Aimé Césaire, "Poetry and Knowledge." James Arnold, in his introduction to the English translation of this essay, describes it as "a rapid overview of modernism in France" and "positively mainstream as a reading of the modern tradition in French poetry."[1] Césaire's hypothesis in this essay is, to all appearances, a repetition of the antirationalist rhetoric of the surrealist movement. It is also overshadowed by the essay *Orphée Noir* (*Black Orpheus*), in which Sartre, four years later, provided the basis for a definition for the negritude movement. Surprisingly, Aimé Césaire, the founding father of negritude, never once mentions the word *negritude* in this essay, which was read as a paper in Haiti—the land where, he once declared, "negritude stood up for the first time." Perhaps, just as Césaire in his *Cahier d'un retour au pays natal* sought to remind Martiniquans of the Caribbean's revolutionary legacy, in Haiti he was reminding his public of the legacy of Caribbean modernism. The politics of "Poetry and Knowledge" are explicit. The political version of this text would appear in the 1955 essay *Discours sur le colonialisme* (published in English as *Discourse on Colonialism*).[2] Yet it is difficult to avoid seeing in Césaire's indictment of Apollonian reason and the inadequacies of scientific materialism an indirect comment on the domination of the northern Caribbean by the United States. By 1944, Haiti had been occupied, Puerto Rico was annexed, and Cuba and the Dominican Republic were under U.S. control. Theoretically, Césaire's paper delivered in September 1944 was no different from the speech given by André Breton in Port-au-Prince at the Rex Cinema in December 1945; Césaire, however, was less interested in the mysticism of Haitian *vaudou* and the practice of the occult.

With Césaire, Caribbean modernism takes on another mask. The mask of plurality and cultural interrelating is removed and a new Caribbean otherness is theorized. What emerges is a poetics of origination—of an elemental Caribbean space outside of time, history, and discourse. In "Poetry and Knowledge," Césaire is articulating, as the title of the essay states, a poetic way of knowing what represents a new beginning—one in which poetry itself is the foundational word and a prelapsarian innocence can be established. Césaire is arguably suggesting in 1944 that the Caribbean and Anglo-Saxon America represent two irreconcilably different notions of culture and human development.

Rather than a rehash of the rhetoric of the European avant-garde, "Poetry and Knowledge" is both profoundly Caribbean and American in its engagement with the problematics of an American identity and the impulse to define a defiant Caribbean other. Césaire's definition of the otherness can be seen as an elaboration of an idea that first emerged in Caribbean poetry in the work of Léon-Gontran Damas of French Guyana. Damas's *Pigments* contains early fantasies of establishing a primal innocence outside of history, discourse, and language itself. Damas's veneration of feeling and expressivity led him to imagine a world of pure presences, a prelapsarian void in which the ideal of being *nègre* could be preserved. For Damas, it is the poet's orphic capacity to reanimate feeling that must be recovered in the face of the distortions of rationality, history, and progress. *Pigments* is a desperate appeal for the emergence of a natural voice of otherness.

"Poetry and Knowledge" is at once an attack on the epistemological deficiency of scientific knowledge and a celebration of a world stripped of contradictions and accumulated experiences. It is about an apocalyptic self-invention, a radical other who, while breaking with an older tradition of modernity and fleeing the oppression of modernization, founds a new, original reality. The negation of history and the return to a primordial time before time is central to a Césarean poetics. This is why the question of knowledge as a closed, rational, authoritative discourse is the target of his 1944 paper.

What is being described by Césaire is an aesthetic of erasure, cancellation. It is not surprising, therefore, that the word *negritude* does not feature in the essay. The definition of negritude as poetics and a politics would be left to Senghor and Sartre, respectively. Césaire's reluctance to theorize or systematize the idea of negritude stems from the need to achieve some kind if ulterior innocence.[3] The magical re-conquest of purity as opposed to the recognition of contact and plu-rality is fundamental to a Césarean poetics and to this particular manifestation of Caribbean modernism.

Césaire's best-known neologism is the word *negritude,* but, ar-guably, his more revealing verbal formulation is the last word of his *Cahier d'un retour au pays natal.* The invented word *verrition* that brings Césaire's epic poem to a startling conclusion is a clear signal of the poetics of erasure that haunts all of Césaire's work. This obscure and suggestive term has an importance that few have understood.[4] It is central to the persistent dream of beginning again—to the impor-tance of invention, "the drive to invent our own way and to rid it of ready made models" that is key to his later resignation from the Com-munist Party (October 1956).[5] In the best translation of Césaire's long poem, the translators Eshelman and Smith give us an important clue to the meaning of this strange, latinate coinage in their introduc-tion. As they reveal in their introduction to the collected poems, "only Césaire himself was in a position to reveal (in a private communica-tion) that 'verrition' . . . had been coined on a Latin verb 'verri,' meaning to sweep, to scrape a surface, and ultimately to scan."[6]

At the end of the *Cahier d'un retour au pays natal,* Césaire invokes "la langue maléfique de la nuit" (the malevolent tongue of the night) that will sweep all before it. The reference here is clearly to the erup-tion of Mount Pelée, which in 1902 destroyed the town of St. Pierre in one explosive night. The fiery tongue of the volcano destroys past relations, stops time, and grounds the possibility of a new space. In this new Caribbean beginning imagined by Césaire, the volcano ut-ters a new world. A new man, a new way of seeing, would, in Cé-saire's utopian vision, be founded on this violent upheaval. *Verrition* is the founding neologism of the new order envisaged by Césaire. Its very artificial nature points to the fact that it would not be grounded in the languages French or Creole; that is, it would not be contami-nated by history. The magical retrieval of purity is inscribed in the ob-scure newness of this invented word.

The close identification of Promethean poet and privileged vol-cano, of founding word and violent upheaval, is clearly stated in the modernist poetics of "Poetry and Knowledge." Early in this essay, Césaire refers to the Adamic ideal of primal innocence that is funda-mental to poetic knowledge. "I even believe that mankind has never been closer to certain truths than in the first days of the species. At the time when mankind discovered with emotion the first sun, the first rain, the first breath, the first moon. At the time when mankind discovered in fear and rapture the throbbing newness of the world."[7] This vision of wonder, exploration, discovery—of a "throbbing newness" before the fall of history, reason, and ideology—is the consequence of the cleansing power of "verrition." Césaire here imagines his heterocosm outside of the contradictions of historical change and the plurality of contact and interaction. Césaire's formulation is impervious to metamorphosis. This almost religious vision is paradoxical, to say the least, coming from someone who was at the time a member of the Communist Party. Césaire's vision represents the other face of Caribbean modernism. His poetry glorifies the nontraditional other in the form of the madman:

> Because we hate you
> and your reason, we claim kinship
> with dementia praecox with the flaming
> madness of persistent cannibalism.[8]

Elsewhere it is the timeless gaze of the child that represents emergence from the purifying flames of the night:

> The night on fire the night untied the dream coerced
> the fire that restores to us the horizon
> of water outrageous to be sure
> a child will half-open the door.[9]

But ultimately, the most potent agent of the transformation, the most idealized transgressive other, is nature itself. The triumph envisaged is that of the primal forest over the machine. It is the destructive force of nature as nonrational other that facilitates Césaire's nostalgia for a time before the time of "the precious vortex: the ego, the id, the world. All the most extraordinary contacts: all the pasts, all the futures."[10]

To the despairing vision of Martinique as a "land without a stele," voiced early in the *Cahier*, Césaire's answer is the blazing monument of the volcano. The ultimate explosive other that can voice the "screams erect in the mute earth" is the symbolic recreation of Mount Pelée as the source of *verrition*. In a revealing admission during an interview with the Guadeloupean novelist Daniel Maximin,

Césaire declares "I always have the feeling that we are born from the mountain, we are born from the volcano. We are the sons of the volcano. I tend to say that if I wish to situate the Martiniquan people, I would say that they are the Peléen people."[11] The volcano then becomes the monumental stele, the upright fire by which an old order is erased and where a new order originates.

The only degree of explosive otherness that the restless poet finds satisfactory is the violent conclusion of the volcano. "Poetry and Knowledge" is unequivocal on this question. The purifying and creative force of natural cataclysm is associated with the poet: "So pregnant with the world, the poet speaks." "In the beginning was the word." "Never did a man believe it more powerfully than poet."[12] The explosive, vegetable uprightness of the poet is advanced in this essay as the salvation of mankind: "But one man is the salvation of humanity, one man puts humanity back in the universal concert, one man unties the human flowering with universal flowering; that man is the poet . . . he has rooted himself in the earth, he has stretched out his arms, he has played with the sun, he has become a tree: he has blossomed, he has sung.[13] As Keith Walker has demonstrated, Césaire's poetry bristles with explosive trees, as the rush of lava or sap creates the possibility of a new eruption of blossoms.[14] Perhaps, the most dramatic example of this explosive *Profession de foi* is the poem "Les pur-sang" (The thoroughbreds), in which the poet-plant-volcano utters "the poet's word, the primal word; rupestral design in the stuff of sound."

> I grow like a plant
> . . . .
> My feet follow the morning meandering
> plant
> my woody limbs circulate strange saps
> plant plant
>
> And I speak
> and my word is peace
> and I speak and my word is earth.[15]

Césaire's poetry does not so much proclaim an ideology as summon a world of otherness into existence. The transforming and purifying force of the volcano releases new possibilities. In the Césarean heterocosm, the new "lemurian being," the yet "undared form," is produced.[16] This new cosmos is ultimately a new mapping—"the world map made for my use"[17] and "the map of spring . . . always to be drawn again."[18] This cartographic impulse that, as we have seen, is fundamental to a modernist poetics is aimed at rejecting the colonialist or imperialist map as a strategy of containment and repression. It also envisages the invention of a new system of representation in which what was unknowable or disfigured in a repressive system of knowledge is given a new prominence in Césaire's new, poetic mapping. However, spatial perceptions in Césaire's new poetry are not by any means the same as those of the end of the nineteenth century. Césaire's new cartography is Adamic—to the same degree that the earlier Caribbean mappings were cosmopolitan, nomadic, and plural.

The *Cahier* serves ultimately as a map that releases the colonial world, through the poetics of *verrition*, from an imperialist vision of closure. It is this rediscovery of a primordial order of things that allows Césaire's poetic cosmos to relate to the rest of the world. Césaire himself has rejected the charge that his imagery is hermetic and idiosyncratic by stating that "all images can be reduced to *primordial images*, which—incrusted in the collective unconscious—are universal, as the language of dreams proves, identical in all peoples beyond the variety of languages and forms of life. Deep down, and the West has no longer forgotten this, the image is the true universal language."[19]

By his own admission, Césaire is not interested in what he seems to see as the surface diversity of language. This lack of interest in linguistic specificity also applies to the poet's conception of the prediscursive nature of the image, outside of historical process, cultural contact, or any pressures of circumstance.[20] The notion of the image as primordial utterance, as a deep-seated universalist syntax, leads Césaire to theorize a poetics based not on diversity but invariance. The poet's task is to plumb the depths of the vital language. Poetry is then reduced to a totalizing code, a closed primordial system that underlies the dissimilarities and complexities that make cultures and languages apparently opaque to each other. Much of the argument of "Poetry and Knowledge" turns on the conception of the poetic image as prerational, universal code. Again and again, Césaire claims that it eliminates contradictions: "the dialectic of the image transcends antinomies" and "when the sun of the image reaches its zenith . . . [a]ccursed complexes dissolve."[21] Poetry, to paraphrase Césaire, is the algebra that generates truth, that makes the world pure, that reveals "the buried knowledge of the ages." Nondiachronic, immutable, poetic expression is a kind of metalanguage.

If this universalizing and reductionist view is true of Césairean language as a whole, it is particularly so in relation to the image of fire, which is a centripetal force in Césaire's poetic universe. The idealizing of the upright fire of the volcano, with its potent, cleansing force permeates Césaire's imagination and forms the link with a politics of violent change. Gaston Bachelard has some perceptive words on the psychology of fire imagery in *La psychanalyse du feu:* "Fire suggests the wish to change, to accelerate time, to bring all life to a conclusion, to its beyond. Then fantasy is truly fascinating and dramatic; it amplifies human destiny; it links the small to the large, the hearth to the volcano, the life of a log in the flames to the life of a world. The fascinated being hears the call of the pyre. For him destruction is more than a change, it is a renewal."[22] In the destructive and reconstructive appeal of the image of fire, we can locate the political implications of a Césarean aesthetic. The poetic word's potential for transforming the world, for producing a new truth (verity is implied in the neologism *verrition*) implies a capacity for action. Césaire's poetry is never contemplative or mimetic but intervenes and invents reality. In Césaire's poetry, however, the force of change is closely associated with the forces of nature. Césaire stoically awaits the explosive liberation of the volcano, and in his later poems this trust in the forces of nature, in what he terms the "calendar of the lagoon" (*calendrier lagunaire*) remains implicit.[23]

Not all who followed Césaire's aesthetic of *verrition* would exhibit the same patient wait for the new utopian order, the idealized heterocosm. Fanon, perhaps, remains closest in sensibility to the poetics of Césaire.[24] His revolutionary calendar does not follow the rhythm of nature but is more disruptive. There has been some attempt to recreate a sanitized version of Fanon in recent times. Edward Said, in his study of imperialist domination and cultures of resistance, *Culture and Imperialism,* focuses on Fanon's theory of national liberation though violent upheaval. Fanon is very much the sung hero of Said's work. Said is very aware of Fanon's conception of imperialist discourse as Manichean and closed. To this extent, the closed codes of rationality attacked in "Poetry and Knowledge" are directly related to Fanon's view of the sign system of the colonial world: "A world divided into compartments, a motionless Manichaeistic world, a world of statues: the statue of the general who carried out the conquest; the statue of the engineer who built the bridge; a world sure of itself, which crushes with its stones the backs flayed by whips; this is the colonial world."[25] The oppressively petrified language of colonialism clearly recalls the three statues of Césaire's *Cahier,* where the conquistador d'Esnambuc, the empress Josephine, and the liberator Schoelcher are frozen in white marble. In order to break free from such a system of codes that marginalizes and ostracizes him, the colonized retreats to a world of dreams where he fantasizes about "muscular prowess . . . of action and of aggression."[26]

At this point, Said seems to want to minimize the emphasis Fanon put on violence in the creation of a new, liberated humanism. He claims, for example, that "it is a misreading of Fanon not to see in him something considerably beyond a celebration of violent conflict . . . the emphasis on 'armed struggle' is at most tactical."[27] Said here clearly wishes to play down the stridency and combativeness of *The Wretched of the Earth* to explore the possibilities of a new consciousness. Indeed, he speculated that the major theoretical influence on Fanon was Lukacs's *History and Class Consciousness,* which appeared in French in 1960, the very year Fanon's work was written. Surprisingly, Said makes no connection between the poetics of violent change in Césaire's poetry and the ideal of convulsive transformation that Césaire's student, Fanon, would espouse in *The Wretched of the Earth.*

Violence is Fanon's political application of the radical monism of Césaire's thought. The heterocosm that could never be concretely realized in dependent, diverse Martinique is imagined in a mythified Algeria. For instance, Fanon's celebration of the cleansing, purifying power of violence can be viewed as an extension of Césaire's idealization of the upright fire:

It so happens that for the colonized people violence, because it constitutes their only work, invests their characters with positive and creative qualities. The practice of violence binds them together as a whole, since each individual forms a violent link in the great chain, a part of the great organism of violence.

Violence is a cleansing force, it frees the native from his inferiority complex and from his despair and inaction; it makes him fearless and restores his self respect.[28]

The imagery of fiery, explosive change as a cleansing, unifying, and illuminating form of group therapy can easily be read as a politics of *verrition*. It leads Fanon to make extraordinary claims for curing the psychological problems of the colonized. What is important here is not so much whether the cure works—even though there is much evidence to the contrary—but the lure of the Césarean ideal of the "precious vortex," of the purifying sensation of "giddy dilation."

Fanon's dream, like Césaire's, is that of restoring the lost paradise. In his euphoric insistence on the ideal of the nation reborn, Fanon is conceptualizing the behavior and culture of the group outside of historical contact and individual idiosyncracies. The interest among contemporary French Caribbean writers in the opacity and diversity of cultures and in the particularisms that need to be recognized in individual societies is very different from the idealistic view advanced by Fanon that all particularisms will be dissolved in the great fiery upheaval of a nationalistic uprising. In his insensitivity to the problematic nature of his conception of the nation, Fanon shares Césaire's lack of interest in cultural specificity or diversity and his desire to reduce the contradictions of specific reality to a tidy, Manichean conception of oppressors and the oppressed. If the Caribbean could be Polynesia, then the entire colonial world could be Algeria.

The persistence of Césairean poetics can be traced outside of the specific context of Martinique and the French Caribbean. Indeed, the project of formulating a Caribbean identity or establishing a presence within a heterogenous American collectivity is often diverted into a nostalgia for a prelapsarian, mythical past. The myth of the Caribbean, African, or pre-Columbian heterocosm is a tempting one. It is this dream of a lost unity in the past that links the Barbadian poet Edward Kamau Brathwaite, for instance, with Aimé Césaire. C. R. L. James was more accurate than he realized when he observed that "there are parts of [Brathwaite's] poem that seem to me to come straight from Aimé Césaire's *Cahier d'un retour au pays natal*. Well, certain things that Césaire says Brathwaite says."[29] Brathwaite's poetic impulse in *The Arrivants* is, like Césaire's, cartographic. He, too, sees the New World as fallen and wants, as does Césaire, to see a new dawn at the end of the wee hours of the morning.

> How will new maps be drafted?
> Who will suggest a new tentative frontier?
> How will the sky dawn now?[30]

Brathwaite also shares Césaire's fascination with the 1902 explosion of Mount Pelée in the poem "Dust": "However, volcanoes as symbols of fiery upheaval have become silent / have shut their red eyes."[31] Brathwaite's early trilogy comes to a predictable conclusion with the appearance of the foundational word: "the word becomes / again a god and walks among us."[32] Brathwaite's modernist poetics affirm the poetic word as the restoration of a primal innocence before the fall, the fulfillment of the quest for new beginnings.

Brathwaite's emphasis on the divine and the numinous is telling. In his work, a Césairean poetics becomes religious; as in Fanon, Césaire's ideas feed a revolutionary ethic. The word for Brathwaite establishes an original coherence. All imperfections, contradictions, and discontinuities fall away as the poetic Word restores a time that is ahistorical, impervious to change. In order to facilitate this emergence of a mystical spirituality, Brathwaite put together an Anglo-American modernist tradition with his adopted Césairean aesthetic. Brathwaite's interest in the ideas of T. S. Eliot is significant in his elaboration of a new spiritual order. Just as for Eliot an earlier Christian and Anglicist order disintegrated under the pressure of materialism in the modern world, so for Brathwaite a sense of the mystical can be located in traditional Africa and its survivals in the New World. Perhaps in the same way that Eliot saw affinities between the English metaphysical poets and the French symbolists, so Brathwaite could find links between a Martiniquan modernist poetics and Eliot's secular theology.

Consequently, Brathwaite's heterocosm is not simply that of a prehistoric past, dateless and primal. Rather, he reconstructs a tradition that is an African equivalent of Eliot's belief in the church, the monarchy and the Great Tradition. If the problem of the fragmented and flawed world could be resolved by the Césairean image, so for Brathwaite wholeness would be retrieved by rhythm and music. This is clearly demonstrated in the final poem of *The Arrivants* and is more generally seen in Brathwaite's interest in various musical forms, from jazz to calypso. Music dissolves the bedeviling historicity of the Caribbean and allows a more ancient, primal rhythm to be retrieved. Poetic rhythm must then aim at echoing a deeper, ancestral rhythm. In celebrating the Guyanese painter Aubrey Williams as the ideal artist, Brathwaite describes the Caribbean modernist as

An ancient artist working in a modern
form. . . . Like a worshipper possessed at

Shango or vodum, as with a jazz
musician, time past and future speak to
the community in the trapped and hunting [*sic*]
moment of awareness. We become the
Maya who were already us. Williams is
the medium.[33]

It is this realization that reality is part of a cyclical pattern that is the
shaping force in Brathwaite's poetic imagination.[34] His work can be
seen as an investigation of the rhythmic continuities that underlie the
chaos and cacophony of surface reality. The title of his essay *History
of the Voice* (1984) is very revealing. It is not a question of voices or
histories or heterogeneity; rather, for Brathwaite, the foundational
rhythmic utterance is what must be traced in the New World; it provides the only answer to the disassociated sensibility provoked by
what, in the poet's view, is the fallen condition of Caribbean man.

Brathwaite's music is not an inclusive chorus. It is uncomfortable
with the ambiguous, opaque, and disparate sounds of the New
World. Like Césaire, he dreams of a therapeutic wholeness, that ancient point where contradictions cease to exist. Yet the historian in
him also senses the importance of the process of creolization in the
Americas. The problem is that he is conceptually ill-equipped to deal
with the radical openness of the creolist model, with its suspicion of
systems of totalization and its insistence on the Caribbean as a profoundly dialogic, conflicting space. It is, therefore, not surprising that
commentators on his work invariably point to the inadequacies of his
model. In *The Empire Writes Back*, we read that Brathwaite's emphasis on "the importance of the African connection has sometimes
obscured his increasing concern with Creolization."[35] Gordon Lewis
is even more precise in pinpointing Brathwaite's methodological defi-
ciencies. For Lewis, Brathwaite's system of classification does not
make a convincing case for a "common, unifying creoledom." "Brathwaite's very system of classification—dealing separately with European, Euro-Creole, Afro-Creole and West Indian segments—implicitly
recognizes the sharp and oftentimes mutually irreconcilable nature of
the groups."[36]

A far more innovative approach to the idea of a creole sensibility
for the literature of the anglophone Caribbean would be found in
Wilson Harris's theories of the cross-cultural imagination. The appeal
of the Caribbean heterocosm does have a powerful effect on those

who experience a sense of homelessness in a heterogenous American collectivity and who consequently, erect a poetic fiction based on both a need to formulate a unique identity and to return to a mythic, organic origin. This need to legitimize difference in the Caribbean is often provoked by a fierce anti-Americanism. For instance, the mythology of a Caribbean otherness was revived by the Cuban literary critic Roberto Fernandez Retamar in his 1971 essay *Caliban,* where he makes a plea for assuming "our condition as Caliban" and "rethinking our history from the *other* side, from the viewpoint of the other protagonist of *The Tempest.*"[37] Fernandez Retamar's celebration of Caribbean marronnage in the figure of Caliban is both a defiant response to Rodó's Arielism as well as an unimaginative extension of the theories of otherness in Césaire and Fanon. The resurgence of this notion in Fernandez Retamar's work demonstrates the seductiveness of one of the major tropes of Caribbean modernism—the island as primeval ground.

The Totalitarian Temptation

My ear pressed to the earth,
I heard tomorrow go by.

—Aimé Césaire, "Les pur-sang"

The utopian impulse behind this theorizing of a Caribbean difference reinforced the idea of the author as the fountainhead of truth, of an authoritative self presiding over a totalized vision and the lure of a nativist politics. As Césaire claims in "Les pur-sang," from his communion with telluric forces he derives the power to see the future. Two years after Césaire delivered his paper on "Poetry and Knowledge" in Port-au-Prince, a young René Depestre proclaimed his own fantasy of mastery, his own vision of purity, not plurality, in which he would hold the seat of power:

Tomorrow when I will be King of my creations
when I will be King of each drop of sweat
I will invent morality for men
virtue for women
a code of conduct for children.[38]

Haitian indigenism is the only fully developed expression of nativist thought and practice based entirely in the Caribbean. Other expressions of literary nativism were centered elsewhere, such as the negritude movement in Paris and the Caribbean Artists Movement (CAM) in London. Indigenism was predicated, as the name implies, on a poetics of difference and on exploring an alternative genealogy to that imposed by Western culture. Haitian otherness became a fiercely nationalistic mask for confronting the nineteen-year occupation of Haiti by the U.S. marines. The poetic nature of this militant anti-American and anti-Enlightenment activism is no coincidence. Indigenism was about beginning again, about creating a new methodology, a new history, where poets would be the keepers of knowledge. The rhetoric of power, therefore, reached well beyond the poetic act to envisage total, political solutions—or perhaps dissolutions—for a new, purified Haiti.

If Césaire based his dream of a heterocosm on an archaic primitivism, the adherents of Haitian indigenism located this primal otherness in the culture of the folk. At its most extreme, the cult of indigenous authenticity meant a celebration of black magic, libidinal impulses, and alcoholic hallucination. Haiti's radicals sought emotional and psychic otherness in the slums of Port-au-Prince and the open space of the Haitian countryside. The Haitian avant-garde remade itself in the image of the Baudelairean *flaneur,* roaming the streets of the capital or penetrating the mysterious bush in search of a bizarre beauty. The desperate radicalism of this generation of Haitian writers is mirrored in the erratic career of the poet Carl Brouard, in whom we not only see the excesses of dissolute nonconformity but the beginnings of a flirtation with totalitarian politics.

The urge to celebrate cultural difference drove Brouard to identify poets as "les extravagants, les bohèmes, les fous" in his poem "Nous."[39] The sites for poetic inspiration ranged from nightclubs, with their stock of prostitutes and drunks, to cannibalistic orgies, with voluptuous, maneating goddesses as can be seen in poems such as "Bouge" and "Hymne à Erzulie."[40] The poet as uninhibited *négre* is the iconoclastic posture adopted by Brouard and others of this generation. What is striking is the way in which this poetics of rupture and violation lead to the belief in the foundational word of the poet and the capacity to base a new social order on a poetic vision.

It is remarkable that among Brouard and his contemporaries there is an absence of any reference to the founding fathers of Haitian independence. Their poetic vision is not historic but ritualistic; it negates time and the complexities of the past. If this strain of Caribbean modernism had a political mentor, it must be the right-wing monarchist Charles Maurras and his movement L'Action Française. Maurras's special kind of antimodernist modernism seems to have had an enormous appeal to Haitian intellectuals. His celebration of the ideal of the nation, of the archaic values of the past, the need for a hierarchial order, and even his anti-Semitism are, arguably, at the roots of the totalitarian impulses that emerge in Haiti in the 1930s. Fascist politics are a hidden dimension to indigenist poetics. Jean Price-Mars in 1928 would cite Maurras's "J'ai tout reçu du sol natal" (I have received everything from my native soil)[41] and it is important to note the influence of Maurras's like-minded contemporary Maurice Barrès on the ideas of the negritude poet Leopold Sedar Senghor.[42]

The temptation of total political solutions is, perhaps, less evident in the indigenist movement than in the ideas of the black nationalist movement Les Griots that succeeded it.[43] By the 1930s, an increasing number of intellectuals were arguing against the merits of a liberal democracy and supporting a politics of "reason and will allied to force."[44] These words from René Piquion were echoed by many of his contemporaries, who expressed great enthusiasm for European fascism. As David Nicholls reminds us, "they saw in fascism . . . an alternative to the liberal democratic model which had widely been accepted as the one which should be followed in Haiti. Many 'noiristes' of this period, with their anti-liberal and authoritarian rhetoric, were advocating a kind of fascism for Haiti."[45] Arguably, these advocates of fascist politics found support for their ideas in the modernist poetics of their contemporaries. Maurras's reactionary rationalism, itself a curious product of European modernism, had a strong appeal among Haitian artists. It is Brouard who most explicitly espoused the Maurrasian cult of authority and a return to the genius of the Haitian *Volk*.

What Brouard preached in the 1930s was not change through revolution but the need for restoration of a mythical past. In the article "Paganisme et Vaudou," he cited the examples of Sparta, Greece, Rome, and ancient China. Brouard is drawn to the ideal that kings in ancient civilizations were *pères de peuples* and the patriarchical king had the absolute authority over life and death. He then sees a direct parallel with the veneration of the *hougan* (priest) in the *Vaudou* cult:

"Certain concepts, certain feelings appear to be universal. If the houmfor is not at the heart of the home, and if the hougan is not necessarily the father, he is venerated by all the family. The climate which in Hellas and Italy required libations to be oil and wine, demands for us, rum and white rum. . . . Let us add that no man of the people drinks his coffee without pouring out some for the ancestors."[46] The Haitian *volksgeist* for Brouard legitimized an authoritarian, patriarchal social structure. In another article, "L'art au service au peuple," Brouard makes his politics more explicit. He boldly claims that the most ignorant peasant "will obey docilely a dictatorship which works for order, truth and the common good because those ideas are inborn. . . . I firmly believe that a people can only reach liberalism slowly, one step at a time."[47] With Brouard, bohemian radicalism had metamorphosed into a fascist primitivism. Eroticism and delirium now yielded to the reconstruction of traditional values, and for an ideal, hierarchical society outside of history. The need to establish an organic, connectedness to reintegrate the self in a pristine totality in Brouard is not simply Rousseauesque; it is ultimately a polemical defence of the imperial state, like of ancient China of Rome, in the face of disorder and incoherence.

The grip that ideals of mastery, control, and symmetry held on Brouard's contemporaries was not always as politically explicit. Even those ideologically opposed to Brouard's fascism were seduced by the retrieval of a terrestrial order, by the restoration of a luminous center from which would emanate a sacred diction, a prelinguistic rhythm, a primal harmony. Jacques Roumain's *Masters of the Dew,* while normally seen as progressive and quite distinct from the ideology of the griot movement, paradoxically reveals an anxiety for establishing a truth beyond words—for literally inscribing a new clearing in the wasted discursive landscape of Haiti. The main protagonist in Roumain's novel is on a quest for a lost paradise, a lost time and vision that will provide an alternative source of knowledge and confer a new set of meanings to the lives of the villagers of Fonds Rouge.

Roumain's novel is curiously situated outside the specificities of Haitian history and social structure; it must be the only Haitian novel that makes no reference to any episode of Haiti's history. The notorious class and color divisions in that society are dealt with only fleetingly. For instance, the only reference to color antagonism is a short reference to workers in Cuba: "One person thought himself white, another was Negro, and there were plenty misunderstandings among us."[48] The predatory Haitian state is reduced to the rural policeman and corrupt market inspectors.

Masters of the Dew does not attempt to come to terms with the teeming and contradictory details of Haitian life; rather it is single-mindedly focused on grounding a new social order. The fathers of Haitian independence are less important here than the new revolutionary genealogy that projects Manuel as the founding father of an alternative, organicist culture. Roumain's novel can, therefore, be seen as an imaginative rewriting of the problems of mastery raised by Durand's "Choucoune." To the crisis of representation and the land's refusal to provide the poet with referential validity, Roumain's imaginative response is a docile, virgin surface on which a new truth can be inscribed, manually, as the name of the novel's protagonist suggests.

The key to full understanding of what Roumain is trying to do in *Masters of the Dew* lies in his use of anthropology in the process of fixing Haitian space. Roberto González Echevarría's comments on the importance of anthropology in Latin American fiction are extremely helpful here. "Anthropology is the mediating element in the modern Latin American narrative because of the place this discipline occupies in the articulation of founding myths by Latin American states . . . the modern Latin American novel transforms Latin American history into an originary myth in order to see itself as other."[49] González Echevarría's argument is that the anthropological discipline is constructed around the need in Western culture to elaborate originary fictions. The Latin American novel uses this model to establish a redemptive otherness. Outside of the hispanophone Americas, Jacques Romain is the best example of the anthropologist-writer. Not only did he study anthropology in Europe in the late 1930s, but he founded the Bureau d'Ethnologie in Haiti in 1941. In 1943, shortly before completing *Masters of the Dew*, he published a study of a sacrificial *Vaudou* ritual, *Le sacrifice du tambour Assotor*. The relationship between the ritualized use of sacrifice to produce a new surface for the *Vaudou* Assotor drum, thereby allowing the gods to speak, bears a striking resemblance to the sacrifice of Manuel in the novel and the creation of a new song for the people of Fonds Rouge.

Consequently, Roumain could be seen as part of that Latin American tradition that allows for the rewriting of time, space, and identity through an anthropological perspective. The official documents of the past, the old chronicles, now give way to a new narrative that has no use for official records—not even for literature or language itself. Roumain's disparaging comments on the language of the Haitian president in the 1930s, Stenio Vincent, are revealing. He dismisses Vincent's language as a "diarrhoea of words, verbal agility."[50] Roumain aims for a new, truth-bearing discourse on which a new beginning can be based. Anthropology seems to have provided him with the kind of totalizing discourse that could assert a new origin for Haitian society, away from the horrors of Western civilization, so fresh in Roumain's mind because of the Occupation and World War II.

In his desire to articulate a new truth about Haitian society, Roumain conceives of a language, or rather a metalanguage, that would reorient the primal images of sun, tree, earth, man, and water. This new discourse is grounded in the land and etched into the surface of the landscape by the cutting edges of various tools. This is first apparent in the Promethean image of men snatching "bright sparks of fire" (27) from the sun, which then cut into the garden's surface through their hoes. Later, Manuel uses his machete to cut the water free from the earth, a direct parallel of which is his own mark left on the deflowered body of Annaise, the receptive, latter-day incarnation of Choucoune. Finally, the water cuts through the landscape like a silvery blade (*mince lame d'argent*), leaving in its wake a new hieroglyph of truth. Thus the language of the novel attempts to bring a rupestral truthfulness to literary French.

The Caribbean heterocosm envisaged by Roumain is intensely related to a genealogical preoccupation with the creator of a founding myth. Into *Masters of the Dew*—his final novel—Roumain pours his deepest longings for a new authority that would be different, unique, autonomous. To this extent, we can describe *Masters of the Dew* as *theogenic,* to use González Echevarría's term for the mythic, genealogical dimension of the *novela de la tierra*.[51] Indeed, one can argue that given the powerful legitimizing authority of Manuel, *Masters of the Dew* can be read as a Caribbean version of the "dictator" novel. The importance of mastery in the novel and the novel's magisterial discourse are related to Manuel's actual paternity. Again, González Echevarría is insightful in discussing this dimension of the Latin American novel. In *The Voice of the Masters,* he points to "the figure of the 'maestro,' who is the possessor and transmitter of knowledge about culture; the figure of the dictator, who wields absolute power and is a hypostasis of the author; the figure of the author . . . who can filter the voice of a primitive 'inarticulate' other and turn it into an intelligible text that is paradoxically endowed with authority by the inarticulate other."[52]

Manuel can be seen as the ultimate authority and the author of a prelapsarian truth in the novel. The close association between Roumain and his protagonist is very obvious in this evocation of Manuel as sovereign voice and master narrator. "Manuel had translated into good Creole the exacting language of the thirsty plain, the plaint of growing things, the promises and mirages of the water. He had led them in advance through their harvest. Their eyes gleamed just from listening to him" (131). The polytheism, the multiple voices of the *Vaudou* religion, are reduced to one voice as Manuel offers the structuring vision, the ordaining voice to the community. His truth is even more indestructible because he dies young. The disembodied voice of the master suggests both an ability to be everywhere all the time and to be the bearer of a truth that is immutable. This truth is the village's new song, unclassifiable, unprecedented, that dictates the rhythm and purpose of the *coumbite.*

The choice of the *coumbite* as the lost ritual that must be revived to redeem the village is a telling one. It is a vital instance of the discursive transformation that is central to the metalanguage Roumain envisaged in a redeemed Fonds Rouge. The *coumbite* is not carnival. Indeed, it emerges as diametrically opposed to the ironic, subversive, and derisive laughter of the carnivalesqe. Ordered, purposeful, and harmonious, the *coumbite* would have met Brouard's criteria for the fundamental ingredients of a Haitian *volksgeist*. In Roumain's novel, the *coumbite* first manifests itself as a fertility rite, with chants that have clearly erotic overtones. The new and improved *coumbite* at the end of the story has no hint of eroticism; the sexual play of the traditional ritual has been replaced by a song venerating Manuel, the now absent founding father "Manuel Jean-Joseph, Oh! Mighty Negro," who is the reincanation of the village's primogenitor, General Johannes Longeannis, who not only founded the community but through whom, we are told, all the villagers are related. The genealogical preoccupations of the novel are evident to the very last line—the "new life . . . stirring" in Annaise as a result of her union with Manuel (168).

Masters of the Dew epitomizes the organicist longings of this phase of Caribbean modernism. Roumain's heterocosm reaches forward to a utopian, prediscursive logos that confers a new intelligibility on the broken, fragmented, fallen world. Haitian—and, arguably,

Caribbean—history begins again with Manuel. Like Césaire's demi-urgic poet, Manuel holds the key to knowledge. It is his Adamic vision that allows the new arcadian order to be realized. What starts off as a dream of liberation from an oppressive Western system of knowledge ends up also asserting a new, closed, hegemonic system of values. One of the ironies of this phase of Caribbean modernism is the way in which a rejection of the tyranny of reason leads to the poetics of closure and authority. In Haiti, the seductive reality of authoritarian politics is not far behind these originary fictions.

The imaginative invention of the Caribbean heterocosm is, perhaps, part of that old dream to herald the triumph of a brave, new world in the Americas. What is particularly interesting about it is the opposition between modernism and the idea of modernity. This is a process that Simon Gikandi associates with a modernist reading of marronnage, a subversive strategy that he, unfortunately, applies to all Caribbean literature and not to one peculiar manifestation of a modernist poetics: "Caribbean writers, in response to their historical marginalisation, have evolved a discourse of alterity which is predicated on a deliberate act of self-displacement from the hegemonic culture and its central tenets. The Maroon is the most visible symbol of this gesture of cultural 'dedoublement.' "[53] The maroon, the Haitian folk, and even the Algerian mujahideen are seen as repositories of this "discourse of alterity." Haiti is reduced to Fonds Rouge. The Caribbean might just be a New World Polynesia. Oscillating between a secular theology and an authoritarian politics, this nostalgia for hierarchical order is the most thoroughgoing attempt in Caribbean thought to constitute a New World other and articulate in absolute terms the voice of otherness.

It is true that the voice of the other can never exist as a distinct, homogenous entity, especially in the Caribbean where the involvement with Europe and the United States is both long-term and intense. Yet the impulse to constitute and express the voice of the other in Caribbean writing arises in situations where an autonomous identity is denied. Self-recognition and the assertion of opacity are the impulses behind the poetics of Césaire, Fanon, Roumain, and other theorists of a Caribbean heterocosm. The U.S. occupation of Haiti, like the morbidly protracted relationship between Martinique and France, encourages the desire to assert difference in the face of dominant Western European models.

There has been some attempt, as we have seen, to dismiss Fanon's theory of violence as tactical and to see Césairean negritude as simply strategic. Indeed, James Clifford makes extraordinary claims for Césairean negritude that ultimately confuse the overall picture of Caribbean modernist practice: "The true heirs of negritude are writers like Carpentier, Guillen, Amado, Vallejo, Cortazar, Márquez. Again negritude is transmuted: it is no longer about roots but about present process in a polyphonous reality."[54] Clifford's predicament is that in his haste to see the Americas in terms of a "New World poetics of continuous transgression and co-operative cultural activity," he misreads the Césairean poetics of *verrition*. He also constructs a list of the "heirs of negritude" that includes those who died before the movement came into being (Vallejo) and those who were ideologically opposed to the aesthetic of the movement (Carpentier). Negritude may be profoundly American in its reaction against the modern, but it should not be confused with other forms of Caribbean modernism that were more obviously based on a "poetics of transgression" and reciprocity. The romance of the ahistorical, organic, whole community complete in itself is almost a period style in Caribbean modernism. By the end of the 1940s, Caribbean thought reenters history. With the rise of the concept of "marvelous realism" in Cuba and Haiti, the ideal of the nativist architext, or archetypal utterance, gives way to the hybrid intertext, or the realization that links with other texts may lie beyond the individual's discursive mastery.

4

A New World Mediterranean: The Novel and Knowledge

Third World Modernism slyly turned the relationship inside out, appropriating the great imperial space of the Mediterranean in order to organize the space of the colonial city

—Fredric Jameson, "Modernism and Imperialism"

Paradigms Lost

In his 1970 lecture "History, Fable and Myth in the Caribbean and Guianas," the Guyanese novelist Wilson Harris proposed that literary, and perhaps, more broadly, imaginative, activity should engage in "a drama of consciousness which reads back through the shock of place and time for omens of capacity."[1] While making an important observation about the potential of the "threshold consciousness," Harris was recognizing literary activity in the Caribbean as a form of reflection and critical thought. Harris's view implies that the most ambitious works of the region can be read as allegory, the text becoming an arena where larger conceptual issues are debated and thought through. If a pattern has been established in this mode of critical reflection, it must turn on the movement from absence to presence, from exile and uprooting to the restoration of a lost, organic communion with the world.

The power and pervasiveness of this trope in the Caribbean is so noticeable that one of the best introductions to French-Caribbean literature, Beverley Ormerod's *Introduction to the French Caribbean Novel*, is organized around the anxiety for origins.[2] Not surprisingly, this work begins with the two texts that most fully articulate a foundational myth—Césaire's *Cahier* and Roumain's *Masters of the Dew*. The particular drama of Caribbean consciousness enacted in Césaire and Roumain is a logocentric poetics. Both propose the fiction of the Caribbean as primal space where Adamic man can begin again. Both after the burning night of the *Cahier* and the cleansing by blood and water of *Masters of the Dew*, a new order emerges based on a system of homogeneity, symmetry, and organic harmony. Both texts are classic expressions of a poetics of alternativity, but as Carlos Fuentes warns, the other, history, fallenness, as it were, are not that easily gotten rid of, because "an isolated community soon perishes; it can become folklore, mania, or specular theatre."[3]

Modernity and modernism make this longing for wholeness in isolation an impossible ideal. As Fuentes continues, "the world needs my alternativity to give it meaning, and I need the difference of others to define myself."[4] As we have seen in the critical literary consciousness of the Caribbean's first independent state, there has existed from the early nineteenth century a tradition of Caribbean modernism that is both skeptical and revisionist. Just as it was vital to ground early Haitian nationalism in nature, the legitimacy of this invented reality soon came under intense interrogation. In the 1930s, the poetics of erasure and rewriting raises once more the tempting possibility of repossessing Caribbean space. The discourse of alterity that dominates Césaire's *Cahier d'un retour au pays natal* and Roumain's *Masters of the Dew* turns on the possibility of making lasting inscriptions on virgin space. In his "Poetry and Knowledge," Césaire after all calls the primal, poetic word a "rupestral design" and "the striking of the mental wave against the rock of the world." Later, the image of durable, revolutionary hieroglyphs and a consequent mastery of Caribbean space is central to Roumain's *Masters of the Dew*, which takes us from the initial image, earth slipping uselessly between fingers, to hands that can become fists and that wield tools in unison and make a collective inscription on the ground.

The restless, demystifying impulse in Caribbean thought inevitably questions this vision of transcendence. The impossibility of absolute knowledge and mastery of primeval New World space is a major theme in the work of the Cuban novelist Alejo Carpentier. The deconstructive force of Carpentier's literary imagination is a vital part of Caribbean modernism. The claim made by González Echevarría for the centrality of Carpenter to a Latin American literary tradition can be made even more strongly within the Caribbean. The following statement is as true of the Caribbean as it is of Latin American writing: "Nature, the landscape, created through its own uniqueness and originality a new and original being who expressed himself or herself in the form of a new and different literature. This ideological safety net lasted up to the work of Borges and Carpentier, more specifically up to *The Lost Steps* (1953), a novel by the Cuban who had undoubtedly been a reader of the Argentinian."[5] The recognition of Carpentier's importance to Caribbean modernism is also apparent in Simon Gikandi's *Writing in Limbo,* which despite its concentration on the anglophone Caribbean includes a chapter on Carpentier.

Carpentier's oeuvre in general and the novel *The Lost Steps* in particular consistently mocks the idea of new beginnings and the dream of absolute mastery of nature. Carpentier's novel can be read as a precise and uncanny response to the fiction of durable inscriptions on the "rock" of Caribbean space. In *The Lost Steps,* the protagonist travels through time and space back to a primeval time. It seems to reenact the journeys of Césaire's and Roumain's texts, but with very different results. Like the works of Césaire and Roumain, Carpentier's novel is based on the dynamics of exile and return, presence and absence. *The Lost Steps* enacts the journey of a first-person narrator from a modern metropolis, a Latin American city, and eventually to the primeval world of an Indian tribe lost in the depths of the Amazon jungle. Each city represents a cultural and historical phase in the history of the Americas. The significance of each of these cultural moments is enhanced by female characters associated with each stage: the protagonist's wife, his mistress, a French intellectual, and ultimately his aboriginal lover Rosario. The symbolic values of these female characters are obvious as the narrator makes his way back to the heartland, significantly called "the valley where time has stopped." The ideal moment of his reintegration into an organic world comes when the protagonist and Rosario become a latter-day Adam and Eve in a jungle paradise. "It was there that we bathed naked, we, the couple in water that splashed and flowed, descending from heights already warmed by the sun, and ran below in beds that the tannin of the tree roots turn yellow. There was no Edenic affectation in this clean, nakedness."[6] The route to this paradise is marked with a V inscribed on a tree trunk. (The V suggests the French *vie,* which indicates the ecstatic discovery of life in its natural form as well as the rebirth of the composer's creative energies.) Yet this fantasy cannot last. As the title implies, the steps leading to this world of pure origins will be lost forever.

The protagonist is driven by a yearning for alternativity, for a wholeness uncontaminated by the West. The pre-Columbian heartland that he discovers is outside of the fallenness of history. In his flight from modernity, the narrator journeys backward toward a primal innocence. Yet as an artist, a musicologist in fact, he is frustrated by his lack of writing materials to give expression to his reawakened creative powers. A search plane finds him and he agrees to return to civilization in order to obtain the materials he needs and make a definitive break with his past. Yet when he tries to return to the heartland, he cannot find the way. The inscriptions on nature that originally led the way are now lost, forever, "the sign covered and the entrance closed" (243). The signs that used to chart the jungle are erased and the narrator must return to the present and to city life. He cannot escape history and his contaminated, American identity. As Glissant observed in a perceptive early comment on *The Lost Steps,* "One must come to terms with the loss of time past, accept one's time, ultimately try to establish the best synthesis of the strengths of this America (rediscovered during the descent in search of time past) and power of the modern world. . . . Ultimately to express, to know that one belongs to one's time. Not one without the other: such is the lesson of *The Lost Steps.*"[7]

The definitive loss of the past and the need to confront modernity, as Glissant observes, constitute a disturbing force of Carpentier's fiction. In *The Lost Steps,* Caribbean modernism shifts from a state of utopian wishfulness to a self-consciously ironic mode. The possibility of erasure and reinscription is profoundly questioned, as Carpentier's protagonist comes to the sad realization that nature can no longer be tagged symbolically or ideologically. Indeed, the novel dramatizes the dilemma of the Caribbean artist: the fact must be faced that the very need to record an image points to an absence of the real thing. The narrator is, as Glissant also comments, "whatever he does, a man of art, of knowledge."[8] Instead of establishing a fiercely autochthonous, poetic certitude in defiance of the uncertainties and ambiguities of New World history, Carpentier explores the possibility of openness to the paradoxes and mysteries of human experience. The creative possibility of the work itself is based on an error, the narrator's mistaken interpretation of a stable heartland and immobile time. Carpentier's protagonist finds that he is as alienated from the city as he is from the heartland, and ambiguously at home in both.

With *The Lost Steps,* Caribbean writing disavows an earlier innocence. Carpentier's novel problematizes the referential validity of the New World heartland. It subverts the authority of the artist and the relationship between artist and work. Ultimately, it raises the question of the dynamic, mestizo identity of the New World, where the journey back to the source is supplanted by a journey inward and outward, backward through time and forward to the present, unceasingly. An anthropologically derived concept of cultural difference is undermined as the novel reenacts the quintessential journey to primal otherness, but one that in Carpentier's fiction is futile.[9]

With Carpentier, the map of the New World becomes labyrinthine and unchartable: the protagonist's itinerary does not lead to authentic experience but to endless permutations or detours from his original intention. Perhaps for the first time in Caribbean fiction, the issue of *errance,* or ceaseless wandering, is raised. The demystification of the traveler, the discoverer, and ultimately the authority of the artist creates in *The Lost Steps* a text that undoes the tradition of the *bildungsroman,* which turns on the *prise de conscience* of the main character. As González Echevarría again perceptively observes, "There are, in fact, no geneses in the novel, only repetitions, rediscoveries, and falsifications. When the protagonist begins to compose music in Santa Monica, it is suggested that Rosario has become pregnant, but he never knows for sure, and then she marries Marcos. Ruth, his own wife, only feigns a pregnancy, and Mouche, his mistress, turns out to be a lesbian. Natural conceptions are fictional or nonexistent."[10] The inability of the protagonist in this novel to reconcile opposites and create new cosmic possibilities from the erasure or transcendence of former contradictions or discontinuities is applied to the ultimate New World traveler in Carpentier's last novel, *The Harp and the Shadow.* Columbus on his deathbed dejectedly recognizes the futility of his quest: "You went into a world that played tricks on you when you thought you had conquered it and which, in reality threw you off course, leaving you neither *here nor there.*"[11] If Carpentier's novel is read as an attempt to subvert the anthropologically based aesthetic of a Roumain or a Césaire in suggesting that no ordinary truth is recuperable from the Caribbean's past and that no aboriginal *Ursprache* can be devised, then *The Lost Steps* must be seen as inaugurating a new stage of critical consciousness in

Caribbean literature. The poetics of the Césairean neologism cannot thereafter create a new, true, language. The inscription on the earth itself is not lasting because the land resists the process of naming. The heartland cannot provide a sanctuary for the modern artist. The appealing symmetries of Roumain's ideologically ordered world now yield a bewildering plurality of signs.

In his questioning of the truthfulness of a certain theoretical practice in the Caribbean, Carpentier not only demystifies the cartographic impulse in Caribbean modernism, but by implication profoundly calls into question the literary act itself. After all, Columbus himself admits that the New World is inexplicable "in the language of the *Odyssey* or in the language of Genesis." In *The Lost Steps*, not only does New World space resist representation, but the text itself, as well as the "author," is denied the power of transcendence. Carpentier's protagonist is as deluded about the organically intact nature of his jungle heartland as he is about his own ability to create an originary voicing of this space. The text as sacred origin is now questioned in this subversion of the primordial status of the creative act. Carpentier almost seems to anticipate the question raised by Michel Foucault in *The Order of Things:*

> The question is no longer: How can experience of nature give rise to necessary judgement? But rather: How can man think what he does not think, inhabit as though by mute occupation something that eludes him, animate with a kind of frozen movement that figure of himself that takes the form of a stubborn exteriority? . . . How can he be the subject of a language that for thousands of years has been formed without him, a language whose organization escapes him, whose meaning sleeps an almost invincible sleep in the words he momentarily activates by means of discourse.[12]

Consequently, not only does Carpentier's protagonist's error lead to physical wandering but also to the realization that accurate narration is itself a phantasm. Thus the poetics of the neologism as originary utterance yields to a poetics that can be described as relational or translational.

Despite the radical implications of Carpentier's thought and deconstructive narrative, he does not follow up on his imaginative daring. González Echevarría states it bluntly: "It was somewhat disappointing at first to discover how ideas were abandoned by Carpentier without being explored to the fullest."[13] *The Lost Steps* implies that the writer has no access to the specific, transcendental truth of the Americas; nature does not reveal itself, does not unveil its secrets to Carpentier's chronicler-cum-musicologist. But Carpentier's thought remained enmeshed in notions of the unique and magical nature of the Caribbean and the Americas. In this regard, we must examine Carpentier's formulation of the theory of "marvelous realism" and its impact on Caribbean writing.

The Marvelous and the Mediterranean

After negritude and indigenism, the theory of marvelous realism can be seen as one of the most valiant attempts to ground otherness in New World space. Carpentier's conception of the marvelous nature of New World reality is yet another permutation of the need to establish a separate and unique American identity. The roots of this foundational fiction have been frequently traced back to primitivist movements in European thought. This myth has also been encouraged in Caribbean writing through the influence of such European intellectuals as André Breton and Pierre Mabille. Yet it is less the tradition of occultism that is important here than the need to envisage the other America in terms of a new matrix of values, a new mythology of Caribbean identity that would end all exile and wandering.

Carpentier is fascinated in much of his work by those authentic populations or communities who are felt to have a particular monopoly on the magical or the marvelous. His depiction of Haiti in *The Kingdom of this World* is clearly an attempt to promote Afro-Caribbean culture as the true, magical heartland of the Caribbean imagination. We learn, with some dismay, that Carpentier's view of Haiti was profoundly influenced by William Seabrook's sensationalist work *The Magic Island*—described by Carpentier as "one of the most beautiful books written during recent times."[14] As González Echevarría correctly observes, "Carpentier searches for the marvelous buried beneath the surface of Latin American consciousness, where African drums beat and Indian amulets rule; in depths where Europe is only a vague memory of a future still to come."[15]

Haiti plays a vital role in Carpentier's special definition of New World alterity. Carpentier visited Haiti in 1943 and could not resist the temptation of seeing Haitian popular culture as the true source of a New World identity. He could easily have been encouraged in this view by radical literary movements in Haiti at this time: the *noiristes* were preoccupied with cultural authenticity and in particular with Haitian *Vaudou*. This is certainly the theme of Carpentier's lecture "L'évolution culturelle de l'Amérique Latine," delivered in Haiti in 1943. This view of the uniquely non-Cartesian nature of Caribbean peoples is developed more fully in his prologue to the novel *The Kingdom of this World* (originally published 1949) and would have an enormous effect on the young Haitian novelist Jacques Stephen Alexis, fifteen or so years later.

Carpentier's prologue focuses on the extraordinary nature of the New World experience. He consistently contrasts the magical nature of Haitian space with the vain attempts to invoke the magical in modern European writing. In the second paragraph of this essay, Carpentier declares that, "after feeling the in no way false enchantment of this Haitian earth, after discovering magic presences on the red road of the Central Plateau, after hearing the drums of Petro and Rada, I was moved to compare this marvelous reality I'd just been living with the exhaustingly vain attempts to arouse the marvelous that characterize certain European literatures of these last thirty years."[16] Indeed, throughout the text, comparisons are made between the imaginatively impoverished artist in Europe and the sense of the marvelous that is naturally grounded in the New World. André Masson's artistic failure is compared with the success of the Cuban painter Wifredo Lam, as are the fantasy structures of Piranesi with the architectural achievements of Henri Christophe. Ultimately, Lautréamont, whose roots in Montevideo explain his instincts for the magical, can only create "a short-lived literary school"; whereas Makandal "has left behind an entire mythology, accompanied by magical hymns, preserved by an entire people, who still sing them at Yoruba ceremonies."[17]

What Carpentier senses in Haiti is not, he feels, unique to the hemisphere's first black republic "but the patrimony of all the Americas." It is this patrimony that tempts Carpentier to argue for a special role for the New World in the history of mankind. It is the newness, the spontaneity, and the cultural syncretism of the Americas that give it an advantage over decadent, cerebralized Europe: "Because of the virginity of its landscape, because of its formation, because of its ontology, because of the Faustian presence of the Indian and the Black, because of the Revelation its recent discovery constituted, because of the fertile racial mixtures it favoured, the Americas are far from having used up their wealth of mythologies."[18] The implication here is that the resources of the marvelous have been used up in Europe. Whereas Europe is calculating and self-reflexive, Carpentier imagines the Americas as the realm of a naturalized otherness.

G. R. Coulthard has pointed to the roots of Carpentier's thought and the Afro-Cuban movement in Oswald Spengler's *Decline of the West*. As he noted in *Race and Colour in Caribbean Literature,* the "super-evaluation of the primitive elements in Caribbean life certainly has its distant roots in Spengler's theories of Western cultural exhaustion."[19] The German philosopher's view was that European civilization was out of touch with the marvelous, or rather had reached that point in its evolution where it had lost touch with the mysterious and the fantastic. The New World, on the other hand, was at that point in its historical evolution where the realm of a marvelous reality could still be explored. The novel *The Kingdom of this World* is described by its author not as fiction but as "based on an extremely rigorous documentation" that proves the existence of the marvelous. This, presumably, would also be true of the journey to the territory of the marvelous made by the narrator-protagonist of *The Lost Steps.* What is striking is not that the Americas are different from Europe but that the former are a revival of a world that Europe has left behind. To be more precise, Europe's Mediterranean origins are replayed in the Caribbean. Gordon Lewis has speculated at length about the possible similarity between the Caribbean and the Mediterranean.[20] Carpentier, however, adds a new dimension to Lewis's view of cultural parallels based on a polyglot, multilingual experience. For Carpentier, Spengler's importance was to have theorized a system of universal history in which patterns of growth and decline can be identified. The Caribbean, therefore, could be construed as belonging to that moment of historical evolution where "their wealth of mythologies . . . are far from (being) used up." In a Spenglerian scheme of things, the Caribbean corresponded to the Mediterranean at the time when Europe still had access to the magical and the marvelous.

The Mediterranean, then, provides in Carpentier's literary universe a matrix of values on which the identity of American otherness could be based. This view of an autonomous American identity was not prelapsarian but included the realities of historical contact and the ideal of racial and cultural hybridity. Despite the effect of the playful, subversive intelligence of Jorge Luis Borges on the Cuban novelist, there remains in Carpentier a longing for a vital originary space. Genealogies do not deteriorate in Carpentier's novels as they do in

Borges, nor does the world become the Library of Babel, filled with mirrors, labyrinths, and false trails. Rather, there is a tendency to idealize, defiantly, New World space. Surprisingly, extraordinarily, the Americas allow the exhausted and inhibited Old World to rediscover its own vital past.

In promoting the ideal of the specificity of the Caribbean and the Americas, Carpentier revives José Martí's concept of *mestizaje,* as has been noted by Amaryll Chamady and more fully explored in Vera Kutzinski's *Sugar Secrets.* Ironically, in the very novel that calls into question the possibility of a communion with the world of lost origins, Carpentier toys with the possibility of envisaging a specific New World identity. In *The Lost Steps* the protagonist is reacting to his father's view of the Americas as historyless. "This so-called New World had become for him a hemisphere without history, alien to the great Mediterranean traditions, a land of Indians and Negroes peopled by the off-scourings of the great nations of Europe" (80). This view is challenged in the novel by the figure of Rosario, who offers the tempting female alternative to a failed patriarch's dream. Rosario is the incarnation of a seductive *mestizaje.* "Several races had met in this woman: Indian in the hair and cheekbones, Mediterranean in the brow and nose, Negro in the heavy shoulders and the breadth of hips. . . . There was no question but that this living sum of races had an aristocracy of her own" (74). The father's negative images are supplanted by a celebratory representation of the true hybrid identity of the Americas.

Rosario is therefore both the feminized, native other and the hybrid inscribed in a universal historical encounter. She is grounded in the reality of a racial and cultural encounter of global proportions that typifies for Carpentier the experience of the New World as a marvelous crossroads. To this extent, the Caribbean's heterogeneity makes it superior to Europe's relatively tame Mediterranean. "For here it had not been the amalgam of related peoples, such as history had fused at certain crossroads of Ulysses' sea, but of the great races of the world, the most widely separated, the most divergent, those which for centuries had ignored the fact that they inhabited the same planet." (75) The narrator's seductive muse becomes the mysterious and seductive alternative to the sterile Eurocentrism of the narrator's father. Rosario begins to embody the jungle world as "she established links with her surroundings" (96)—a world the narrator can neither classify or explain and which, like Rosario, was governed by forces "whose workings were obscure and, besides, were beyond man's understanding" (162–63).

With the narrator's failure to possess Rosario, a major crisis is created in the novel. A curious solution is, however, offered by the Greek miner Yannes, who is a "reader of Homer" and presents his copy of the *Odyssey* to the narrator (169). This "living Ulysses," as he is described, is what is left of the narrator's fascination with the New World's affinities with the Mediterranean. If the narrator's return to paradise is foiled, he has not abandoned his desire to retrieve a Mediterranean identity for the Americas. Indeed, Yannes emerges as a mentor superior to the narrator's father. The relationship between the two men at the end of the novel has been expressed as homoerotic. But this is going too far. This interpretation, expressed in Kutzinski's rather reductionist view of gender relations in *Sugar's Secrets,* obscures the larger issue of Carpentier's reformulation of a New World genealogy that went far beyond a narrowly defensive nativism.[22] It would be far more useful to see Yannes as the guide that leads our narrator out of the jungle, and the erotic fantasies generated by nature, to the city, where old dreams of pure origins are abandoned and Rosario's Mediterranean legacy can be lived as an ongoing process.

The recovery of Caribbean history is the main objective of the later novel *Explosion in a Cathedral* (first edition 1962). The extent to which the Caribbean continues to be imagined as a Mediterranean encounter is made explicit in Esteban's words. He speaks of "this Caribbean Mediterranean" where

> the blending of characteristics had for many thousands of years been in process within the ambit of the peoples of the sea. Here, after long being scattered, the descendants of the lost tribes had met again, to mingle their accents and their lineaments, to produce new strains mixing and commixing, degenerating regenerating, a temporary enlightenment followed by a leap backwards into the darkness, in an interminable proliferation of new profiles, new accents and proportions.[23]

This description of Caribbean history is striking in its inherent formlessness, multiplicity, and unpredictability. Nothing seems to harden into a particular pattern. The process is one of dissolution and shaping, destruction and reconstruction, that does not yield to a coherent system. Perhaps Carpentier abandons the quest for explanation, simply accepting the fact that "New Worlds had to be lived before they could be analyzed."

In this way, it could be said that Carpentier ultimately relegates, or rather promotes, the experience of the Americas to the realm of the naturally mysterious. The writer's inability to impose names or meaning on this world, to play the romantic role of Adam giving names to virgin space, yields to a sense of the baroque as the true order of the Americas. In this Carpentier seems to anticipate Gilles Deleuze's definition of the baroque in terms of a process of folding: "The Baroque does not refer to an essence, but rather to an operation function, to a characteristic. It endlessly creates folds. It does not invent. . . . But it twists and turns the folds, takes them to infinity, fold upon fold, fold after fold. The characteristics of the Baroque is the fold that goes on to infinity."[24] Fluid, profuse, open-ended, and repetitive, New World space is not primeval and resists being mastered symbolically. In *Explosion in a Cathedral,* the atavistic longing for a feminized hinterland yields to a ceaseless roaming of the Caribbean Sea. Reading the *Odyssey* is transformed into living the *Odyssey. The Manatee,* the name of the ship that takes the narrator out of the jungle in *The Lost Steps,* seems echoed in the later novel's musings on the mermaid, as a New World symbol of the sea. In this world where manatees are taken for mermaids, naming is a precarious exercise. Esteban now creates a language of symbiosis, radically different from the Césairean neologism: "The language of these islands had made use of agglutinations, verbal ambiguity of things which participated in several essences at once."[25] In the novel, Esteban dutifully keeps an inventory of flora and fauna. His classification of the marvels of the Caribbean depends on the juxtaposition of heterogenous items invariably joined by hyphens; for instance, acacia-bracelets and tiger-fish. This interest in naming an amalgamated reality that already comes with names, histories, traditions, intensifies as Carpentier takes an increasing interest in urban architecture. As González Echevarría observes, Carpentier discovers a "melange of styles" in Havana. In that city, the process of repetition and recombination exists concretely. The New World reality is one that already bears several names and, by extension, any act if naming is essentially one of renaming. As González Echevarría further observes, Carpentier then prescribes this new baroque style for all writing in the Americas.[26] Already, what is suggested here is a poetics of infinite translation: no text or word has primordial status and is nothing but the representation of things that have already been represented.

Whereas the theory of marvelous realism has an enormous impact on Latin American literature, the only Caribbean country to respond explicitly to Carpentier's ideas was, not surprisingly, Haiti.[27] It was in Haiti, after all, that Carpentier's ideas were first formulated and, perhaps, first disseminated. René Depestre makes reference in his article "Le réel merveilleux haitien" to Carpentier's lecture and the effect it had on its audience.[28] Depestre clearly sees "le realisme merveilleux" as a compensatory fantasy that allows the spirit of the Haitian people to endure their nightmarish plight. For Depestre, marvelous realism is really a kind of romantic atavism; it is grounded in a poetics of alterity that allows the Haitian poet to produce an image of Haiti that functioned as an alternative to the Christian West. Ultimately, Depestre is interested in using "le réel merveilleux" to celebrate the ceremony of the Bois Caiman in 1791 as a founding myth for Haiti that epitomizes cultural difference.

Carpentier's ideas were used in a far more original way by Depestre's contemporary Jacques Stephen Alexis, Curiously, Alexis never made any reference to Carpentier in his theoretical writing.[29] This silence is surprising since he had been exposed to Carpentier's ideas and even used the term *marvelous realism,* which if it were not invented by the Cuban novelist had been popularized by him in the 1940s. Alexis borrows from Carpentier the Spenglerian view of history. The West was now in a phase of decadence in accordance with Spengler's theory of the cycles of history and the Caribbean was in a state of exuberant youthfulness. The words used by Alexis in his two majors essays, "Du réalisme merveilleux des Haitiens" and "Où va le roman," to describe Western art are *exhausted, anaemic, alienated,* and *cold.* In this regard, he echoes Carpentier's mocking of the surrealists' art as cold-blooded and contrived. In contrast, the art of Haiti was "a new wine that we novelists of young cultures have to offer the world."[30] Alexis also takes from Carpentier the concept of the Caribbean's identity as that of a New World Mediterranean: "When you think for instance that around the Caribbean Basin and the gulf of Mexico a veritable Central American Mediterranean, the different nations that live there have experienced in the past similar conditions for being populated and for migration . . . you cannot be surprised by the fact that they are experiencing a confluence of their diverse national cultures."[31] Alexis was, thereby, proposing for Haiti not a national or racial identity but essentially a zonal one. He actually saw this process of "zonal confluence" as a larger global pattern that caused individual cultural traits to weaken over time and fuse to form new hybrid varieties:

> Moreover, a zonal confluence of cultures is not peculiar to Central and Latin America, all the nations of Western Europe seem to have embarked on a process of interpenetration of diverse national cultures and in all the major regions of the globe, you notice the same phenomenon. . . . One must wonder in the face of this confluence of national cultures in zones, if we are not witnessing in today's world the beginning of the creation of zonal cultures which, at a higher level, would dominate national cultures.[32]

This view of globalized cultural interpenetration, coming from a writer whose intellectual culture tended to be fiercely nationalistic and delivered at a conference devoted to racial solidarity, is certainly a "masterpiece of daring and tact."[33] It is based on a concept of culture as a process of ceaseless metamorphosis that makes Carpentier more the precursor to Alexis than was Roumain, whose work manifested an anxiety to recover lost origins. In 1956, Alexis was attempting to resist the idea of Haitian culture as esoteric other; rather, culture was a dynamic process that was ongoing and could not be reversed. As Alexis stated, "Culture is an unceasing becoming whose origins are lost in the night of time past and whose evolution fades into the mists of the future."[35]

In Alexis's novels, which can be considered massive inventories of specific periods of Haitian history, it is culture as process and transformation that is privileged. In such a system, negritude, with its single-minded devotion to cultural retention, remains little more than a compensatory fantasy in the face of the hegemonic claims of Europe. The world presented is one of multiple voices and unceasing change. In this, Alexis shares Carpentier's fascination with music as the most natural and expressive emanation of New World space. The very title of Alexis's novel *Les arbres musciens* indicates this, and the forest in the novel is invariably expressed in terms of music and sound:

"The canticle of canticles of the earth wandered through harmony and disharmony, wound and unwound its sounds, its semiquavers, its arpeggios, its polyphony."[35] And: "The forest whistles and hums unceasingly with the wind twisting its way between the gnarled tree trunks. The entire forest is a massive organ which modulates with its multiple voices."[36] In both of these excerpts, the music is not one of simple pastoral harmony but of "multiple voices" and a "polyphony" of sounds. One of Alexis's characters goes so far as to see "this wild polyphony" as superior to "the motets of Italian cantors of the 14th century."

In Alexis's novels it is the quest for mastery or control that is doomed to failure. In *Les arbres musciens,* those characters driven by an almost libidinal impulse to devour or dominate, such as Edgard Osmin or his brother Diogene, or the U.S. ambassador, for that matter, are doomed to fail. It is those characters who are capable of adaptation and transformation who survive the catastrophy of the present. In *Les arbres musciens,* this is clearly exemplified by the orphan Gonaibo, who leaves the forest behind at the end of the novel. It is also exemplified by the son of the peasant Theagene Melon, who also leaves the world of his father behind. This fascination with change and urbanization is perhaps strongest in Alexis's last novel, *L'espace d'un cillement.*[37] Set in Port-au-Prince, the protagonists in this story are not Haitian but Cuban. La Nina Estrellita is a prostitute and El Caucho is the son of a Haitian mother and a Cuban father. The story is about the woman's awakening social and political consciousness and the man's involvement in the trade-union movement in Port-au-Prince. In Alexis's work, an aesthetic *prise de position* always implies a political ethic.

In his definition of Caribbean culture as part of that of the Americas, Alexis was not interested in strange juxtapositions of incongruous items or cultural patterns. Alexis forgoes the surrealist practice of violent juxtapositions for a notion of cultural fusion. As he argues in his essay on marvelous realism, "fusion would be even more accelerated in this land where everything was to be rebuilt."[38] The marvelous becomes the ultimate transgressive force in Haiti's culture; it is the marvelous as baroque metamorphosis that produces new cultural forms. The role of the artist was to chart and to encourage this process of transgressive change. It is important to remember that the work Alexis never managed to complete was entitled *La Chine miraculeuse.* It seems clear that his sense of the miraculous and the marvelous was closely allied with the realistic, especially the politically realistic.

In 1956, Alexis, inspired by Carpentier's sense of a transcendental marvelous, was theorizing a new idea of Caribbean time and space that would liberate the region from an asphyxiating series of colonial, anticolonial, and national constructs. Despite its longing for fusion, there is something unfinalized about Haitian and Caribbean identity in Alexis's theory of zonal ethnogenesis, and this lack of finality easily identifies it with a modernist suspicion of systems of mastering and an exploration of a more interrelational concept of historical change. The appropriation of the Mediterranean as Caribbean space may have its limitations, clinging as it did to the idea of apocalyptic nature as a release from the weight of history, but it is a significant step in the discursive repositioning of the Caribbean.

The Twilight of the New World

In an unwittingly direct response to Fredric Jameson's claim that one of the main cartographic projects of Third World modernism was "appropriating the great imperial space of the Mediterranean," Derek Walcott, referring in his 1992 Nobel lecture to Joyce's use of the *Odyssey* as a map for reading Dublin, describes Port of Spain as

> so racially various that the cultures of the world—the Asiatic, the Mediterranean, the European, the African—would be represented in it, its humane variety more exciting than Joyce's Dublin. Its citizens would intermarry as they chose, from instinct, not tradition, until their children find it increasingly futile to trace that genealogy. . . . This is Port of Spain to me, a city ideal in its commercial and human proportions, where a citizen is a walker and not a pedestrian, and this is how Athens may have been before it became a cultural echo.[39]

If Carpentier's hero in *The Lost Steps* loses his way in the jungle and is forced to live in one the American cities from which he feels alienated, Walcott consciously chooses the Caribbean's experience of modernity, the city of the other America, as an exemplary zone of exchange and interrelating. The relationship between Athens and Port of Spain and the definition of their citizens as "walkers" suggest his interrogation of historical time and ancestral origins and an exploration of the sense of wonder that he sees as fundamental to the New World psyche.

The importance of Walcott's vision of the Caribbean city as polyglot and indeterminate can be shown if it is contrasted with Fanon's view of the neurotic Caribbean city in *Black Skin, White Masks*. For Fanon, the heart of Fort-de-France is a petrified, regimented space called the Savannah.

> Imagine a square about 600 feet long and 125 feet wide, its sides bounded by worm-eaten tamarind trees, one end marked by the huge war memorial (the nation's gratitude to its children), the other by the Central Hotel; a miserable tract of uneven cobbles, pebbles that roll away under one's feet; and, amid all this, three or four hundred young fellows are walking up and down, greeting one another, grouping—no they never form groups, they go on walking.[40]

The symbolic heart of Fanon's city is a stony arena, constricting and sterile. Walkers are forced into narrow paths and obliged to repeat, endlessly, the same pattern, which is dictated by the totalitarian square. Nature has been banished and the life of the group is frozen into a desperate mimicry watched over by the "huge war memorial." For Fanon, the colonial city is a morbid world, a poisonous adjunct of the metropolitan city.

Walcott's Caribbean city is anything but an uncreative adjunct or parody of metropolitan culture. The Caribbean city is a bold recreation of the fragments of other cultures. His insistence is consistently on the brilliant nonoriginality of Caribbean culture. His emphasis is not genealogical but intercultural. As Walcott puts it, "Break a vase, and the love that reassembles the fragments is stronger than the love which took its symmetry for granted when it was whole. . . . Antillean art is this restoration of our shattered histories, our shards of vocabulary. . . . And this is the exact process of the making of poetry, or what should not be called its 'making' but its remaking."[41] In Walcott's equal emphasis on the freshness, the novelty of this New World recreation, the "walkers" in his city can just as easily be called "wakers." Within this space, as Walcott puts it, "the body moves like a walking, waking island."[42]

In Walcott's poetic universe, the Mediterranean symbolizes an intercultural matrix, the geographic correlative to the Caribbean archipelago. This is the poet's strategy for wresting the Caribbean Islands free from the stereotypes of fragmentation and dependency. The Caribbean then emerges as quintessential American space, profuse, baroque, and creolizing. It is not the horror of privation that Walcott evokes but its virtues, as he observes, "In the Antilles poverty is poetry with a 'v', *une vie,* a condition of life as well as of imagination."[43] This "condition of imagination" is based on a re-creative response, on an aesthetic of juxtaposition of heterogenous items, on verbal agglutinations. As we have seen, this is also the view of Carpentier in *Explosion in a Cathedral.* Walcott, too, is equally interested in the hyphenating function of the New World imagination. Rei Terada, in a wonderfully insightful reading of Walcott's poetry, points to his frequent use of "pivots," "hinges," "stitches." As Terada observes, in Walcott's *Omeros,* "books have seams and semes. Walcott's swift a poetic seamstress, cross-stitches beginning to end. . . . The swift's hyphenating function is finally the faculty of poetic language itself, scanning disparate textual features."[44]

Walcott's relation to Carpentier is not as explicit as Alexis's. However, his awareness of Carpentier's work and in particular that crucial novel *The Lost Steps* is apparent in the epigraph to section 2 of *Another Life.* Walcott is drawn to Carpentier's imaginative struggle with seeing the New World purely in Adamic terms, and like Carpentier he senses that an intimate and idyllic identification with nature cannot shut out the ironies of New World history and the clamouring voices of the Caribbean. Arguably, Walcott represents for Caribbean poetry the possibility of breaking free from the transcendental vision of a poetics of *verrition* and exploring what Glissant would later term the poetics of transversality. If there is a master theme in Walcott's work, it must be the enactment and the reenactment of the confrontation of transcendental purity and transversal contingency. It is in this context that we must position his increasing preoccupation with the possibility of the re-creation of a Graeco-Hellenic Caribbean, a Homeric America. The imaginative construct of the Mediterranean allows the poet to resist the flight into nature and the temptations of erasure that haunted an earlier generation. It is the move away from the temptation of new beginnings, of pastoral plenitude, tellingly dramatized in the autobiographical poem *Another Life,* that provides that capacity to exploit the emancipatory trope of a Caribbean twilight. The magical and liberating fantasy of a Caribbean twilight provides a clear epistemological break between Walcott and his Caribbean counterparts in my chapter 3, who longed for the light of an Adamic dawn.

To this extent, Walcott's poetic impulse can be considered translational in the same way that Carpentier's fictional world is seen as representing things that in themselves are representations. Just as original inscriptions are lost in the flood at the end of the Cuban novelist's
The Lost Steps, Walcott's aesthetic is translational and intertextual
rather than essentialist and foundational. He fits into Pérez Firmat's
definition of the "critical criollist." In his discussion of Cuban literature, Firmat makes a difference between critical and primitive creolization: "The critical criollist has a less ambitious but more realistic
aim: he wants to inflect, rather than efface, European culture. Thus
he seeks a relative, relational 'originality' rather than an absolute,
pristine 'aboriginality'. . . . One is a foundational enterprise, the other
is a translational enterprise."[45] In his preoccupation with hyphenating and re-creation, Walcott clearly qualifies himself as a critical criollist." He also has raised the specific issue of translation in one of his
best-known essays, "The Muse of History," when in praising the
Mediterranean dimension of the work of St. John Perse and Aimé Césaire he asserts that the poetry has "the appearance of translation
from an older epic."[46]

Walcott's vision of the New World Mediterranean allows us to explore the relation between the translational and a creole transversality. In the literature of the anglophone Caribbean, the debate sur-
rounding creolization is much older than Walcott and is tied to a
refutation of the image of uncreative dependency that has been attached to the Caribbean. Two theoretical positions have traditionally
seen the region as fragmented and dependent. The plantation school
of theorists have so insisted on the structures of domination and the
conformity of the majority that there is little possibility of grasping
and exploring the creative resistance that the plantation might
spawn. Equally pessimistic a view is that of Caribbean pluralism,
which focuses on the fragmentation and division in plantation
society. Whether the Caribbean people are seen as a subject group or
as stranded groups, these theoretical models demonstrate little interest in the active role of Caribbean people. Herein lies the major importance of the idea of creolization for the Caribbean.

It is perhaps no coincidence that creolization concentrates on culture and is usually defended by artists. Their focus is invariably on
the inadequacies of a rigidly socioeconomic interpretation of relationships in plantation society. From the outset, the argument for
creolization was based on relations and interactions between indi-

viduals and groups. Indeed, not only did the creole model depend on the collective as opposed to the individual, it also was less interested in direct challenges to the system than in cultural resistance within a context of domination. For the proponents of creolization, it is less the externally driven explicit rebellion of the maroon that is noteworthy; it is rather the internal, psychic processes that allowed groups not only to endure but to actively engage in a more subtle, re-creative response to a hegemonic system. The plantation and plural-society models underestimate the capacities of those caught in the system to generate a new culture. Brathwaite, both poet and historian, made a case for a new dynamic in plantation society. He criticized traditional models as simplistic and raised the issue of the transformative power of a collective *imaginaire:* "The plantation . . . does not contain all that is planted. Therefore, it is essential that our concepts and models, when made and applied, should be applied not only to the outer field of reality, but to our inscapes equally."[47]

It was, perhaps, the poet in Brathwaite that made him so acutely sensitive to "inscapes." Yet he may have been too much of a historian to explore fully the implications of his observations. The exploration of inscapes and Caribbean space as a re-creative ground is more fully realized in the work of such writers as Claude McKay and C. L. R. James. For instance, in the work of McKay, the question of hybridity and exile are problematized. *Home,* in his autobiography *A long Way from Home* (1937), does not refer to Clarendon but to Harlem, a community of migrants and displaced people. Similarly, his novel of postemancipation Jamaica, *Banana Bottom* (1933), develops the ideas of the hybrid personality whose legitimacy is equal to that of the native inhabitant. Already McKay seems to have sensed that the ideal of an organic, traditional community, safe from the unrelenting spread of modernity, was a self-indulgent fantasy.

The issue of creole culture formation within a global, modernizing context is given greater theoretical formulation in the works of C. L. R. James. James is clearly fascinated by the way in which the group or team can retake power within a situation of domination. In his work, the dominated community is not docile or passive, despite the fact that there is no possibility of escape to an elsewhere outside of the prevailing system. This idea is first raised in his early historical study of the Haitian revolution. In *The Black Jacobins* (1938), James is drawn to the figure of Toussaint-Louverture and his vision of the

Haitian revolution within a global culture. Toussaint-Louverture, in James's view, does not wish to create a maroon state but to transform Haiti into a modern revolutionary state, just as the *sans culottes* had done in France. What is striking here is the concept of revolutionary change within a global culture, and that it is not a nativist plea for isolation and an atavistic return to tradition.

This issue becomes even more evident in *Beyond a Boundary* (1963), James's celebrated study of the game of cricket. In the first few lines of this work, James focuses his attention on a much over-looked detail—that his home town, "like all towns and villages on the island, . . . possessed a recreation ground."[48] The recreative and re-creative possibilities of this space, or field of play, is the most star-tling aspect of James's study of cricket. The code of conduct that dominates this field of play is harsh and Victorian. Under the um-pires' watchful, repressive eyes, the puritanical code of self-restraint and reticence is enforced in a tropical environment. But the "re-creation ground" allows for a level of dramatic, creative performance that ultimately disrupts and subverts the rules of the game. Cricket falls into that area of human activity and experience that, in James's words, "my history and my politics did not seem to cover."[49] He is struck by the passion of "the common people" for "organized sport and games." Cricket then emerges as a paradigm for those areas of Caribbean life that are normally overlooked by historians and soci-ologists. To this extent, the relationship between carnival and social transformation that a later generation would explore is not unrelated to James's insight into play, performance, and the transformation of the social *imaginaire*.

James, like Walcott, relates cultural practices in the West Indies to those of ancient Greece. James goes so far as to confess he be-lieved "that if when I left school I had gone into the society of An-cient Greece I would have been more at home than ever I had been since. It was a fantasy for me, it had meaning."[50] He saw in the re-lation between sports, drama, and democracy a universal ideal that was more his heritage than anything that had come down from that class-ridden, colonial power Great Britain. The Athens-Tunapuna rela-tionship is already explored thirty years prior to Derek Walcott's Nobel lecture. The cricket field is conceptualized as a primal modern and modernist space, where boundaries, both real and figurative, are fre-quently and creatively transgressed. James's treatment of resistance to the tyranny of the system through play seems almost to anticipate Mikhail Bakhtin's examination of the roots of travesty and parody in early Greece.[51] Cricket represented, as it were, a creative polyglossia in the face of the centralizing, monologic discourse of the colonial system.

The question of the relationship between a translational sensibility and the emergence of a creole culture is again implied in James's model. It is in this regard that postmodernity has been of significant value in providing a theoretical and philosophical basis for the somewhat undertheorized idea of creolization. Formed within a context of domination and subordination, creolization is an unceasing process that does not result in homogeneity but creative contention and interaction. This is precisely the interpretation of the text that is elaborated by the theoreticians of deconstruction. Bakhtin's own theorizing raises the question of representation by asserting that a given utterance may not actually represent reality but be the representation of a previous "speech act" about a given reality; hence, his interest in the process of parody and travesty. The deconstruction of the notion of the original, of the concept of a unified, transcendental beginning, is the main focus of the ideas of Michel Foucault and Jacques Derrida. Their notion of the text as continually shifting—"at play," as it were—seems to have enormous implications for the construction of a model for social and cultural creolization. The translational impulse then becomes the only reality, as it allows further room for play, improvization, and extension of the boundaries of the permissible. In Derrida's view, God emerges as the ultimate deconstructionist by creating the Tower of Babel; thenceforth, no one tongue can be imposed, and all mankind is obliged to submit to a plurality of languages.[52]

Walcott's vision of the New World Mediterranean is inextricably bound up with the idea of Babel. In his celebration of Port of Spain, he speaks of a "downtown Babel of shop signs and streets, mongrelized, polyglot, a ferment without a history, like heaven. Because that is what such a city is, in the New World, a writer's heaven."[53] Here the "complex polyglossia" that was, as Bakhtin observed, "characteristic of Hellenism" is rediscovered in the Caribbean.[54] Port of Spain becomes, for Walcott, a particularly carnivalesque field of play, an exuberant, dramatic bazaar of languages and styles—the quintessential heart of the other America.

This imaginative geography penetrates the creative crepuscularity of Walcott's poetry, which is so profoundly synchronic and relational. The hyphenating impulse that Terada examines facilitates the linking of worlds, genres, and styles; therefore, Walcott's poems can be seen as playgrounds for innumerable, irreverent acts of subversion. Perhaps Walcott's verse should not be read as poems at all—at least in the strict definition of the genre—but as an indeterminate form that constantly drifts toward the novel. Walcott himself notes in "The Muse of History" that "the primal imagination in West Indian literature is "crucially evolving in West Indian fiction."[55]

An important clue to the significance of Walcott's observation is the idea elaborated by Bakhtin that prose fiction does greater justice to the polyglossic nature of social and linguistic experience than the canonical genres of poetry and drama. The novel's anticanonical potential derives from the parody and travesty that Bakhtin locates in Greek farce. He refers, for instance, to the comic Hercules, "the monstrous glutton, the playboy, the drunk and scrapper, but essentially Hercules the madman." The element of comic mimicry, he continues, "forces us to experience those sides of the object that are not otherwise included in a given genre or a given style."[56] It should, then, come as no surprise that Walcott's poetry should favor the long narrative form or that the epic poem *Omeros* should be divided into sixty-four chapters in seven books.

Perhaps the most dramatic example of the parodic mode in Walcott's verse is to be found in "Spoiler's Return." The Calypsonian's name is perfectly suited to the image of the parodic and parasitic figure: "So, crown and mitre me Bedbug the First— / the gift of mockery with which I'm cursed."[57] The persona of the poem emerges as joker, thief, and vermin. The mode of satire and mimicry that is highly developed in this poem makes Walcott, in the Bakhtinian sense, a true heir of the parodic forms of the Greeks. This produces a new artistic and linguistic consciousness that Walcott would see as perfectly suited to the New World as a whole and to an archipelago of islands in particular. As Bakhtin explained, "Linguistic consciousness—parodying the direct word, direct style, exploring its limits, its absurd sides, the face specific to an era—constituted itself *outside* this direct word. . . . A new mode developed for working creatively with language: the creating artist began to look at language from the outside, with another's eyes. . . . The creating consciousness stands, as it were, on the boundary line between languages and styles."[58] Bakhtin's observations radically overturn the opposition between native and exile, local and foreign. It is the foreignness of native speech, the creative outsiderness of the poet, that releases the power of the creating consciousness. Caribbean polyglossia, like its Hellenic predecessor, facilitates the condition that frees artistic consciousness "from the tyranny of its own language and its myth of language."

As Terada explains in her perceptive examination of Walcott—a study that both paradoxically omits Walcott's emphasis on the Mediterranean matrix and makes no real use of Bakhtin—the creole and the universal are creatively juxtaposed in the poetry. "Walcott's internationalism is the other side of his creolization. By entering English Walcott feels St. Lucian contours as though he were an outsider, exploring its creole etiologies; but the English he enters is in turn creole. For the genuinely polyglossic poet outside and inside lose their conventional meanings."[59] It is within this flux of linguistic forms and styles that Walcott constructs his "Twilight," an ideal of Caribbean creole identity. This quest for self-definition is given a significant reformulation by Walcott. In "The Schooner Flight," his wandering narrator, Shabine, who is racially indeterminate, sets off on a romantic quest "for one island that heals with its harbour and guiltless horizon." However, his search is futile. As he realizes, "[t]here are so many islands as the stars at night." The earth itself is merely one "island in archipelagos of stars."[60] In the same way that the islands of the archipelago have broken away from the mainland and are cast adrift on the Caribbean Sea, so no fixed home or stable essence can be identified for Walcott's "fortunate traveller."

Like Carpentier in *The Lost Steps*, Walcott enacts the drama of displacement and the impossibility of possessing any ultimate truth in the poem "The Light of the World." Rosario is as elusive as the beautiful, anonymous woman on the "transport" in his poem. The poet is a traveler among other travelers, a wanderer in a community of transients. However, his state of being transported, physically and emotionally, comes to an end. "They went on in their transport, they left me on earth."[61] The relationship between the poet and the beautiful woman on the bus has a direct parallel in a short story by Gabriel García Márquez, "Sleeping Beauty and the Airplane." Like Walcott, García Márquez is enacting the experience of the New World traveler. In García Márquez's story, the woman leaves without revealing her secret. The story ends with "Sleeping Beauty" disappearing into "the Amazon jungle of New York."[62] For García

Márquez as for Walcott, the Caribbean city represents a new forest of symbols.

For Walcott, to be a Caribbean poet in the Americas is to be the ultimate kind of poet. The only parallel situation, geographically, is to be found in the Aegean Sea, which also produced a wealth of cultural and artistic diversity. As Walcott explains, "I think that an archipelago, whether Greek or West Indian, is bound to be a fertile area, particularly if it is a bridge between continents, and a variety of people settle there."[63] The symbolic power of the Mediterranean in Walcott's imagination can perhaps best be described, in Bakhtinian terms, as chronotopic. As a governing motif, the chronotope of the Mediterranean forms a kind of gravitational center in Walcott's imagination. It is not a foundational myth but rather an idea that allows the exploration of a number of complex issues in Caribbean literature. It is as if the promise of the polyglossia of the Aegean Sea is not so much fulfilled by Europe as by the Caribbean. For Walcott, as for Carpentier and Alexis, the route to self-discovery in the other America lay through the repossession of Mediterranean space.

Through the Mediterranean as intertextual matrix, a number of powerful tropes enter Caribbean writing: the field of play, the city as a polyglot Athens, the Babel of the Caribbean Sea, the magic of the twilight, and the futility of the flight into nature. This would signify an epistemological rupture with the earlier search for an aboriginal identity, for pastoral seclusion. Increasingly, urban vitality, street performance, and the maelstrom of the crowd will enter Caribbean writing. A new, antipastoral modernism will attempt to create an art form from the dissonance, incongruity, and chaos of modernity. Such an implication of this new sensibility is precisely described by Jonathan Raban in *Soft City:*

> The idea of the city as encyclopedia or emporium is a useful
> one . . . (it) suggests the special randomness of the city's diversity: it
> hints that, compared with other books or communities, the logic of
> the city is not the kind which lends itself to straightforward narration
> or to continuous page by page reading. At the same time, it does
> imply that the city is a repository of knowledge, although no single
> reader or citizen can command the whole of that knowledge.[64]

5

Fields of Play: Parody and the Postmodern

But America is not a novel, it is a comedy of errors.

—Guiliermo Cabrera Infante, *Mea Cuba*

One of the basic impulses in Caribbean thought is undeniably the need to reconceptualize power. The fascination with worlds of closure; the need to ground a new society on a visionary discourse; the exploration of a foundational poetics; Césaire's conception of poetry as "rupestral inscription"—all these manifestations of the desire to establish a new authority, to repossess time and space. It is no coincidence that this pursuit of an ordering and ordaining vision is essentially a poetic one. In his passionate defence of poetry *The Bow and the Lyre*, Octavio Paz in a fuller way than Césaire, his counterpart in the other America, celebrates poetry as "the disincarnate word" and the "poet's mission" as "the need to re-establish the original word."[1] Paz's text is essentially self-serving since he proclaims the value of poetry over prose: the latter is condemned as a profane compromise with rationality.

As an unrepentant modernist, Paz refuses to acknowledge equally important but perhaps less visible manifestations of the postmodern in the Americas. However, as can be sensed in as early a writer as Oswald Durand, the deconstructive substratum that sees power as elusive and all knowledge as infinite is already apparent. The gradual shift from poetry to prose, from poetic vision to novelistic discourse, marks the liberation of the substratum of postmodernity in the other America. The turn to prose, not as an extension of "the disincarnate word" but as an exploration of the carnal, the ambiguous, and the heterogenous, marks the epistemological rupture with the poetic and revolutionary dream of a utopian reunion of word and world.

In understanding this shift from the poetic to what Mikhail Bakhtin would call the parodic, Bakhtin is a far more reliable guide than Paz. Bakhtin, writing in the Soviet Union in the 1920s, when an old aristocratic order had fallen and social, geographical, and cultural borders were becoming erased, was acutely sensitive to the importance of the mingling of codes and the impossibility of transcendent visions. His interest in the early "parodic-travestying forms" of classical literature that "prepared the ground for the novel" is of vital importance to understanding the emergence of a novelistic discourse in the Caribbean. The liberation of Caribbean prose is closely tied to Bakhtin's assertion that early parodic forms mark a break with epic poetry because "they liberated the object from the power of language in which it had become entangled as if in a net; they destroyed the homogenizing power of myth over language; they freed consciousness from the power of the direct word."[2] Away from the homophony of poetry to the polyphony of the novel, Bakhtin traces the collapse of an absolute order and the emergence of a new linguistic festivity.

The emergence of the postmodern in the novel has already been explored in Alejo Carpentier and traced in C. R. L. James's notion of the "recreation field" and the mock-heroic style that emerges in the later work of the Caribbean's most novelistic poet, Derek Walcott. It is not only the turn to prose that is impotant here but the creative possibilities that exist between powerlessness and play. Even though this is yet to be investigated, there is a practice of the postmodern in the Caribbean that is not related to the concept of postmodernity in industrialized societies. The turbulence, the diversity, the indeterminacy left in the wake of the collapse of the plantation as a production site is no doubt key to the application of the postmodern to the Caribbean archipelago.[3]

In the emergence of a Caribbean postmodernity, the female writers of the region have played a vital role. This pattern is by no means unique to the Caribbean. As Linda Hutcheon observes in *A Poetics of Postmodernism*, "women have helped develop the postmodern, valuing of the margins and the ex-centric as a way out of the power problematic of centers."[4] However, the contesting of the text as a site for the conjunction of power and knowledge is central to traditions of writing by Caribbean women. In this regard, they reanimate the relationship between the postmodern and the novel that, Bakhtin argues, is at the very foundation of the genre: "The novel begins by presuming a verbal and semantic decentering of the ideological world, a certain linguistic homelessness of literary consciousness, which no longer possesses a sacrosanct and unitary linguistic medium for containing ideological thought."[5] The novel may not have begun in this way in the Caribbean, but the "decentering of the ideological world" certainly marks the beginning of a female literary tradition in the Caribbean.

The Female Grotesque

With good reason, women writers are acutely aware of the negative, and even neurotic, consequences of powerlessness. It should then come as no surprise that the strength of their contribution to Caribbean literature lies in their capacity to interrogate and demystify systems of total explanation. Nor should it be surprising that this contribution has been at its most creative in the novel, with that form's powerful decentering possibilities. It is no coincidence that the preferred form for female novelists is not that of conventional realism; rather, their literary production is dominated by the first-person monologue, the diary, the epistolary novel, the ramblings of the neurotic, or the unreliable reminiscence of the aged. Their characters, too, are invariably poised between past and future, life and death, heaven and earth. The great danger in critically assessing this practice of writing has been the temptation to essentialize, by either privileging the victim as the voice, if it is collective anguish, or by asserting the counterorder of a matriarchy.

Yet this tradition is arguably at its best when it takes an irreverent stand against all totalizing and centering systems. It is in this regard that the contribution of women writers to a Caribbean poetics is most significant. It is also from this perspective that the short story "Folie" (Madness) by the Haitian novelist Marie Chauvet can be seen as a major statement on Caribbean writing as a whole, and a perhaps unprecedented exploration of a Bakhtinian poetics of "parodic-travestying forms." This might seem paradoxical since "Folie" is the least-noticed story of Chauvet's pathbreaking *Amour, Colère, Folie.*

The subversive force of Chauvet's "Folie" can be seen as the culmination, or at least the most extreme manifestation of a deconstructive impulse that is apparent in her earlier work. In an essay, Joan Dayan argues very perceptively that Chauvet's novels demonstrate a refusal to idealize and tend rather to "detail the pressing needs of abject lives."[6] Dayan is acutely sensitive to the ambiguities of Chauvet's earlier work of fiction *Fonds des Nègres* (1961), which she sees as a subversive response to that legendary creation of heroic modernism from Haiti's literary avant-garde, Jacques Roumain's *Governeurs de la rosée*:

> In Roumain's book hope returns with the arrival of Manuel, the worker, to his native land, where the peasants who have no "esprit" and do not know, will be redeemed by the intellectual who knows. Although that possible renewal is fraught with ambiguity . . . Manuel dies a hero. In *Fonds des Nègres,* the promise embodied in the dreams of Papa Beauville comes with the visit of Marie-Ange to a land in which she has no intention of remaining. The story of why she does finally remain undermines any claim to heroics.[7]

Unfortunately, despite Dayan's perceptiveness, "Folie" gets short shrift in this essay, as it does, equally and perhaps even more surprisingly, in Dayan's short study entitled "Reading Women in the Caribbean: Marie Chauvet's *Love, Anger, Madness.*[8] In the latter essay, Dayan justifiably makes a claim for the literary rehabilitation of Chauvet and offers thoughtful readings of "Love" and "Anger." "Madness," one suspects, is ignored, almost completely, because this third tale contains no female protagonist who corresponds to Claire or Rose in the other two stories.

The place in Haitian literature of *Amour, Colère, Folie,* Chauvet's fourth work, has been, and still is, very uncertain. Once published, in 1968, this work was seen by Haitian critics as too daring politically and too critical of the Haitian bourgeoisie to receive public acclaim. For Chauvet, divorce, exile, and silence followed in quick succession. However, this trilogy, and "Folie" in particular, must mark both the most powerful assault on literary modernism in the Caribbean and the full-blown emergence of a postmodernist poetics.

It is hard to think of another writer in the Caribbean who explores the claustrophobic world of the grotesque as fully as Chauvet does in her trilogy. To the same extent that female characters tend to represent ground, and invariably open ground, Chauvet's protagonists represent grotto or cloistered space. The grotto-esque, as it were, is readily apparent physically in the first story, "Amour," in which Claire, the main character, locks herself away in her bedroom, and aesthetically in the use of an interior monologue sustained through her poisonous and caustic personal diary.

To take Dayan's comparison between *Fonds* and Roumain's *Gouverneurs* even further, Annaise's virgin fecundity and grounded femininity in Roumain's novel metamorphoses into a monstrous childlessness and a shameful genealogy in "Amour." For that matter, Claire is as different from Annaise as she is from Simone Schwarz-Bart's Telumée in *The Bridge of Beyond,* a narrative dominated by the metonymical force of the whisps of smoke from Telumée's pipe. Schwarz-Bart's character is a disincarnate, Ariel-like figure capable of disintegrating material reality into almost Mallarméan smoke rings, whereas Claire is the embodiment of a freakish carnality. One is tempted to see a relationship between Claire's body and Chauvet's view of the Haitian body politic, with its emaciated peasantry, incestuous bourgeoisie, and repressive politics.

"Amour" also turns on the relationship between Claire's bedroom and the street, with a related link between writing and action. Claire not only locks herself away but locks away her anger and potential for action in her diary, in which she fantasizes about violence, murder, and suicide. Unexpectedly, at the end of the story, Claire ventures outside to commit an apparently revolutionary act. She stabs Caledu, the army commander, who has wreaked havoc on the town. This act is, to say the least, an ambiguous one and a travesty of what Fanon would have seen as liberating violence. The act of writing in "Amour" does not lead to change but remains self-involved. From the outset of her trilogy, Chauvet is slyly subverting the pretensions of the modernist avant-garde. Caledu is stabbed with a double-edged letter opener, a wickedly ironic weapon for effecting political transformation. Not surprisingly, at the story's end Claire does not join the rebels in the street but retreats to the security of her grotto-bedroom and the self-indulgent fantasies of her pen.

Like "Amour," "Folie" is set in a small provincial town in a country where mistrust and paranoia are ubiquitous. The tale is told by one of four mad poets who have barricaded themselves in a foul-smelling, vermin-infested room for protection from an invasion of devils. In this story pandemonium, literally, reigns. As in the other stories in the trilogy, the town is under the control of a sinister military commander called Cravache. In "Folie," Cravache suspects the mad poets of subversive activities because they go around the town shouting "Aux armes!"—part of the poem "L'Alarme," written in the late nineteenth century by the Haitian poet Massillon Coicou.

Written eleven years after François Duvalier came to power and seven years after the execution by Duvalier of Jacques Stephen Alexis, after he and a few others attempted to land clandestinely in Haiti with the hope of overthrowing Duvalier, "Folie" focuses on the nightmare of the Duvalierist state and—perhaps the work's most important aspect—tackles the disturbing reality of writing in a brutal, authoritarian system. The reference to Coicou is by no means incidental. Coicou (1867–1908) was considered one of the most politically *engagé,* and greatest, writers of patriotic verse in nineteenth-century Haiti because of his book of poems *Poésies Nationales,* published in 1892, Chauvet's mad poets attempt in their own pathetic way to imitate Coicou. They succeed in a way they would never have imagined or desired: Coicou and his two brothers were executed by firing squad in 1908 by a paranoid President Nord Alexis, and "Folie" ends with René and his brother poets André and Simon about to be executed by firing squad. History repeats itself in "Folie" with a wretched pointlessness as the poets become martyrs futilely; they have no hope of either overthrowing the state or of provoking revolt among the dispossessed.

Unlike Chauvet's earlier *Fonds des nègres,* which essentially is a peasant novel, *Amour, Colère, Folie* deals with the provincial bourgeoisie and, "Folie" even more explicitly than "Amour," the issue of literary commitment. In so doing, "Folie" holds up to ridicule the legend of the Haitian avant-garde. René, the main protagonist, oscillates between a self-assertive exhibitionism and its opposite, paranoid voyeurism. His fantasies are of worlds of endless vistas, of panoramic horizons. In reality, he is forced to look through a keyhole or a partly opened door to see what is taking place outside. The modernist myth of the poet as exerting creative dominance over the world through an Adamic naming is mocked, René being incapable of playing such a role. The logocentric paradigm and, perhaps, by extension, the ideal of the paternal creator, is undone in these tales of literary impotence.

René's unsuccessful attempt to inhabit or to be housed in a grand old tradition finds a direct equivalent in the dilapidated house that he cannot fully possess and within which he is barricaded into one, foul-smelling room. This room is a prisonhouse for his fevered mind—as much mental as physical space. It would be difficult in all of Caribbean literature to find a more poignant image of the degraded nature of a literary tradition based on the visionary, transcendental power of the poetic world. Indeed, the story seems constantly to link physical debility and poetic fervor. André's incessant scratching of an unhealed wound seems as much to do with poetic desire (the itch to write) as with the wound. Similarly, Jacques, as described by André, is physically entrapped by verse: "Caught in the trap of rhyme. He has fallen into the trap and can no longer get out. He can no longer run to escape rhyme. His legs are crippled. The mechanism of the trap has been unleashed and cut off his legs up to the thighs."[9]

Fantasy serves as a compensatory impulse in this story. René attempts to suppress his persistent sense of paralysis and impotence by dreaming of himself as a liberator. He summons up an old nationalist image of "ancestral majesty" as a way of resisting the invasion of devils: "I go forward, draped in ancestral majesty and with a kick open this door and walk up to them. Dessalines, Petion, Toussaint, Christophe! I call on our indomitable heroes for assistance" (336). However, this display of nationalist fervor is pointless in René's situation, and his dream of liberating the town is ultimately self-serving—a way of trying to win recognition for himself from the (inaccessible) love of his life, Cecile: "When I have liberated the town, Cecile will stretch out her hand to me. My name will resound in the four corners of the world. Do you know René? The great René who conquered the devils? Have you read his poems? I shall conquer the devils" (348).

René, as victim, dreams of domination; he is no different from the authoritarian political culture that created the atmosphere of suspicion and terror in the first place. Here Chauvet has put her finger on the disturbing reality that suggests that in every intellectual and writer there lurks the monster of all Haitian intellectuals, François Duvalier. As Laennec Hurbon put it, "In each intellectual as in each political leader, one can see the emergence of nothing but the phantom of Duvalier."[10]

It is perhaps not excessive to see in René's descent into madness the ludicrous extreme of the modernist legend of the avant-garde artist and its wild utopian fantasies. Just as the avant-garde created no generalized *prise de conscience,* so René and his fellow poets are cut off from the rest of society. They are alienated from both the bourgeoisie they despise and the masses—people described as poor wretches "gone to earth somewhere, in the hills, without water or provisions, without Vaudou drum or dance, without white rum or moonshine" (357). Indeed, "Folie" seems to suggest the tragic end of Haiti as a national community. It is ironic that the first Caribbean state to begin the experiment of creating a modern nation-state should here be so tellingly demonstrating the tragic impossibility of a national entity. The only mother in the story is René's, and she is the epitome of the degraded, exploitative relationships that exist in that society. Almost enslaved to a wealthy landowner by her own parents, she is raped. The child of mixed blood she produces is disowned by his father and yet desperately longs for the father's recognition. Socially and culturally dysfunctional, René personifies the flaws of the Haitian artist and intellectual.

René yearns for a time when ideas mattered, when words could change the world, and a poem could start a revolution. Such a time no longer exists—perhaps never really existed. René high-mindedly looks down on the philistines around him and nurtures a blind nostalgia for the romantic ideal of the poet as the cutting edge of consciousness. René cherishes the ideal of the artist as exemplary risk-taker, whose authority is obtained at immense physical and moral cost. Like Claire, he despises others because they remain in servile bondage to social and political reality. Yet Chauvet's story suggests that he and his malnourished brethren are themselves enslaved, to a romantic tradition they have eagerly adopted but that stifles and paralyses them. René's education seems to have given him a taste for the ideal of the *poète maudit* and the notion of artistic genius. "Mozart, the German, was my brother beyond blood, beyond the centuries and distance. A hyphenating link between races as were Villon, Baudelaire and Rimbaud. . . . Poet of damnation! Poet of imitation! Black poet shaped by France! Where is your tongue? White rum was mine! In order to forget, I got drunk night and day. Like Villon, like Baudelaire, like Rimbaud" (373–74). To fit this image he imagines his room is a *mansarde* (garret), despite that paradoxically it opens onto the street. The cruelly parodic nature of Chauvet's fiction reads like a defiant send-up of the heroics of modernism as defined in such texts as Césaire's *Poetry and Knowledge* and in the idealism of such writers of the generation of 1946 as Depestre and Alexis.[11]

René's dream is one of release from both demonic reality and his parochial society, but he cannot transcend the world of clogged, unyielding matter that surrounds him. The devils—physical debauchery, defiled space—represent the other extreme of René's asceticism. The binary oppositions of body and spirit, evil and good, darkness and light, are all powerful in René's Manichean imagination. The dark forces that pursue him have as much to do with the state police as with his acute sense of the world's fallenness. Consequently, and not surprisingly, he resorts to the mystical and the magical as a form of therapy. He predictably falls back on his childhood *Vaudou* beliefs and reduces Christian beliefs to the apocalyptic vision of the book of Revelation.

René's psychic agony finds escape in an esoteric spirituality that is nourished by faith in a world reborn, freed of evil. Huddled together in a filthy room, René and his friends are like a tiny, extremist sect that feeds on images of martyrdom and apocalyptic rebirth. They dream of a wrathful God, who with fire and brimstone will create order from the prevailing chaos. The entire story seems, at times, scripted in the language of the book of Revelation, from the first lines that suggest the claustrophobic entombment of the grotesque—"It was as if, suddenly, the convulsed earth, ravaged by a horrible cataclysm had opened and swallowed us"—to the last images of celestial ascent—"And it is then that the sky softly opened and I saw descending angels with shiny wings who took us in their arms and bore us away singing (428). The images of disorder, invariably, in the Bible, linked to the sea, are repeated in René's vision of cosmic disorder: "Its ravaging waves lift up abandoned sail boats and they are gnashed together like teeth" (341). These are the fantasies of impotence as rational political hope fails and marginalization and vulnerability provoke suprarational visions. Conventionally, in Caribbean literature, it is the peasantry who are shown to be afflicted by magicoreligious beliefs. In "Folie," Chauvet extended this dubious honor to the Haitian artist and intellectual.

Salvation is the story associated with an impossible purity. The world of "Folie" is one of unyielding and putrefying matter. The struggle between angels and demons will inevitably be resolved in favor of the latter. Imaginative activity becomes, in this hothouse atmosphere, a kind of ritualized incantation, magical formulae to provide escape from a demonic reality. René is haunted by the fear that his consciousness will disappear and he will fall silent. His answer is a desperate loquaciousness. His companions are caught in equally desperate mental games: "Jacques' blind gaze and his hand racing across the paper distract my thoughts from their purpose. The bovine inactivity of André gets on my nerves. He is always sitting, his arms hanging loosely, his mouth open unless he has his hands clasped muttering prayers" (370). In "Folie," we have a strange tribute to literary activity. Cravache and his police think the poets are the source of subversion and they therefore destroy the creators of words. The poets see words as creating an alternative world, or more precisely a multiplicity of worlds, that allows them to escape state control. Yet neither state paranoia nor poetic self-delusion are enough to salvage literary activity that seems headed for either pointless verbal excess or, the other extreme, passive silence.

If writing cannot bestow a state of grace, it is because of its profoundly unreliable and misleading nature. Writing in "Amour" is the equivalent of masturbatory fantasy. In "Folie," René's spiritual project, his belief in the purifying potential of language, his almost prudish longing for symmetry, comes up against a reality of profane multiple transformations—what Bakhtin classified as the *carnival grotesque*. Despite, or perhaps because of, René's majestic sense of his self-importance, the prevalent mood of the story is that of tragic farce. The mocking, derisive spirit of the carnivalesque is suggested in the epigraph to the story, where the identities of king and madman are deliberately blurred. Questions haunt the tale: Is wisdom a form of madness and vice versa? Could it be that the demonic forces of Duvalierism had finally created a grotesque orgy of equality in a society divided by class, color, and ideology?

"Folie" provides an illustration of the "peculiar logic" of the carnivalesque. As Bakhtin put it, "the peculiar logic of the 'inside out,' of the 'turnabout,' of a continual shifting from top to bottom, from front to rear, of numerous parodies and travesties, humiliations, profanations, comic crownings and uncrownings."[12] The story itself seems to follow the general pattern of the carnival. The first part is gruesome masquerade with devils in the street; when the carnival ends, with the throwing of a Molotov cocktail, the second part leads to the martyrdom of the poets and the dream of resurrection. This parallel is directly mentioned in the preceding story, "Colère," in which the mother is caught up in a carnival band and "pushed, manhandled by the crowd, prisoner of its exuberance" (264). However, as in "Folie" Chauvet's perspective in "Colère" is ultimately pessimistic. This is not the "joyous relativity" of the Rabelaisian carnival in Bakhtin's definition; the carnival offers only "the illusion of freedom." For Chauvet, Haitian society had become a ludicrous nightmare from which Haitian writing would never awake.

Amour, Colère, Folie was to be the last work published during Chauvet's lifetime. Her legacy would be understood only by a later generation of writers living in exile. It is tempting, for instance, to see a relationship between Chauvet's trilogy and Dany Laferrière's notorious short novel *Comment faire l'amour avec un nègre sans se fatiguer* (How to make love to a black man without getting tired), first published in 1985. Not only does Laferrière's title echo Chauvet's word *amour*, it also replicates the primal scene of the grotto-esque, of writers shut away in a tiny, filthy room. The word *crasseux* (filthy) recurs constantly in the text in relation to the room. "This room is really filthy. I keep repeating this but it is true."[13] The same hothouse atmosphere of fevered imaginations, religious mysticism, and scatological obsessions, prevails. Laferrière's characters are also cut off from the world. As his narrator-protagonist confesses, the writers have "nothing that links us with the damn planet" (35). As in Chauvet, the devil is present. This time he lives upstairs and both men also await "impatiently, breathlessly, the end of the world. The private apocalypse" (15). However, unlike Chauvet's hapless poets, Laferrière's characters experience an exile that is external, not internal. Laferrière, as much as Chauvet, is mocking the complacency and highmindedness of a certain tradition in Caribbean writing. He is, in fact, more explicit and courageous than Chauvet in deflating literary pretentiousness. The main character in his novel has a frequent sexual partner, whom he labels Miz Literature. The dark, irreverent humor of the novel extends to the typewriter on which the novel is being composed. He cleans the machine with petroleum jelly and types on the table he also uses for having sex (55). He describes the act of writing in explicitly sexual terms: "I type frantically. The Remington is jubilant. It spurts all over. I type. I cannot go on. I type. I am exhausted. I climax. I collapse on the table, next to my typewriter, my head between my arms" (176). The rebirth he longs for is one not in the arms of singing angels but in literary fame (163). The novel is about the gestation of his work—a work that is part sex manual, part diary, part anthology of sexual escapades. Laferrière's novel is postideological and obviously postmodern in the self-referential nature of its narrative and its sustained parody of practically every literary movement in the Caribbean.

Inspired by Henry Miller and Charles Bukowski, Laferrière's novel may well be one of the most provocative manifestation of the post-modern in Caribbean literature. As in Chauvet, writers are protago-nists who attempt a desperately ludicrous rearguard action against encroaching chaos. The text cannot provide a symbolic order to resist the chaos on the outside. The text is mere words, merely textual—or, to follow the spirit of Laferrière's novel, the textual is merely sexual.

Maryse Condé may be the only major female novelist other than Chauvet to pursue the postmodern vein in Caribbean writing. Her vi-sion is less gloomy than Chauvet's and less shocking than Laferrière's, but her appreciation of Chauvet's trilogy is telling in her critical text *Les parole des femmes*. She recognizes the intimate relationship be-tween "Folie" and the other stories. She sees them in terms of the pro-gressive disintegration of the family—almost an allegory of the frag-mentation of Caribbean society. In "Folie" she observes "the family has disappeared. There remain three men, symbolically a Black, a White, a Mulatto, who have taken refuge in the only form of life pos-sible, madness, and are already marked for destruction."[14] This process of disintegration, which is pathological in Chauvet, is revis-ited in a more Rabelaisian fashion in Condé's work.

It is impossible to read Condé without noticing a pervasive subver-sive laughter. It would be unfair to describe this laughter as merely ludic, just playfully postmodern. The recourse to laughter is, perhaps, best explained in this incisive observation by Bridget Jones, writing on Condé's early plays: "She takes a welcome pleasure in resisting racial and ideological stereotypes in order to present fallible, incon-sistent human beings. The creaking of bed-springs tends to replace the rattling of machetes."[15] In Bakhtinian terms, the lower stratum— the lower *body*—is a powerful deflating force that undoes the prud-ery and high-mindedness of ideological and, perhaps more specifi-cally, patriarchal orders. As Bakhtin writes, and Condé illustrates, "The lower stratum is always laughing." In a real way, the works of Condé are often ironic enactments of a bodily drama.

While Chauvet and Laferrière reduce the literary to the scatologi-cal, Condé explores what can be termed an aesthetic of the grotesque. As defined by Bakhtin, such an aesthetic focuses on the fact that "the events of the grotesque sphere are always developed on the boundary dividing one body from the other and, as it were, at their points of in-tersection."[16] The propensity of sexual relationships to lead to complications is a major element in Condé from her work's earliest days. The protagonist in *Heremakhonon* (1976) has affairs with a Guadeloupean, a French architect, and an African politician. Each relationship creates an intensifying pattern of moral and ideological ambiguity. Her moral dilemma is ultimately so overwhelming that she retreats. Her sexual adventures represent a kind of truth in the novel; they liberate her from her father's repressive puritanism and from the delusion of a socialist utopia in Africa.[17]

This sexual iconoclasm of the early work yields later to a general rejection of any transcendental truth or originary discourse. The libidinal impulse in *Heremakhonon* seems powerful enough to undermine any cohesive sense of self as a unity. The disorder unleashed in Condé's corporeal dramas leads away from an archetypal self to a multiplicity of selves. Corporeal discourse here moves away from establishing roots and claiming territory; it favors horizontal transformations, crossing boundaries of race, ideology, and moral stricture. This phase in the evolution of Condé's corporeal dramas is the single most noticeable feature of her African saga *Ségou* (1987). Compared with *Heremakhonon*, one text may be more recognizably historical than the other, but we see the same multiplicity of characters and the strange encounters that sustain and dismantle groups of individuals.

This particular vision of corporeal multiplicity and the emancipating presence of the other may have reached its high point in Condé's 1989 *La traversée de la mangrove* (Crossing the mangrove). In this novel, the demystifying thrust of Condé's imagination is at its most intense. The mysterious nature of the central character of the work is the key to its main theme, which must be the ambiguous origins of Caribbean and New World societies. No one will ever learn the identity of Francis Sancher, the absent patriarch of the novel, but we hear a multiplicity of diverse accounts, a proliferation of language as intense as the intertwining of bodies in other novels, that has resulted from his impact on the community of Rivière au Sel. The narrative, more experimental than anything attempted previously by the author, moves from subverting the patriarchal ancestor to suggesting the absence of any ordered genealogical pattern in the emergence of Caribbean societies.

This novel is as much about Sancher as it is about the inexplicable power of the arbitrary stranger. Critical attention has been paid to the Faulknerian aspects of this novel, but here I want to bring out the sense in which *La traversée de la mangrove* is the result of the inexorable skepticism that has driven Condé's entire literary project. This dimension to her literary endeavor, facilitated in the text by the mocking, comic, and solemn ambiance of the Caribbean wake, places her squarely in the parodic, postmodern mode, so visible previously in Chauvet's "Folie." It also makes Condé into one of the quintessential practitioners of the postmodern narrative in the Caribbean. The symbolic presence of that other variation of the grotesque, the mangrove of the title, is an important key to the meaning of the work. It is impossible to cross or master the mangrove. As the character Vilma observes, "You do not cross the mangrove swamp. You become impaled on the roots of the mangroves. You are sucked in and suffocated by the brackish water."[18] Consequently, no totalizing system or master narrative is possible in such a world. Condé here restates her distrust of ideological and theoretical constructs. In the novel she cannot resist a critique of the *créolité* movement, which she clearly sees as attempting to create a false ideological construct from a process that is open, unpredictable, and always in a state of becoming. As one character exclaims, "Our society is a mixed society. I reject the word "creole" that some are using."[19]

Perhaps, in the same way that Chauvet's parodic aesthetic finds an echo in Laferrière, Condé's merciless deconstruction of the hegemonic and patriarchal self finds an equivalent in the work of Raphael Confiant. The impossible crossing (*traversée*) of Condé's narrative becomes the paradoxical crossing of Confiant's unrelenting interrogation of Césaire—*Aimé Césaire, une traversée paradoxale du siècle* (A paradoxical crossing of the century).[20] Confiant's provoking attack on the putative father of the Martiniquan people interestingly also contains at the end a celebration of the mangrove—to be more exact, "Mangrove-Martinique," with its "mangrove-language" (creole) and "mangrove-culture" (créolité). Confiant, the incarnation of that "unstable mosaic" of the racially composite Caribbean, in the 1990s has become the most daring exponent of the parodic in Caribbean literature. There is an understandable tendency to associate his work closely with that of the other theoretician of créolité, Patrick Chamoiseau; however, the explosively parodic and postmodern dimension of Confiant's work reveals that he has more in common with Ishmael Reed, Guillermo Cabrera Infante, and Luis Rafael Sanchez than with his French-speaking contemporaries.[21] Indeed, because of his irreverence, one is even tempted to treat Confiant as postcreole.

There is a real difference between Confiant, the solemn polemicist and militant who is a signatory to *Eloge de la créolité*, the manifesto of the créolité movement, and a regular, fiery columnist in the weekly magazine *Antilla*, and the author of wildly comic works such as *Le nègre et l'amiral* (1988), *Eau de café* (1991), and *L'allée des soupirs* (1994). The most precise and profound description that has been advanced regarding Confiant has been made by Laurent Sabbah, who in a postface to Confiant's *Basin des ouragans* (1994) describes the author as "le clown de la créolité" (créolité's clown).[22]

The mocking tone of Confiant's work is apparent in his first novel in French, *Le nègre et l'amiral*. The names of the main protagonists, Rigobert (*le nègre*) and Robert (*l'amiral*), already suggests the mocking (*rigoler*) of Admiral Robert. The same parodic impulse puts together in one narrative Josephine, Napoleon's first wife, and Josephine Baker. Perhaps more importantly, this comic thrust is aimed at writing itself. Here we see that element of self-reflexitivity in Confiant that suggests an awareness of the ephemeral nature of all literary endeavor. This novel is a book of texts, in that it is both intertextual and about the creation of texts. As much as anything else, the narrative concerns the fortunes of a writer, Amedée Mauville, who undergoes the influence of André Breton and Aimé Césaire and seems to practice automatic writing: "Amedee sat down at the table . . . and sheets of paper in hand, blackened them . . . without even trying to reread."[23] Ultimately this act of narration yields little more than "little black sticks on white paper."[24] Here, the use of the *mise en abime* technique of the narrative that enacts the writing of itself echoes that of Laferrière in *Comment faire l'amour avec un nègre sans se fatiguer*.

Indeed, Confiant is particularly fond of the use of subtexts—of narratives within narratives. This procedure reaches a mischievous high point in 1994—a wildly prolific year for him—in his novel *L'allée des soupirs*, which has as its subtext an ongoing conversation about the nature of French-Caribbean writing. Inevitably, what is said in this dialogue forces the reader to reflect on the novel itself. The debate over the authentic form of literary expression in the Caribbean is conducted by a fifty-year-old Martiniquan poet, Jean Symphorien, and a white, foreign critic, Jacquou Chartier, whose name suggests both Cartier, the explorer, and the creole word for parrot, *jacquot*. The loquacious foreign adventurer has gone native and in the novel defends the cause of créolité. He asserts at various points in the debate, "the grotesque is the insular version of the American baroque";[25] "modern man will be creole or will not be"; "the creole novel will be cacophonic or it will not be." In Chartier's incessant babbling, all the main ideas of créolité are parodied, whereas the local poet defends French and pastoral poetry in the face of Chartier's solemn pronouncements. Confiant demonstrates an exasperation with the attempt of intellectuals and critics to devise a rhetoric of closure to appropriate the creative act by imposing their academic definitions. Ultimately he reduces this theoretical debate to the absurd and the scatological when the final physical battle between Symphorien and Chartier is disrupted by a contest between two local champions of public defecation, the grotesque alter egos of the literary figures (383). As the champions of excretion relieve themselves before a group of gleeful spectators, the literary figures, purged of their high-minded theories, become reconciled. In Confiant's work the body always has the last word.[26]

Confiant appears to be the Caribbean writer who has explored most consciously the grotesque idea of language as bodily secretion. Against the puritanical rigor of the official and the established, Confiant juxtaposes the excremental and the obscene. This parodic vein in Caribbean writing, which owes much to Chauvet's pathbreaking trilogy, calls language and the literary act into question and reduces everything to matter. This view of the world as absolutely material, absolutely carnal, undercuts any idealistic dualism separating the literary from the real, consciousness from matter, mind from body. It is not surprising that this tradition should result in a rejuvenation of language, making it more immediate and sensory. The poetics of the organic and the orgiastic seem here more important than any linguistic scrutiny of the accuracy of Confiant's use of creole. It is also worth noting that the Czech novelist Milan Kundera has championed the work of Chamoiseau, although temperamentally, he is closer to the life-enhancing, manic laughter of Confiant.

Street Plays

It is difficult not to notice the importance of the street as a primal and problematic site in modern Caribbean writing. A fundamental departure from the world of the pastoral, the street is, in a conventional sense, profoundly unpoetic. It is the zone of the public self, the collective consciousness. The street represents movement, chaos, and anonymity. From his earliest work, V. S. Naipaul could sense the street's ability to confer a liberating anonymity on the individual in the crowd and to create the possibility of discarding the constricting hierarchies and relationships of parochial postplantation Trinidad. As his protagonist in *The Mimic Men* reflects, "I stepped out into the street and was alone, free of mother and sisters, without a father: myself alone. The camera was in the sky. I was a man apart, disentangled from the camouflage of people. The street, usually to me so dull, was now an avenue to wonder."[27] The street becomes a scene of open existential possibilities, of a new pathway to errancy and the marvelous. Naipaul is, however, often uncomfortable with this disorder, and perhaps all his fiction is about trying to reestablish some order within ever-increasing circles of chaos.[28]

Naipaul's anxiety about the street and the anonymous crowd was not shared by those Haitian iconoclasts who, from the 1930s, saw themselves as latter-day versions of the Baudelairean *flaneur*.[29] As opposed to Roumain, who persisted with the pastoral ideal, the poet Brouard, for example, was drawn to the novelty and the seaminess of Port-au-Prince at night. The promenades of André Breton's *L'amour fou* and Louis Aragon's *Le paysan de Paris* were replayed in Brouard's poems, which frequently invoked his nocturnal wanderings through the Haitian capital. For Brouard, the only real world was that of the night, with its capacity to render the familiar strange and shocking. Nocturnal Port-au-Prince seemed to have a particular capacity to create these effects because of its bizarre juxtaposition of the archaic, the sordid, the mysterious, and the dilapidated. Brouard epitomized the dissolute, uninhibited *poète nègre* who sought every opportunity to repudiate the world of bourgeois respectability from which he came.

Sexual adventure was a vital aspect of Brouard's antiestablishment feeling. His muse, as he defiantly proclaimed, was the street prostitute. The primal scene for his nocturnal fantasies was invariably the sordid rum shop with its bizarre encounters, as can be seen in the *danse macabre* of the melancholy prostitutes in the prose poem "Bouge."[30] There is something remarkably and monstrously anti-Rousseauesque about Brouard's promenades. His poems are essentially enactments of sexual desire. Even his *Vaudou* poems do not seem, even faintly, religious, rather are they evocations of sexual rapture. For instance, his "Hymme à Erzulie," published in 1934, does not present the goddess as Mother Africa but as the incarnation of cannibalistic lust.

> Anthropophagos Goddess of Pleasure
> And riches
>
> .　.　.　.
>
> flesh soft to the touch like velvet
> humble flesh
> joyous
> sad
> shuddering
> throbbing
> heartbreaking
> flesh more beautiful than soul
> because one day
> no one will smell it without holding his nose.[31]

It is evident that the yearning for freedom from the encroachments of bourgeois respectability led to the violation of sexual taboos. Nature hardly matters. Brouard's world is one of intensity, profusion, and promiscuity as he haunts the labyrinthine night-world of Port-au-Prince. In Brouard's imagination there is a thin and often blurred line between permanent revolution and perpetual orgy, between convulsive political change and Dionysian explosiveness. The use of eroticism as a path to liberation, pioneered by Brouard in Haiti in the 1930s, is important to understanding the attempts at a politics of the erotic in a later poet like René Depestre. The temptation to see in eroticism the potential for radical change is thoughtfully explored by Susan Sontag in her essay "The Pornographic Imagination." Pornography, she explains, can be a legitimate form of avant-garde activity because of its capacity to enact "extreme forms of human consciousness," which can ultimately result in the salutary effects of "psychic dislocation."[32] In Brouard's case, this desire for absolute liberation would lead to no collective *prise de conscience* and would, because of his role as an apologist for *noirisme,* usher in the Duvalierist dictatorship that would deny even the most basic freedoms to Haitian society. Brouard, the evangelist of the erotic, turned to religious proselytization in the last years before his final descent into madness.

Brouard remains a pathetic but exemplary figure in the Caribbean because of this almost evangelical quest for salvation through erotic *défoulement.* A significant aspect of this quest is its location in the amoral, ahistorical site of the town's inviting low life. The contribution made by René Depestre to this theme in Caribbean writing appears to be the globalization of Brouard's quest, which Depestre terms *géolibertinage*. Port-au-Prince has been replaced by Paris, as Depestre's *érotomane* narrator surveys his urban field of transgressive play. "Paris, ripe, fertile, promised me infinite new fields to plough. Paris offered me the spectacle of the curvaceousness, mother of all exotic, life-giving folds whose waves crashed against the shell of my thirst for the absolute" (my translation).[33] The scale of Brouard's sexual exploits has been enlarged; however, the essential project remains the same. Sex is the ultimate weapon against a world of hypocrisy, phoniness, and repressions—his miraculous weapon aimed at the self-righteous, Christian West. Ultimately, this crusade transcends narrow ideological boundaries as the artist finds himself hostile to both the puritanical Left and the repressive Right.

So far, the critic who seems to have paid the most serious attention to the erotic politics of Depestre's oeuvre is Bridget Jones, in "Comrade Eros: The Erotic Vein in the Writing of René Depestre." She raises a question that is fundamental to his pursuit of a transgressive poetics. One is tempted, she notes, to "wonder whether the erotic dimension in Depestre's work does not also function almost as a safety valve, creating a reserved area—a garden of delight—where he has no obligation to express a party line."[34]

Depestre's love poetry has taken him from the early Eluard-inspired hymns to pagan sensuality and to the later fantasies of dramatic and frequent sexual fulfillment that owe much to influences such as Pierre Mabille, André Breton, and Georges Bataille. Depestre's later work seems permanently locked in the mode of joyous eroticism, which can be read as a compensatory fantasy for impotence in other arenas. Indeed, his use of the carnivalesque in the novel *Hadriana dans tous mes rêves* (Hadriana in my every dream), published in 1988, is very telling. The carnival, for Depestre, is a means of escaping history, as we see in the extravagant juxtapositions that dominate the carnival, put on as a wake for the zombified Hadriana. The drought, decay, and human waste that afflict Jacmel cannot be solved by another *coumbite,* as was the case with Fonds Rouge, but by the return of a nubile, white Erzulie. In the same way that Cuba once served as an escape from repressive Haiti, Jamaica now provides Depestre with an escape from the false and hypocritical world of Cuba. The narrator is reunited with his beloved Hadriana in Jamaica, where he defiantly celebrates the joys of historylessness, since "love has no history." Depestre, in his later work, has publicly bidden farewell to his dreams of revolution. In the poem "Adieu à la Revolution," he confesses that "I have ceased to be a 'black poet' on the lookout at the gate of *casa de las Americas*."[35] His recent short stories, *Eros dans un train chinois* (1990), the second volume in an erotic trilogy, are the continuing adventures of the sexual libertine in lands where tradition or ideology are powerful restrictive forces. These tales have produced admiring reactions from Milan Kundera, who praises "the black poet with his head full of crazy sex-dreams crossing the great communist desert, puritanical beyond belief, where the smallest erotic license had a terrible price."[36]

However, this may be the very contradiction that Depestre cannot resolve. His sexual exploits may produce a kind of narcissistic revenge but, in the end, change nothing. There seems to have been at least fleeting awareness of the futility of this new sexual mapmaking that turns everything and everyone into objects of curiosity. His refusal to be located in space and time, his anonymity, seem to heighten his ecstasy. In his confessional tale "Mémoires de géolibertinage," the narrator, a would-be Icarus, looks down from the Eiffel Tower in a moment of hubris but is cautioned by a voice that says, "The global womanizing that you thought you drew from nowhere is just another trick of Europe's, another of this country's farces."[37] Such disquieting clairvoyance ultimately does not prevail against the temptation to be the ubiquitous voyeur, as noted earlier a latter-day erotic incarnation of the Baudelairean *flaneur,* a connoisseur of carnal delights but profoundly disengaged from social reality. It is as if the grounded Annaise of Roumain's earlier political parable had been transformed into the groundless Hadriana of Depestre's novel, written four decades later and enacting a desperate, late phase of Caribbean modernism.

The real René lives the aftermath of Chauvet's fictitious René and seems to have achieved what Naipaul, another famous Caribbean exile, calls "the Buddhist ideal of non-attachment, not signing petitions, not disturbed by national or international issues."[38] However, the lure of the street does not always lead to self-indulgent *geolibertinage*. Perhaps, we can make a distinction between the harmlessly ludic enterprise of a Depestre and the "deep play," to use Clifford Geertz's expression, of another tendency in Caribbean writing. The use of street ritual, especially that of carnival, in Caribbean writing suggests an immensely creative interest in a master trope of Caribbean literature equivalent to the use of the *coumbite* in Roumain's novel *Gouverneurs de la rosée* (Masters of the dew).

Geertz enticingly proposes a reading of ritual as artistic form. What he claims for the Balinese cockfight has significant implications for any literary treatment of ritual. He suggests that the defamiliarizing potential of the literary project overlaps interestingly with any expressive group activity because both work by "disarranging semantic contexts in such a way that properties conventionally ascribed to certain things are unconventionally ascribed to others, which are then seen actually to possess them."[39] Caribbean writers have been tempted by the use of play as a corrective to the restrictions of the everyday world. For instance, C. L. R. James uses cricket in precisely this way. Indeed, Geertz would see cricket as "deep play" and agree with James that cricket can be treated as an artistic form.

Geertz's three criteria for judging ritual as an artistic form are identical with those of James. Geertz focuses on "immediate dramatic shape . . . metaphoric content and social context."[40] James asserts that "cricket is first and foremost a dramatic spectacle. . . . The second major consideration . . . is the relation between event and design," and "value to the spectator."[41] James's *Beyond a Boundary* appeared ten years before Geertz's yet the theorizing is practically the same. What both James and Geertz share is a common interest in public spectacle's ability to influence group consciousness, to alter sensibility in the way art forms are supposed to.

Interestingly, James's point regarding cricket as play moves it away from drama to spectacle. James speculates that cricket is, perhaps, "the only game in which the end result is not of great importance" and that the players are always "trafficking in the elemental human activities, qualities and emotions."[42] There is, consequently, no need to read the game as continuous text. James even goes so far as to say that the "finer points" and subtle shadings are less important than primal sensation, even excess, grandiloquence, and intensity of feeling. In taking cricket in the direction of pantomime, James offers a provoking Caribbean rereading of a game normally associated with respectability, decorum, and reticence. Indeed, James has pulled together the two key rituals in the anglophone Caribbean, cricket and carnival. The latter can then be seen as an extreme and explicit manifestation of what is implicit in cricket: the discontinuous text, the free play of signifiers, the primal nature of sensation, and the transgression of boundaries.

The relationship between sport and the street, fair play and deep play—that is, the carnivalization of cricket or vice versa—is key to understanding the massive recent interest by Caribbean writers in the spectacle of carnival. Some of the best writing on the element of the carnivalesque in cricket done since James's book is Richard Burton's essay "Cricket, Carnival and Street Culture." Burton's focus is primarily on the street culture shared by both carnival and cricket: "Carnival is a phenomenon of the street, and it is also to the street that, in the first instance, West Indian cricket belongs."[43] We are again seeing the liberating possibilities of the street as field of play at work here. He concentrates on the sublimating, defusing potential of the game and less on James's speculations on performance and catharsis.

Cricket can indeed function as compensatory fantasy. The most striking literary expression of cricket as Calibanesque reversal is Kamau Brathwaite's poetic psychodrama "Rites," in which the crowd feels empowered because of the performance of the batsmen, "as if *they wheelin* de willow / as if was *them* had the power."[44] The use of carnival by a younger generation, however, attempts to disentangle the Caribbean social imaginary from a constant and reflex struggle to beat the colonizer at the latter's own game. In using carnival as the ritual of choice, more recent writers focus on the flamboyantly recreative possibilities of street culture.

As would be expected, a list of those who use the ritual of carnival in their work would be dominated by Trinidadian writers; however, the literary exploration of carnival is by no means restricted to Trinidadians. Carnival is a tempting trope for Caribbean writers because it so obviously facilitates an exploration of a free flow of time and space as well as the permutations, randomness, and eclecticism that are central to the cultural diversity of the Americas. For instance, two works published in 1985, *Mémoires d'isles,* a play by the Martiniquan ethnologist Ina Césaire, and *Carnival,* a novel by the Guyanese surveyor-turned-writer Wilson Harris, demonstrate the extent to which the metaphor of carnival facilitates the Caribbean writer's intentions.

In Ina Césaire's play, carnival initially offers a mental space that permits two old women to explore the past through their personal reminiscences. They are presented as *diablesses* in a carnival jump-up. This allows them, in the manner of Bakhtinian grotesque, to step out of their restrictive social identities, as mulatto schoolmistress and black urban dweller. Harris's novel simply permits a more explicit exploration of the commonplaces of his fiction, which has always contained an important element of the carnivalesque. The metaphor of carnival with its promise of the "androgynous miracle of . . . revolution," simply facilitates more openly the game-playing, masking, and indeterminacy that characterizes an oeuvre that has defiantly stood outside the conventions of literary realism. Carnival becomes the ultimate metaphor of the labyrinthine space that permits the transcendence of old boundaries and defamiliarizes a world made dull by habit and ideology.

In contrast to Harris's somewhat abstract manipulation of the carnival metaphor, for Trinidadian writers carnival takes on a significance that is more culturally and socially grounded in local questions of identity. Perhaps the use of carnival as street theater is a response by a younger generation of writers to the problem posed by Naipaul's evocation of the troubling yet liberating anonymity of the street. The street, for Naipaul, seems the first step in his career of exile and wandering; in writers like Lawrence Scott and Willie Chen, the street carnival leads back to Trinidad and the possibility of participation, at least temporarily, in a community formed outside of the constrictions of race, politics, and nation. It is no coincidence that Scott, a French Creole, and Willi Chen, of Chinese ancestry, both come from minority groups that need a new, imaginary social order in which to function freely. Carnival functions here as a disruptive ground allowing for the temporary creation of a supranational synthesis.

Scott's novel *Witchbroom* attempts to present the history of Trinidad from a white Creole perspective. The novel is archly postmodern. It constantly winks at the reader and, perhaps more disturbingly, the literary critic. Scott has obviously read his Walcott, Marquez, and Barthes, and wants us to know this. His novel, which is self-consciously intertextual and polyphonic, seems to respond to Barthes's prescription that the modern text must become a multidimensional space that facilitates a variety of literary codes. Scott's narrator/protagonist is another emblem of the postmodern—the hermaphrodite. Lavren, whose name is sexually ambiguous and echoes the French *la voix*, (the voice) and *la voie* (the way), defies conventional binary divisions. In Scott's words, "s/he hung between genders.

S/he trembled between loves and desires. S/he was pigmented between races."[45] Lavren seems to be the apotheosis of the more conservatively composite Bita Plant in McKay's *Banana Bottom,* the most extreme attempt to imagine a new, synthetic, creole identity.

Not surprisingly, there is a description of carnival in *Witchbroom.* Scott projects carnival as the collective manifestation of the ambiguities of his exemplary hero/heroine: "There is no hierarchy in carnival; no colour, no class, no race, no gender . . . all may cross over and inhabit the other. Mas can come from any house, any alleyway, up Belmont so, down Dry River, even up Lady Chancellor and St. Clair, where the rich come out at last and can pretend to be black."[46] If this exemplary view of carnival in Scott's novel is compared with Barthes's view of wrestling as a form of baroque excess, the similarities between the Trinidadian novelist and the French theorist's celebration of a transgressive and kinetic aesthetic becomes evident. "The rhythm of wrestling . . . is that of rhetorical amplification: the emotional magniloquence, the repeated paroxysms, the exasperation of the retorts that can only find their natural outcome in the most baroque confusion . . . a final *charivari,* a sort of unrestrained fantasia where the rules, the laws of the genre, the referee's censoring and the limits of the ring are abolished, swept away by a triumphant disorder."[47] For both writers, the "baroque confusion" of these spectacles is a rhetorical tactic that frees Barthes from a poetics of the static and the repressed and Scott from the constricting polarizations of Trinidadian society.

Scott's postmodernist idealizing of carnival as the ultimate manifestation of a collective, multiracial, classless community is even more explicit in the short story "King Sailor One J'Ouvert Morning." In this tale, the main character—like Lavren, in *Witchbroom,* a member of family named Monagas—chooses to play King Sailor and not Jabjab because the former is more becoming and suited to his color and class. However, in the crush of carnival he finds himself in the wrong band and ends up pushing a bass pan. The story ends with a joyous shedding of social trappings: "He had to laugh for truth as he looked at his King Sailor shirt tied around his neck and his bell-bottom pants rolled up to his knees. He laughed and said to himself as he pushed the pan right back into the pan yard. 'Like I play Jabjab after all.' "[48] The symbolic transformation of the King Sailor costume points to a final unmasking that makes possible a new, utopian national ideal for multiethnic Trinidad. Perhaps Scott is not that much of a postmodernist, since there is a prescriptiveness and a didactic impulse lurking in his manipulation of the carnival ritual.

In another short story with a carnival theme, Chen comes up with a very different insight into that public ritual. "King of the Carnival" is about the extent to which tensions and rivalries in Trinidad's society are carried over into the carnival. In Chen's tale, in the costume competition a traditional outfit worn by a black Trinidadian loses to a modern robot costume worn by a white masquerader. Chen's evocation of the clash between technology, consumerism, modernity, and a traditional, popular form of self-empowerment immediately recalls Earl Lovelace's novel *The Dragon Can't Dance*, about which there will be more discussion below. Indeed, Chen's main character is called Santo Lovelace and his costume is that of a dancing dragon.[49] However, Chen's story is not a mere repetition of Lovelace but a rereading and problematizing of carnival as ritual of resistance. In his excellent study of nationalism in writing from Trinidad, Stephano Harney has a perceptive discussion of Chen's work in which he distinguishes the modernist impulse in Lovelace from the postmodernist doubts of Chen. "Chen's stories," he argues, "reveal the error of the will to nationalism, the impossibility of its task."[50]

Lovelace's novel (1979) remains an exemplary display of Caribbean modernism in its treatment of carnival as a ritual for collective self-scrutiny and the reconceptualizing of the community. In *The Dragon Can't Dance*, Lovelace, a Trinidadian, traces major changes in the island's recent history: the movement from country to town, the growth of the black-power ideology, the greater visibility of East Indians, and the rapid spread of consumerism and modernization in that society. The ground has now become one of mocking self-sacrifice, Calvary hill with its false saviors, and the dragon an emblem of the traditional past that must be transformed under the pressures of the present. The strength of Lovelace's work is that, unlike the facile celebratory thrust of Scott's view, he focuses on the persistent conflicts between street and yard, modern and traditional, between the queens of the world on the inside and the kings of carnival. The outcasts of the hill of Calvary effect a kind of self-realization through disruption, displacement, and recognizing the presence of others among them.[51]

In Lovelace's novel, both traditional carnival as well as traditional revolution must yield to some new strategy that combines powerlessness and resistance, overt consent with new forms of opposition and self-preservation. Lovelace gives no clear answer as to how these issues will be resolved, but it is in the street-centered culture of carnival that the future seems to lie. Harney is again insightful when he remarks that there is a will to truth in Lovelace; the novelist is attempting to write the nation into existence. "Lovelace writes about the role of the writer in stitching together a national costume, a costume that is habitable for all citizens, poor and rich, male and female, African and Indian."[51] It is this belief in the power of the individual to challenge state culture and for the creative artist to push beyond a traditional, essentialist truth that reveal the extent to which Lovelace is practicing a modernist poetics that is visible again and again in the Caribbean. Toward the end of the novel, Lovelace's protagonist, Aldrick, philosophizes: "One is saved by one's self, as a faith, a hope. . . . Each man had the responsibility for his own living, had the responsibility for the world he lived in and to claim himself and to grow and to grow and to grow."[52] The ultimate question is, How does this modernist homily stand up to the collapse of the modernist experience elsewhere in the Caribbean? How does Lovelace's optimistic hero sound next to the wild babbling of Chauvet's failed poets?

The quest for "realplaying" as opposed to "réel-playing" in the novel (as in *réel merveilleux*), a true self, an authentic identity beyond history, nation, and tradition is poignantly evoked in Lovelace's treatment of the ambiguities of carnival as emancipatory ground. *The Dragon Can't Dance* both represents an epistemological break with the tradition of a prescriptively pastoral discourse and enacts the anxieties of a foundational poetics in the Caribbean text. His narrative depicts the cynical manipulation of creoleness and carnival in the "All o' we is one" slogan shrewdly invoked whenever the power structure is threatened. As a provisional answer, Lovelace falls back on the warrior ethic, a kind of latter-day maroon practice, that enables the heroic loner to prevail against the moral and ideological void that postindependence Trinidad represents.

The existential quest for individual truth within the context of the disjunctures and ambiguities of carnivalized space is explained by the modernist critic Marshall Berman as the archetypal struggle of the individual against the maelstrom of modernity—what he call "the moving chaos" of urban life. Anarchistic, irrational, contradictory, the modern urban environment of nineteenth-century Paris can be seen as the equivalent of the chaotic, carnivalized maelstrom of Lovelace's postindependence Trinidad. Berman explains: "The man in the modern street, thrown into this maelstrom, is driven back on his own resources—often on resources he never knew he had—and forced to stretch them desperately in order to survive. In order to cross the moving chaos he must attune and adapt himself to its moves, must learn not merely to keep up with it but stay at least a step ahead. He must become adept at . . . sudden abrupt, jagged twists and shifts—not only with his legs and his body, but with his mind and sensibility as well."[53] Lovelace's project of self-formation is the only valid task that Aldrick (surnamed Prospect) identifies in the "moving chaos" of modern Trinidad. But what if Prospect, read allegorically as the modern West Indian, finds that he has no prospects and cannot "attune" and "adapt" to the contingent, multiethnic space of modern Trinidad? What if the chaos is not easily traversed or transcended, as the free play of identities in Willi Chen's fiction suggests? What if the carnival does not stop but remains, permanently and maddeningly deconstructive and unregimented? Neither the defiantly antipostmodern Berman nor Lovelace, the heroic modernist, has the answer. For the beginning of a creative response to this dilemma, we must turn to what is arguably the most disruptively modernized Caribbean territory, Martinique, and the poetics of errancy and ambivalence inaugurated by Glissant, which has emerged full-blown in the Créolité movement.

6

A Poetics of Liminality:
Another Caribbean Fin de Siècle

At the centre, an urban logic that is Western, linear, strong like
the French language. From the margin, the open profusion of
the creole in the logic of Texaco. Blending two languages, the
creole town speaks secretly a new tongue and no longer fears
Babel.

—Patrick Chamoiseau, *Texaco*

Maroons of the Macadam

Since our reading of the Caribbean as "the other America"
began with Haiti, it should not be surprising that it
should end with an examination of contemporary Martinique. Haiti
and Martinique are exemplary Caribbean societies because they represent two extremes of Caribbean and, arguably, Latin American cultural and political reality. Haiti was the first Caribbean state to declare itself other and define itself in terms of a new self-consciousness
that required an international recognition that was impossible at the
time. Martinique has, on the other hand, never had the opportunity
to declare itself other. It has had an almost unbroken relationship
with the metropole and has been totally integrated into the French
system after becoming an overseas department in a national plebiscite
in 1946.[1] Both societies, therefore, represent the extreme alternatives
that, in one way or another, confront the other America, caught as
they are between the poles of impoverished isolation and chronic
dependency.

As the twentieth century draws to a close, however, both societies
have undergone new and unpredictable developments that make

them more similar than one would expect and, perhaps, representative of the social and cultural transformation that faces the region as a whole. The pressures of migration and a proportionate loss, through underdevelopment, of an interior or heartland have created radical changes in Haiti and Martinique. The case of Haiti's ecological disaster is notorious: the ground has literally and symbolically been eroded through underdevelopment and deforestation. In Martinique, overdevelopment has created a similar crisis; whereas in Haiti the topsoil has been washed away, in Martinique it has been bulldozed and asphalted over. The phenomenon of *betonisation* (the spread of concrete) is such a pervasive and defining feature of modernization in Martinique that Burton has wittily and lucidly observed that the entire landscape has been so swallowed up that "there is no 'hors-plantation'—to adapt a famous pronouncement."[2] It is one of the ironies of the turn of the century that Martinique, the island that consumes the most Yoplait yogurt per capita in the hemisphere, and Haiti, where one-sixth of the population depends on USAID for nutrition, should face a similar dilemma with regard to the preservation of a hinterland.

Concurrent with the gradual disappearance of farmland—traditionally the element that kept people from leaving rural areas—migration has created large overseas and urban populations. These diaspora communities are significant enough to be recognized both demographically and in colloquial speech—in the case of Haiti as that nation's tenth department and, in the case of Martiniquans living in Paris, as *la troisième île* (the third island). The experience of these communities, along with the spread of the media, communication technology, and the ease of travel, are causing the notions of exile, belonging, and cultural difference to be rethought. Again, the phenomenon of modernization and the intensely migratory nature of Caribbean space are creating an unprecedented hybridization of both societies. Both on the inside and the outside, notions like exile, rootedness, and resistance must undergo radical reconsideration.

One of the distinguishing features of Martiniquan intellectual culture is its experience of modernity. In Haiti, the experiment in creating a modern state was quickly undermined when the counterrevolution set in under the presidency of Jean-Pierre Boyer. If the early experiment in modernization in Haiti was inspired by the changes wrought by the French Revolution, in the twentieth century the Russian Revolution created a similar impact in Haitian thought. Yet the dream of modernizing Haitian society for a card-carrying Communist like Jacques Roumain remains utopian and arguably naive. For instance, the scene at the end of his *Masters of the Dew,* with its light-flooded plain and the radiant, mobilized workers accomplishing the *grands travaux* that would usher in the dawn of collective egalitarianism, has all the subtlety of an official, larger-than-life political poster. But the experience of modernity has always been more complex and arguably less naive in Martinique.

For instance, if we examine the end of Césaire's *Notebook of a Return to the Native Land* we find not the shadowless field of Roumain's novel but a suggestion that modernization means leaving behind a closed, suffocating world and embracing a new realm of paradox. The "great black hole" comes along with vertiginous ascent and lasso of stars. Modernization in Césairean thought is a Faustian pact. It opens new vistas for a stagnant, feudal society and releases new sources of energy, but this new dynamism is also accompanied by the forces of darkness and the underworld. This vision of paradox and contradiction is explored in its pseudo-Faustian dimension in the essay "Poetry and Knowledge," which ends with a panorama of "strange cities, extraordinary countrysides, worlds twisted, crushed, torn apart, the cosmos given back to chaos, order given back to disorder, being given over to becoming, everywhere the absurd, everywhere the incoherent, the demential. And at the end of all that! What is there? Failure! No . . . the modern idea of energetic forces in matter that cunningly wait to ambush our quietude."[3]

The Faustian wager seems to have found concrete realities in 1946. Departmentalization would institute a special relationship with the metropole that would transform Martinique from colonial backwater to island plunged into a whirlwind of change, as the denouement of *Cahier,* Césaire's epic poem, envisions. Once this adventure began, there would be no hope of turning back. Indeed, one of the more arresting ambiguities of Césaire's poetic vision is the fact that the clarifying fire of the Césairean volcano would eventually make negritude itself an obscurantist and obsolete ideology. The idea of preserving some kind of essentialist racial difference in a world where, to use Césaire's own words, the "absurd," "the incoherent," "the demential" are omnipresent was to say the least problematic. Rapid and intense modernization, therefore, became the sine qua non of the contemporary Martiniquan experience. No current account of this overseas department can avoid dealing with the "systematic derangement" of the development process, as the sociologist André Lucrèce put it in his recent short study of modernity in Martinique.[4]

The hold extended over Martinique in particular and France's overseas departments as a whole by a disruptive modernizing process is very much a feature of the metropole's international policy. As Robert Aldrich and John Connell explain in their *France's Overseas Frontier,* "the DOM-TOMS represent a particularly important component of [France's] internationalist policy. They provide the sites for the space station in Guyana and nuclear testing in French Polynesia and are 'windows on the World' in their respective regions, show places for the French political system, culture and technological sophistication."[5] The example cited by Aldrich and Connell of the Centre Spatial Guyanais at Kourou, French Guyana, is a telling and perhaps exemplary one. The space program—proof of France's ultimate technological achievement—is sited in an artificial clearing in the Guyanese rain forest. It is a dramatic illustration of the intrusive, transformative power of modern technology in a local environment.

The experience of the overseas departments is part of that secularizing, desanctifying process that is an essential aspect of modernization. As Walter Benjamin put it, modernization depleted human experience and created "the disintegration of the aura in the experience of shock."[6] The disappearance of ritual, the sacred, from art in a world afflicted by what Benjamin termed *Erlebnis* is a major dilemma for the artist in the face of intrusive and pervasive material development. Marshall Berman points out that this is as true of Baudelaire as it is true of the developing world; however, what Benjamin saw as depleted experience and jeopardized values, Berman conceived as the flowering of the spirit of modernism. In his examination of Baudelaire, for instance, Berman points out that the poet's "best Parisian writing belongs to the precise historical moment when, under the authority of Napoleon III and direction of Haussmann, the city was being systematically torn apart and rebuilt. Even as Baudelaire worked in Paris, the work of its modernization was going on alongside him and over his head and under his feet."[7] Berman's point is that this "historical moment" is paradigmatic for the experience of modernity, in that a static, stratified, and self-enclosed society was being torn down and something unpredictably new was rising from the rubble of municipal demolition. He further argues that the first poet to celebrate this new urban dynamism and unprecedented diversity in city life was Baudelaire. Similarly, the most important subject and site for modern Caribbean writing are the creative disorder and the undomesticated frontier zone represented by new urban enclaves. Much recent Caribbean writing can be interpreted as experimentations in mapping a new urban space that is contingent, nomadic, and diverse. Fredric Jameson makes the point that the emergence of a modernist aesthetic in the Third World is not possible because earlier

> there the face of imperialism is brute force naked power, open exploitation; but there also the mapping of the imperialist world system remains structurally incomplete, for the colonial subject will be unable to register the peculiar transformations of First World or metropolitan life which accompany the imperial relationship. Nor will it, from the point of view of the colonized, be of any interest to register those new realities, which are the private concern of the masters, and which a colonized culture must simply refuse and repudiate.[8]

Jameson is too categorical and sweeping in this generalization about the need of the colonial culture to "repudiate" issues created by imperialism, which "are the private concern of the masters." He consequently finds the creative "Third World" response to the representational problems posed by imperialist modernization in the "exceptional situation" of Ireland and in the writing of James Joyce.

We already have some idea of the impact on the writing of the Caribbean of writing from the "exceptional situation" of Ireland. Perhaps the best example of the influence of the work of Joyce on a Caribbean writer is that of Cuba's Cabrera Infante. His *Three Trapped Tigers* set out to transform Havana in the late 1950s in the same way that *Ulysses* represented Dublin at the beginning of the twentieth century. No doubt the modernization, or more precisely the Americanization, of Havana at the time would create circumstances favorable to adapting Joyce's literary inventiveness to an eclectic urban culture in the Caribbean. Perhaps in a similar way the writing of Virginia Woolf left an indelible mark on Gabriel García Márquez, as has been pointed out by Michael Bell. The long, wandering sentences of *Mrs. Dalloway*, Bell argues, lead inexorably to the rhetorical extravagance of *One Hundred Years of Solitude*.[9]

Martinique's metamorphosis from colony to department marks the movement from "the open exploitation" of an early imperialist practice to an "exceptional situation" in which there is "overlap and co-existence between . . . incommensurable realities which are those of the Lord and of the bondsmen altogether, those of the metropolis and of the colony simultaneously."[10] In this combination of the reality of the developed world and the underlying structures of underdevelopment, a new kind of creative energy is released that will create an art form from the incongruities and dissonances of urban space. It is no coincidence that the writer who best expresses the aesthetic "possibilities" of this new urban experience is Patrick Chamoiseau. Chamoiseau was born and raised in Martinique's capital Fort-de-France, which makes him radically different from his literary predecessors. It also makes him acutely sensitive to the need for a new mapping, a new spatial language, to deal with the experience of what he terms the "ville créole."

Chamoiseau's work did not always reflect the aesthetic inventiveness and the linguistic extravagance of such novels as *Chronique des sept misères* (Chronicle of seven miseries) (1982) and *Texaco* (1992). His early play *Manman Dlo contre la fée Carabosse,* written in 1977, *Carabosse,* for instance, rather conventionally pits a symbol of telluric sapience, Manman Dlo, Queen of the Lézarde River, against the Graeco-Latin spirit Carabosse. This play is almost Glissant rewritten in the manner of a negritude polemic. Carabosse, for instance, "imprisons the land in an architecture of steel; decomposes Nature and forces Life into new channels."[11] In this pointedly nationalistic allegory, the colonizing project of the evil foreign fairy is foiled when the divinity, who is not only indigenous but antochthonous, unleashes the forces of nature, sweeping all before them. Carabosse learns the salutary lesson that "nothing controls the water! Nothing can tame it," and Manman Dlo counsels her daughter, "Never cut yourself of from the Earth."[12] In its depiction of Martinique as an organic community that preexisted the invasive forces of modernity, this play is a naive exercise in wishful thinking.

Mercifully, Chamoiseau's later work abandons this more conventional and fanciful modernist fantasy of organic wholeness triumphing over alienating and nihilistic materialism for an exploration of the themes of adaptation and contact. The novel *Chronique des sept misères* is an important transitional text. In this novel "la fée Carabosse" is still malevolently present in the form of various state officials but Maman Dlo has been excised from the script. Consequently, the make-believe autochthonous community symbolized previously by Maman Dlo is replaced by a liminal community of *driveurs,* who instead of heroically and improbably resisting the advance of modern technology devise strategies of opposition and adaptation. The *driveurs* do not represent some primordial community lost in the heartland but the Martiniquan nation in embryo, shaped by history and contact. This point is cogently argued by Burton, who sees the activities of the main characters in Chamoiseau's novel as essentially maneuvring within the dominant system: "*Chronique des sept misères* suggests that, in contemporary Martinique, self-marginalization is no longer an option for the simple reason the margins themselves have been drawn in to the centre. . . . But what the novel also shows is that there is significant, if limited, room for manoeuvre on the lowlands themselves, not least in the capital city itself."[13]

Despite its superficial similarity to Marshall Berman's ideal of the human spirit that needs to keep in step, literally, with the moving chaos of the maelstrom of the *ville créole,* Chamoiseau's narrative is not an instance of triumphalist modernism. He focuses on a group of *djobeurs* (handymen) who use their wheelbarrows to transport goods in the market. Unlike Lovelace's dragonmaker, who is a romantic symbol of the sovereign individual and transcendent will, Chamoiseau's "seven miseries" are border figures. Their habitat is the liminal space of the town market. As much chronicler of the world of the *djobeur,* Chamoiseau is an ethnologist of a mobile, pragmatic, yet dependent group that is neither assimilated by the modern state nor made up of hapless castaways, passively succumbing to invasive materialism. The index of the ability of Chamoiseau's characters to find some kind of equilibrium in urban Martinique is in their capacity or incapacity in handling the wheelbarrow. As an artefact, the wheelbarrow offers important clues to understanding the mentality of the *djobeurs;* in their political and cultural situation, it is rich with symbolic resonances. The barrow can be interpreted as an attempt to resolve the contradictions of the daily lives of the *djobeurs,* both on the imaginative and practical levels. It can be seen as an expression of the precarious, liminal space that these freelancing hustlers inhabit, since it both draws on the symbolic hegemonic order they live in and reveals their capacity for improvisation, or bricolage. Perhaps a musical parallel to this reconstructed artifact is the steel pan in Trinidad, which, constructed from metal containers, in the urban environment of Port of Spain in the 1940s grew to represent the emergence of creolized local traditions. We are told on the first page of Chamoiseau's narrative that the *djobeurs* are "wealthy only because of a wheelbarrow and their ability to handle it."[14] Later we are given instructions as to how it is constructed. The inability to maneuvre this equipment or to repair it can have disastrous results: one character, incapable of fixing the wheel on his barrow, quickly loses his hold on reality and ends up in the mental asylum, where he dies.

Certain qualities are indispensable for the practitioners of this precarious trade. During a competition among the *djobeurs,* the reader is initiated into an alternative world of reading and understanding Fort-de-France: "To triumph there was a matter of genius because you had to calculate as precisely as possible the speed, the length of step, to handle the heavy wheelbarrow like a feather so as not to hurt anyone, not miss an opening. This required a perfect knowledge of the district, the dimensions of each street, and above all, an ability to react to the unexpected" (89). Many critics have with good reason concentrated on the linguistic inventiveness of Chamoiseau's text, but the artefact of the wheelbarrow gives us equally great insight into the social imaginary of this group. The tool they create is a kind of interlectal language or idiom that borrows from and yet allows for self-expression with the prevailing hegemonic linguistic system.[15] The dominant prevailing system is based on the language of modernization. The *djobeurs* response is a kind of individualized, concrete speech, or *parole,* that has its own intonation, inflection, and idiosyncrasy. The artefact then becomes a symbolic act that is both unique yet part of shared culture. It is characteristic of the interlectal space that produces it.

It would be misleading to portray Chamoiseau's characters, his seven miseries, as social rebels. It is true that their existence challenges the status quo, but this is neither conscious nor sustained. Their behavior does have primordial roots in the tradition of *la petite maronne,* or small-scale marronage, which meant periodic absenteeism from the plantation, not negation of the system. It signifies the importance to a creole culture of survival in that liminal space in the interstices between *morne* (hill) and plain, maroon negation and plantation enslavement. But the *djobeur* can in no way alter the course of history or counter the massive changes sweeping Maritiniquan society. One cannot read into Chamoiseau's work the nationalist allegory that emerges from his early play. This does not mean that his *djobeur* is the Caribbean equivalent of the pathologically nationless *pachuco,* the Mexican migrant who anonymously roams the streets of the United States and whom Octavio Paz in *The Labyrinth of Solitude* associates with an extreme manifestation of the Mexican personality.[16] The Martiniquan *djobeur* embodies the irrepressible creole sensibility and its capacity for improvisation, similar to what Glissant in *Caribbean Discourse* traced in the creative transformations of the official French bumper sticker. However, this capacity is not sustained, nor is it attached to any definable group politics. The *djobeurs* are singular, but this singularity is subdued and does not endure. Chamoiseau consequently ensures that we do not see his main protagonist in heroic terms. Pipi, despite his title as king of the *djobeurs*, his family name Soleil, and his supernatural beginnings as the firstborn of a virgin, is less than majestic. As if the name Pipi, his alias, meaning urine, was not deflating enough, he is described as effete (in Chamoiseau's words, *zoclik* and *bancal*), a late developer, always in need of female guidance and, in his spectacular love affair with Marguerite Jupiter, is desperately in need of aphrodisiacs. Indeed, during his relationship with Jupiter, he takes on the role of mothering her children and begins a vegetable garden. He cultivates this garden according to a chaotic natural order, or rather disorder. In this regard, Pipi as *jardinier créole* is manifestly different from Roumain's vision of the gardener as ideologically driven "master of the dew." Chamoiseau is suggesting that this lack of an identifiable manliness, or for that matter, capacity for mastery, may well be the source of Pipi's strength, which lies in the realm of the disruptively carnivalesque.

In his exploration of the *djobeur*'s capacity for unceasing self-invention, Chamoiseau suggests that no ideology or model can capture the ever-shifting street culture of the Martiniquan *macadam*. In so doing, he rereads two of the major tropes of Caribbean literature, the maroon and the forest. The primordial figure and his primeval space are given a revisionist treatment by Chamoiseau. He reminds us in his autobiographical work *Anton d'enfance* (Bygone days of childhood) that island space, because of its visible limitations, could easily be traversed by roads or systems or discourses that indiscriminately subsume everything under a universal sameness. Resistance, therefore, takes the form of constant flux and displacement, thus creating new traces, detours in this process of *drivage* and errancy. As Chamoiseau puts it, "To take the straight path was not the best way of getting to places, and if the traces twisted and turned through the woods, you had to twist and turn with them. . . . You had to take the traces, scramble their order with the irrationality of a runaway."[17] The

djobeur as urban maroon continues this process of twisting and turning as an oppositional, subversive tactic, "supple, accessible to everyone, open to good fortune and careful of the wind . . . the *djobeur*
fears becoming stiff and losing his adaptability."[18]

In this evocation of the emancipatory, transgressive spirit of
créolité, Chamoiseau focuses on the ultimate colonial space, the
town, as a new forest of symbols for the urban maroon. Not the official knowledge but an alternative way of knowing how to combine,
scramble, and improvise is the key to survival in Fort-de-France. At
one point, these two kinds of knowledge are contrasted in the novel
as the postman, Ti-joge, has a contest with Pipi as to who knows the
town better. Pipi's maroon irrationality wins out over the postman's
more official reading of urban space. Chamoiseau points out that it is
the nature of the evolution of the colonial town that makes it open to
the improvisatory tactics of the *djobeurs*. Chamoiseau's *ville créole*—
or to borrow Confiant's formulation, a *ville mangrove*—is made of
layers and layers of structures that were originally constructed on
swampy terrain.

> Such urban knowledge was rare in this town born from a disease-
> ridden swamp but judged suitable by Governor Du Parquet for siting
> the next fort of the King. On the The land first torn away from this
> hell they built a church. The mangrove was destroyed and they built
> houses which had to be rebuilt each time it was flooded. Despite the
> town of Saint-Pierre, which shone with a thousand fires, people came
> from everywhere to inhabit this new-born site. (93, my translation)

Two of the features that stand out in this description of the emergence of Fort-de-France are the recurrent image of the swamp and the
contrast with the older, more traditional city of Saint-Pierre. The latter seems very much a product of plantation Martinique, whereas
Fort-de-France represents a rupture with a rigid, hierarchical past.
Equally important is the constant reference to the mangrove, which
suggests, in the new town, not a rigidly conformist space, not
grounded in a foundational poetics, but one that is constantly being
made and remade. Indeed, the process of *betonisation* does not suppress the primal swamp, which is part of the mythology of this new
urban enclave.

This image of the urban mangrove, or Marshall Berman's oxy-
moronic expression "mire of the macadam," returns with even greater

force in Chamoiseau's most ambitious novel to date, *Texaco*. As in *Chronique des sept misères, Texaco,* as the title suggests, emphasizes the shaping force of urban space. The main character of *Texaco* is not a divinity of dark, occult powers but an enigmatic *femme-matador*—in many ways the female equivalent of the *djobeurs* of the earlier *Chronique*—who as the keeper of the community's memories emerges as the mother of the precarious Martiniquan nation. In both novels, the structuring force of language in the face of extinction is pervasive. In *Chronique des sept misères,* the stream of gossip, rumor, and stories that comes from the bar of choice, Chez Chinotte, makes this meeting place as significant as the vegetable market where the *djobeurs* earn their livelihood. It also contrasts these spaces of exuberant orality with the regimented world of the written. This bar is lost through fire, at very much the same time that the market begins to collapse because of the Europeanization of the local economy. The hegemony of the written prevails under the authority of Césaire, modern Martinique's patriarch, founder, and author. The question of the linguistic reality of *Texaco* is an important one—so much so, it is tempting to conclude that, to paraphrase Lacan's famous dictum, the *ville creole* is structured like a language.

The theme of *Texaco* is apparently that of the founding of a city. Chamoiseau seems to have taken seriously the advice from Glissant, printed as an epigraph to *Texaco,* "Gibier . . . tu n'es qu'un neg-bouk: c'est de la qu'il faut parler" (Game bird . . . you are really a town boy: it is about there that you must speak). Periodization in the narrative is subject to the rhythms of building materials. The Era of Thatch is followed by the Era of Planks that in turn is succeeded by the Era of Prefabrication, then the Era of Concrete. The text itself is structured in terms of three, sometimes spuriously official, subtexts from the personal chronicle of the female protagonist, Marie Sophie Laborieuse's notebooks, the correspondence of a town planner, and the author's correspondence. To this extent, the text, too, like the dwellings of the main characters, seems almost an edifice of heterogeneous materials.

These texts are as much tied to the structuring of narrative as they are to the founding of the town of Texaco itself; writing is intimately related to founding. However, since much of the writing is a parody of archival models, it questions and undermines, like the mangrove itself, the solidity of the Era of Concrete. Ultimately *Texaco* is, despite its apparent thematic interest, neither a genealogical novel nor a novel about archival truth; it is not about exercising authority over territory or about hoarding an authentic truth. What *Texaco* does, in its own, more wholesome way, is echo the outrageous combination, which we have seen in Confiant's *L'allée de soupirs*, of feces and writing. What Chamoiseau seems to be doing in *Texaco* is not so much providing a recorded, official history for Martinique as giving expression to a world on the edge of the written, saturated in orality, where the spontaneity, playfulness, and immediacy of the spoken pervade the entire narrative. As the Marqueur de Paroles, the narrator, himself warns the native informant, or perhaps informer, "You must fight against writing: it turns into indecency, the inexpressible reality of the spoken."[19]

Yet this is not, like Chamoiseau's earlier texts, a simple exercise in privileging the spoken over the written. The written, elaborately represented here in terms of the filing and classification of the texts by the Bibliotheque Schoelcher, also exercises a powerful attraction. The role of the character Ti-Cirique in the novel is to defend the importance of the written: "He got into the habit, when time permitted, to sit with me and read my notebooks, correct my homework, give meaning to my sentences. He gave me access to his vocabulary, stirring in me a taste for accuracy in language which I forever found difficult to master. Then he spoke to me of the mass of interwoven texts that was Literature, a single manifold sound that pulled together the languages of the world, peoples and lives" (356–57). Chamoiseau's heroine emerges as a perplexed chronicler. Rather than polarizing his argument in terms of the written over the spoken, or vice versa, Chamoiseau ranges promiscuously between both extremes.

Texaco enacts an almost Lacanian drama of symbolic order confronted by defining disorder. The prototypical *ville créole* is structured like a language, in that it not so much fixes binary extremes but has an infinite capacity for recombinations and permutations. Texaco, the town, is symbolically a *ville mangrove* and therefore treacherous terrain on which to ground a foundational text. Chamoiseau's heroine longs for a form of expression that would combine the elements of the preconscious, unconscious, and conscious. She asks: "Oiseau Cham, does there exist writing informed by the spoken, and by moments of silence, and which remains alive, turning in circles, circulating all the while, irrigating unceasingly with life what has been written before, and one which reinvents the circle each time the way spirals do?" (354). In her appeal for a language that is circular, repetitive, and more intuitive, Chamoiseau's heroine is raising an issue that runs deep in Caribbean literature. It was, perhaps, first raised with great eloquence in Césaire's longing for a prediscursive space. Chamoiseau distinguishes himself from Césaire by envisaging a dialectical relationship between written and spoken.

Texaco raises the possibility of a language that eschews linearity and clarity and that is organically tied to the sensuous experience— that feeds on the corporeal and the actual. This collective experience is tied to the individual life of Marie Sophie Laborieuse. She is drawn to the written word because she senses approaching death and feels the need to record the totality of her knowledge. Her memory is not always reliable, however, and, in any case, she fears that Texaco will die in her notebooks while in reality it is not yet complete. "Texaco is dying in my notebooks while the real Texaco was yet to be finished" (353). If writing is death, then Texaco, which remains beyond representation, will be always incomplete, always being built. Literature's temptation to totalization is confronted by the *ville créole's* resistance to closure. Perhaps it is summed up in the slipperiness of the word Texaco itself. The word is neither French nor creole but the trade name for a U.S. oil company, a symptom of the international language of modernization. If anything, Chamoiseau's novel reterritorializes the extraterritorial trademark Texaco within the mangrove space of Martinique. At its best, Chamoiseau's work is an attempt to come to terms with the compelling momentum of modernization in the Caribbean, with all the risks this process entails. As the enlightened *urbaniste* warns, "But there is danger in the town; it becomes a megalopolis . . . on the ruins of the nation-state, it rises monstrously multinational, transnational, supranational, cosmopolitan" (390).

Texaco is dedicated to Edouard Glissant, whose ideas as we shall see, are critical to understanding Martinique's experience of the modern, particularly in terms of his theorizing of errancy and transversality as fundamental to understanding a creole culture. It is also dedicated to Vera Kundera, whose husband, Milan Kundera, makes an observation on Czech culture that seems relevant to Martinique's relation to the modern and overlaps with many of Glissant's ideas on small states and their roles within a global process of modernization. Kundera argues that "small Central European countries have, at the beginning of the twentieth century, become important centers for world culture. All these small countries have shown a dynamism typical of young nations . . . and have supplied a new and surprising vision of the world which, often enough, shocks through the lucidity of its relentless skepticism born of defeat and experiences painful to a degree unknown to bigger peoples."[20] Martinique at the end of the twentieth century is a "small country" irrevocably inserted within a modern, global culture. This in part explains the disproportion between its size and the intensity of its intellectual life. The wrenching, and at times draconian, imposition of modernization, Césaire's Faustian wager in 1946, has forced a turn-of-the-century writer like Chamoiseau to attune himself to the chaotic, urbanized, overdeveloped world that Martinique has become. It is from what was once thought to be an unlikely environment that the only dynamic literary movement in the region at the present time, the Martiniquan créolité movement, springs.

From Folds to Fractals

> Serene slab cast down here from
> Some obscure catastrophe.
>
> —Stéphane Mallarmé, "Le Tombeau d'Edgar Poe"

In choosing to focus his attention on the "maroons of the *macadam*" in his novels, Chamoiseau projects a liminal urban culture as paradigmatic for the modern Caribbean. The preoccupations of a turn-of-the-century generation of writers have, consequently, shifted in a decisive manner from the evocation of the other America as heterocosmic space. This ideal, which suggested a mythic world, outside of time, whose values were antithetical to the modern world, was highly favored during the heyday of the negritude movement. But in a larger sense, there is something quintessentially American about this idea. The vision of a redemptive wilderness, a pristine sanctuary that offered a refuge from fallen civilization, is as true of the heroic evocation of the American frontier as it is of the world of the *morne*.[21]

With Chamoiseau and the créolité movement, the maroon's heroic isolation is deemed to be an inadequate response to the process of rapid interculturaltion taking place in Martinique. As we see in *Texaco*, "The maroons stared at the plantation blacks with their eyes wide open, envious of their knowledge of these events. Already free, proud, they somehow felt marginalised from the general momentum of things."[22] A passage such as this marks a break with the negritude movement's image of the romantic maroon and all those images of the sovereign self in Caribbean writing and places a creative new emphasis on the pedestrian, muted survival of the plantation slave. The larger implications of this revisionist view is that the heroic isolation of the frontier has been supplanted by the process of creolization and, arguably, Americanization, in threshold communities. The poetics of liminality have taken the place of the pieties of maroonism. The liminal community now constitutes a new internal frontier, a site of transgression and growth.

The poetics of liminality in contemporary Martinique should, perhaps, be considered within the broader, global interest in cultural contact and interpenetration. Writers as supposedly diverse as the Mexican Octavio Paz and the Anglo-Indian Salman Rushdie share a common interest in what the latter calls the "experience of uprooting, disjuncture and metamorphosis (slow or rapid, painful or pleasurable) . . . from which can be derived a metaphor for all humanity."[23] Similar concerns have been articulated by the Ghanaian Anthony Appiah (*In My Father's House*, 1992) and the Bulgarian Tzvetan Todorov (*On Human Diversity*, 1993). Increasingly, the idea of liminality forms the basis for defining the Caribbean. A remarkable example of such a study is Lauren Derby's "Haitians, Magic and Money: Raza and Society in the Haitian American Borderlands 1900 to 1937." Her study offers a fascinating insight into the relationship between the borderlands as transgressive, undomesticated space and the state as a center of power and territorialization.[24]

The Caribbean writer who has so far given the most thoroughgoing and subtle treatment of the poetics of liminality is Glissant. From very early in his career, Glissant focused on the need to make an epistemological break with the poetics of erasure, practiced by an earlier generation, and to devise a more deconstructive, less closed model for Caribbean thought. Such a rupture with a previous generation's poetics would mean a shift from the ideal of a heterocosmic point outside of time and space to the quest for a continuum within time and space—in Glissant's language, the shift from transcendence to transversality. In the late 1950s, such a model is devised by Glissant in his notion of reality as a series of folds. This model, which was both structurally repetitive and yet continuously metamorphosing, gives all of Glissant's work a phenomenological unity. Later systems of philosophical thought devised by Glissant would consistently draw on the structuring force of this model and lend an imaginative coherence to Glissant's entire oeuvre.

Perhaps his first explicit reference to the importance of the idea of reality as a series of folds was made in 1957 in his critique of the use of the novel for anticolonial protest. He felt that the potential of the novel form would be fulfilled only when it was free of the polemical and the prophetic and when it could follow the minute, secretive variations within reality. "It will no longer need to be prophetic about reality since the novel is more suited to following reality in its tiniest infoldings. It will no longer need to be schematic about reality . . . since the novel is more capable of exploring the thousand and one variations within reality."[25] Reality is, therefore, conceived in terms of an iterative model with its twists, turns, mirroring, dislocations, diversions, and reversions.

This image is rooted, perhaps, in Glissant's early interest in Mallarmé's poetic ideas.[26] The importance of images of folds as a key pattern in Mallarmé's imaginary universe has already been fully explored by Jean-Pierre Richard.[27] Folds in Mallarmé's conception of self-expression represent the infinite capacity for slippage that exists between reality and consciousness. Folds then become a pattern of relational lines that do not stabilize objective reality but simply establish a series of encounters in which meaning is continuously made and unmade. The folds of a fan or a book emerge as objective manifestations of this unceasing game of presence and absence. What Glissant seems to have drawn from this complex web of imagery is the belief, to paraphrase Mallarmé's famous dictum, that the world is made to end up as a series of folds.

Glissant's first books of poetry in the 1950s can be read as early performances of this aesthetic of the fold, in which neither absolute exterior nor a coherent interiority prevails but consciousness is evoked twisting progressively and regressively between both extremes. For instance, *Un champ d'iles* (first published 1952) is an exploration of precisely such a self-reflexive activity, in which longing and desire multiply images of the field of islands that is the Caribbean. "From this room where you are now coiled within life's spread wings, the day suddenly departs, shedding its bloom, towards a language which is lost, and then takes hold."[28] Even if Glissant tends to see Mallarmé's poetic project as ultimately narcissistic and precious, one would be hard put not to see echoes of Mallarmé in these images of light fading in the room, veiled longings and the encroachment of the formless dark. Glissant's early verse is Mallarméan in that it evokes states of consciousness that nervously shift between the boundaries of self and world, inside and outside. The ebb and flow of the sea become the Caribbean poet's imaginative equivalent of the opening or closing of the Mallarméan fan or book.[29]

From the late 1950s, Glissant's work moves from the intense interiority of the early poems to an exploration of the image of multiple infolding in terms of the specific realities of Caribbean space. His first novel, *The Ripening* (*La Lézarde*), which won the Prix Renaudot in 1958, is constructed around the image of multiple asymmetrical recurrences. The novel itself is a retelling, that is a version of a traditional tale of two men who hated each other but traveled together down a river; the tale is repeated in 1945, with a new range of meanings, and yet again in the novel's retelling. Its central image of the river is a tangle of folds whose secretive, elusive meanings the protagonists in the novel must decipher. The truth of this coiling motif is performed, as it were, by the group of activists in the snaking line of dancers at the end.[30] The plot of the novel is made up equally of a series of journeys, whose tangled trajectories yield a kind of truth: "Four separate movements. But unleashed from a single subterranean source, like a wind fighting itself and turning against itself which finds in this contradiction the true meaning of its howling cry. Like a stubborn root whose very proliferation becomes an obstacle and which in its multiple growth must conquer itself before growing directly, across rock and sand, towards the loose soil calling out to it."[31]

Consequently, Glissant's entire oeuvre can be read not as a series of "orphic explanations" but as a sequence of reading and unreading, where, as it were, *lire* and *delire* construct and undo each other in turn. Certainly, one aspect of Glissant's interest in delirium is manifested in terms of his own texts, which continuously undergo a process of rereading and reinterpretation. As he once declared, "The project of literary creation or, what comes down to the same thing, that of knowing is flexibly sustained around a fixed axis. . . . In my case, I do not write essays or books occasioned by circumstances: what I write is most often, at least I strive for this, centrally focused."[32] Even a superficial knowledge of Glissant's work allows the reader to have a sense of the six novels, seven books of poetry, and four books of essays as products of a continuous monitoring and drifting that makes each utterance part of the pattern of secretive infolding and mobile thresholds. This pattern is reflected in the titles of his two last major works, *Les grands chaos* (1994) and *Tout-monde* (1993).

Glissant himself has called attention to this pattern in his essays by attempting, particularly in *Caribbean Discourse*, to theorize a creole transversality and, most recently, by invoking Felix Guattari's and Gilles Deleuze's poetics of the rhizome. In *Poétique de la Relation*, Glissant elaborates on the idea of the rhizome in the context of his concept of resistance and interrelating, opacity and openness. "The concept of rhizome would therefore retain the reality of rooting, but eschew the idea of a totalizing root. Rhizomatic thought would adhere to the principle of what I define as a poetics of relating, according to which a identity shaped in relation to the Other."[33] There is an important overlap here between Glissant's theory of a relational poetics and Deleuze's concept of the centrality of the other's presence. As Deleuze explains: "We must attach a great importance to the notion of the Other as structure: not at all a particular 'form' inside a perceptual field . . . but rather a system which conditions the functioning of the entire perceptual field in general."[34] Deleuze's ideas are part of that current global concern with the fate of cultural diversity within a global universalization of culture. This is the main impetus behind Todorov's massive investigation of French thought, *On Human Diversity*, in which he examines various attempts "to conceptualize the diversity of peoples and the unity of the human race at one and the same time."[35] For Glissant, Martinique's experience of its relationship with Europe is an acute example of the complex relational experience of the other America as a whole.

The evolution of the pattern of continuous infolding into a full-blown poetics in Glissant's thought represents a decisive break with the preoccupation with *enracinement*, filiation, and a foundational poetics that have dominated Caribbean thought for the better part of this century. With Glissant's ideas, the traditional literary canon is disrupted and a new light is shed on the significance of the "classics" of Caribbean writing. As Richard Burton accurately observes: "With *Le discours antillais* and *Poétique de la Relation*, French West Indian thought has undergone an epistemological shift of major importance: identity is no longer imagined as a single tree rooted in the landscape (as it is in such classics of West Indian literature as Césaire's *Cahier d'un retour au pays natal*, Jacques Roumain's *Gouverneurs de la rosée* (1946), [and] Jacques Stephen Alexis' *Les arbres musiciens* (1957)."[36] Indeed, Glissant replaces these stalwarts of the French-Caribbean literary canon with writers from the Americas who are by no means exclusively French. Glissant's alternative canon takes in, among others, the problematic white Guadeloupean creole St. John Perse, the Cuban Alejo Carpentier, the southern novelist from Mississippi William Faulkner, and more recently the St. Lucian poet Derek Walcott. Glissant sees in the work of these writers the alternative epistemology that drives his redefinition of Caribbean thought.

In Glissant's complex and continuously, or rather sinuously, evolving theoretical writing, the two works that stand out are those singled out by Burton. In these lengthy and nuanced reflections on the experience of the Americas in general and the Caribbean in particular, Glissant focuses on the mutually interdependent notions of relation, or interrelating, and resistance, or the capacity to retain cultural diversity. His view is that resistance "stubbornly persists" even in situations of extreme assimilation. In examining the balance between "relation" and resistance in *Caribbean Discourse,* he optimistically concludes

> The Caribbean constitutes, in fact, a field of relationships whose shared similarities I have tried to point out. A threatened reality that nevertheless stubbornly persists. And in this reality, Guadeloupe and Martinique seem even more threatened by the universal manifestation of cultural contact that is called assimilation. They are deviated from their natural course of development, zombified within their world, yet resisting an overwhelming force, given the means used to achieve successful assimilation. Colonization has therefore not had the success that was apparent at first sight. The irresistible pressure to imitate comes up against the areas of resistance whose problem is that, in a literally fragmented context, nothing holds them together.[37]

Much of this speculation as to the capacity of the overseas departments to survive depends on what Glissant terms "the right to be different" and the manifestation of difference in terms of strategies of opacity.

As Todorov notes in his discussion of the ideas of Lévi-Strauss in *On Human Diversity,* diversity is threatened globally because of cultural homogenization. "If communication accelerates, then differences are blurred and we advance toward the universalization of culture . . . the disappearance of differences would be fatal for all cultures, not simply for the most easily influenced among them."[38] This anxiety is almost at the heart of Glissant's *Caribbean Discourse*. Unlike Lévi-Strauss, Glissant cannot opt for a rejection of intercultural communication. Glissant's hypothesis is that cultural interrelating does not lead to inevitable destruction of diversity. Glissant would agree, however, with Todorov, who suggests that in individual situations of cultural homogenization, "differences are displaced and transformed; they do not disappear."[39]

In Glissant's theory, relating and resistance do not collide as oppositional forces but are better understood in terms of twisting thresholds of contact that do not allow tensions to be resolved in an absolute manner but redistribute, on the one hand, the forces of consent and coercion, and on the other, the reaction of subterfuge and opposition. What is vital to understanding Caribbean culture, and in particular Martiniquan culture, is the analysis of those folds, or interstitial zones, where the complex and unpredictable infolding takes place. In this regard, Glissant is as fascinated with this subtle process of interrelating in Martinique as he is with the other permutation of this liminal world in the metropole. To conceive of the Caribbean otherwise would be, in Glissant's view, a refusal to take into account its "irruption into modernity."[40] Consequently, Glissant visualizes the Caribbean as an unceasing struggle between the reductionist forces of homogenization, or sameness, and the capacity for resistance that is found in cultural opacity.

The area in which this dialectic between outside and inside is most fully investigated is that of language. Within the poetics of the creole language, Glissant discovers the persistent detour toward opacity that is a vital instrument in resisting transparency and universalization. Creole is a particularly fertile area of investigation for Glissant because it is not a traditional language but the product of contact; consequently, it best reflects the pattern of camouflage, subterfuge, and displacement of meaning that exists in that unstable frontier between the official and the unofficial, the foreign and the local. The only oral equivalent that Glissant cites is that of the speech of black Americans. Here again language enacts the detours and ruses that are the tactics of an opaque poetics in "the doubling of the voice, the echo placed behind the speaker is repeat and amplify his speech."[41]

Ultimately Glissant sees in these procedures the basis for a counter-poetics in literature. He praises the creole storyteller's use of "the procedure of repetition, of doubling back of reversion, of oral performance. The techniques of listing used in Saint John Perse's poetics and that I use a lot in my work, those interminable lists that attempt to exhaust reality not in a formulaic way but by accumulation, accumulation used precisely like a rhetorical device."[42]

Whereas *Caribbean Discourse* raises these issues in a diffuse and free-ranging way, the later book of essays *Poétique de la Relation* does so in a more focused and thoroughgoing fashion. In a passing reference to the interrelationship between the two texts, Glissant himself describes the latter as "the reconstituted echo, or the spiraling reiteration" of the earlier work. He thereby applies to his own oeuvre the techniques of *redoublement* and *ressassment* advocated earlier and eschews the linearity and clarity normally associated with the essay form. Indeed, in *Poétique de la Relation* Glissant actually enacts linguistically the dialects of inside and outside, of fusion and fission, in his litany of *binarités dépassables* at the end of the book. In this list, a comma signifies relating, a hyphen opposition, and a colon a consequential relationship. Hyphen, colon, and comma, therefore, become the linguistic markers for the pattern of inclusion and exclusion, consent and negation, and multiplying arabesques that resonate through all of Glissant's works.

Poétique de la Relation is paradoxically most interesting in its pursuit of the concept of opacity. The book could perhaps just as easily be called *Poétique de l'opacité*. The declaration that haunts all these essays can be found in the one entitled "Pour l'opacité," in which we find the observation, "The theory of difference is a precious one."[43] This seems a startling observation by Glissant, who is quite justifiably credited with attacking negritude for being trapped in notions of racial difference and whose ideas have always explored openness to the outside and the other. Given Martinique's historical inability to declare itself other in political terms, theorizing otherness is an inevitable and constant preoccupation among the department's intellectuals and writers. However, Glissant could certainly have made his declaration less controversial had he simply made *theory* a plural noun.

Previous notions of difference had been grounded in a mythical hinterland. Not only is Glissant acutely sensitive to the inadequacies of this nostalgia for an *arrière-pays* but he has observed that, far from providing a form of resistance, such a myth of resistance has been neutralized by the hegemonic spread of French intellectual culture. As Glissant notes in *Caribbean Discourse,* negritude is "regularly defended by the French representatives. (at international conferences) undoubtedly because they find in it the ambiguous generosity of the "generalizing theories" they so like to defend."[45] The capacity of the French system to officalize and absorb forms of radical dissent poses a challenge to Glissant's new theory of opacity, as does his recognition that there is no possibility of literally or symbolically grounding a theory of difference in Martinique. His notion of opacity is an attempt to revisit this problematic of difference, but in terms of the precariousness and inscrutability of the assertion of resistance. In *Poétique de la Relation,* he offers a nonessentialist, nonreductionist theory of opacity as a force countering the relentless spread of cultural sameness: "Against this reductionist transparencies an impulse toward opacity is at work. No longer that which once encompassed and reactivated the mystery of filiation but another: taking care of precarious points of growth which are linked (without being intertwined, that is to say fused) within the open perspective of inter-relating. We therefore term opacity that which protects Diversity."[46]

As it is true of many of Glissant's enigmatic assertions, this theory of difference as diversity is as elusive as it is rich in imaginative possibilities. Opacity emerges as a central thread, or more precisely a fluctuating force, within a network (*trame*) of horizontal encounters (*étendue*). Martinique's experience of modernity as ever-intensifying contact with the encroachment of a universalizing culture is seen as an extreme instance of a larger global condition. This Glissant describes as the contemporary *chaos-monde.* In such a world, neither order nor disorder dominates, but the sinuous unfolding of lines of interactive forces. "The chaos-world is neither fusion nor confusion: it neither recognizes uniformity nor amalgamation—all-consuming assimilation—nor inchoate formlessness. Chaos is not " 'Chaotic.' "[47] Glissant's profound interest in the phenomenological pattern of folding has again manifested itself, this time in the fascination of modern physics with broken dynamic symmetry. His shift from folds to fractals represents the use of a modern scientific model to refute the hypothesis that the world is evolving, or rather devolving, toward an all-encompassing transcendental sameness.

He goes so far as to say that science and poetry are similarly unstable systems. They both value accident and error, latency and mutation, disorder and chance. "In both cases the system . . . accepts the accident, is sensitive to its coming transcendence." In a later essay in *Poétique de la Relation,* Glissant returns to this question of error in relation to the computer. Here the computer's virus becomes the salutary seed of disorder within the system. "The virus would reveal the fractal propensity of the system; it would be the sign of the intrusion of chaos, that is the undeniable proof of the asynchronous nature of the system."[48] Consequently, a poetics of folding is confirmed by science that now permits poetry to become a form of cognition. "In its furthest reaches, the science of chaos eschews the powerful hold of the linear, conceives of the possibility of analyzing the indeterminate, measuring the accidental. Scientific knowledge . . . in this way develops one of the techniques of poetry, facilitating the longstanding ambition of poetry to establish itself as a form of knowledge."[49]

Poétique de la Relation constantly refers to the frenetic pace of the end of the twentieth century (*la précipitation historique*), from which no culture is insulated and where cultural confluence is inevitable. Glissant, therefore, theorizes opacity as a deposit or sediment that is accumulated from irreversible, unceasing cultural interrelating. This deposit is first formed within the space where contact is made. "Sediment is thus first and foremost the country where the tangle of the plot begins for you."[50] Opacity is an integral part of the system of sinuous infolding, a virus that keeps the process of relating dynamic and unstable. The right to opacity as advocated by Glissant is as necessary as it is an inscrutable aspect of one's experience: "opacity, all the silt deposited by peoples, fertile silt but to be honest inscrutable, unexplored even today and most often denied or camouflaged, whose insistent presence we cannot but feel."[51] In the dark, looming slab of the Diamond Rock, off the coast of Martinique, Glissant seems to visualize a creole opacity, inscrutable yet accessible, volcanic yet marine. This mysterious monolith appears as the inscrutable marker, as in Mallarmé's poem to Edgar Allan Poe, of some obscure catastrophe.

Opacity is also tied to Glissant's vision of the secret connections within the other America. *Poétique de la Relation* revisits the idea of multiple movement tied to a subterranean force, already seen in Glissant's first novel *La Lézarde.* The two epigraphs for these essays, taken from the Caribbean poets Edward Brathwaite and Derek Walcott, suggest the shaping "transversality" of submarine currents. This image is more fully developed in Glissant's most recent novel, *Tout-monde*. One character imagines that

> in the north of the country, the fire of Mont Pelée in its secret vol-
> canic turbulence, and the lava reaching in the distance the fresh
> water and the salt water each in turn, and this twofold liquid flowed
> under the land of Martinique to surface in the mangrove of
> Lamentin, converging with another stream coming down from Vau-
> clin in the south. . . . And this network branched out at various
> points to the beaches of the south of the country, at Diamant and Pe-
> tite Anse, and it could well be that it flowed under the sea, through
> the Canal of St. Lucia in the south and the Canal of Dominica in the
> north, converging (in the north) with the force of Soufrière in Guade-
> loupe and that (in the south) of Castries and of other hills and moun-
> tains scattered as far as the Andes in Venezuela. (My translation)[52]

Opacity, then, like the Freudian unconscious, cannot be seen directly but remains in this fiery liquid of the volcano, binding the islands together and even joining the continents. The New World mapping continues, "and perhaps it connected in a Great Flood one continent to the other, the Guyanas to Yucatan, through this string of craters dispersed among tiny islands."[53]

Glissant ultimately redefines Caribbean space in terms of complex, self-regulating systems of adaptation and opposition: "It is to this point that we must return: to what generates our cultures, to the dynamism of their inter-relating contents, to better appreciate this disorder and to adapt our actions to it."[54] In the same way that the Lezarde River conferred a spatiality on the pattern of constant infolding in the 1950s, now Glissant locates in the beach at Diamant and the town of Fort-de-France systems of self-regulating adaptation. For instance, at Diamant in the south of Martinique he sees evidence of the secret trade conducted with the dark magma from the island's volcanic north. It is not the explosive force of Mont Pelée that is evoked here but its repressed, hidden fire. "And I imagine these sombre waves coating the sea's depths, transporting to the wind-blown space before me what the smoldering intensity of the North has perfected from inscrutable dark and ashes."[55] This beach, which functions as frontier and not heartland, is obviously a mental topography. Glissant here suggests the power of the forces of latency, repression, and sublimation that makes the fragile space of the beach immune to systematic order, a supersyncretic allegory of Caribbean space.

The image of buried order of meaning is repeated in Glissant's reference to the *ville créole*. Like the black beach at Diamant, Fort-de-France is unsettled space because of its beginnings as a mangrove. It is volatile, unstable, beneath the symbolic order of *betonisation*. Writing of Foyal, the local name for Martinique's capital, Glissant says, "Foyal is not what you see, all this concrete, there is a secret Foyal by day and by night with its regulars as it were the initiated, lively neighbourhoods all around the nucleus where the town is pulled together, no this is not a tiny French enclave from the Atlantic . . . it is really a creole town from the Caribbean."[56] The name Foyal is the town's local name, derived from the original Fort Royal. It is also a zone of centripetal and centrifugal forces because of the unstable nature of its gravitational center.

Glissant's ideas have unleashed the power of new conceptual categories in the turn-of-the-century Caribbean. These categories form the context for conceiving of the American identity of the Caribbean. In *Caribbean Discourse,* Glissant refers to the Caribbean Sea as the "estuary of the Americas"; it is where the alluvium of the New World experience is deposited.[57] And it is in Martinique that the American experience exists at its most threatened, yet at its most intensely lived. As fragile, liminal space, Martinique is the point where the Caribbean, perhaps most intensely, confronts, in its most disruptive manifestation, the overwhelming form of modernity. It is there that paradigms are being redefined and old definitions put to rest. If the overseas department of Martinique represents a center, a *lieu-commun,* for radical redefinitions, it does so only temporarily, since the main thrust of these ideas is skeptical of all centers, of definitive constructs. For the present, however, it remains the site of the latest, and one of the most daring, attempts to bridge narrative and cognitive, politics and poetics, in an effort to invent a new idiom for negotiating the complex experience of identity in "the other America."

Conclusion: View of Twilight in the Tropics

"God damn it!" he shouted. "Macondo is surrounded by water on all sides."

—Gabriel García Márquez, *One Hundred Years of Solitude*

In Gabriel García Márquez's novel *One Hundred Years of Solitude,* the tellingly named José Arcadio Buendia one fine day founds his Arcadian promised land on what he declares is an island called Macondo. Buendia's fantasy island, isolated in time and space, at least in his imagination, facilitates a dream of self-invention, of establishing authority over the jungle, of achieving a heroic sovereignty. Outside of history and geography, the island of Macondo enacts an elemental New World drama, that of discovery, foundation, and the establishment of a new origin in the tangled jungle of competing discourses. But in Márquez's wonderfully ironic novel, this myth of new beginnings is dismantled as the wandering pilgrim Buendia and his descendants will discover that this island Macondo is a mirage. Márquez critically rereads this foundational myth by allowing history to intrude in Buendia's island sanctuary, with its rebellions, plagues, and crime. By the second half of the novel, Macondo has become nothing more than a tropical dystopia of heat and dust.

In this brillant parody of yet another New World discoverer whose quest for origins is thwarted by history, Márquez is not simply offering a thoroughgoing critique of the need for rootedness and the quest for new beginnings in the Americas; as much as anything else, he is calling our attention to the relationship between man and nature in the New World imagination. The longing for the lost heartland, the need for redemptive ground, and the romantic flight into nature are enacted by the Buendias in what they take to be island space. As we have seen, this desire for an absolute elsewhere is a product of anxieties created by the triumph of modernity of Western society. Buendia's quest is a paradigm of the attempt to establish authenticity and recover lost values. The discursive source of Buendia's fantasy is exoticism. The appeal of difference, of alternative worlds, of a restorative primitivism is an inevitable consequence of an exoticist discourse within which the ultimate referent is the tropical island; it is in the tropical island space that the exoticist project exists in its purest and most thoroughgoing manifestation. Privileged island space, in limbo, in a climate as distinct from that of Europe as one can imagine, becomes the ground for a utopian self-sufficiency and a prelapsarian union with nature. The evocation of the hidden island, free from all care and hardship, is, for instance, the central idea behind Michel Tournier's rewriting of the Crusoe myth in his *Friday or the Other Island*. In his rewriting of Defoe's canonical text, Tournier goes beyond that of his eighteenth-century predecessor to reproduce the exoticist project in a full-blown way. Crusoe's adventures are tellingly grounded on a tropical island he names Speranza. The novel's French subtitle, "les limbes du Pacifique," explicitly refers to the island as an absolute elsewhere lost in limbo. The subtitle in the English translation, "the Other Island," indicates the island that Crusoe comes to discover after he abandons his dream of colonization. This other island is a Macondoesque dream space. It is prelinguistic, prehistorical, presocial, and Crusoe attempts to dwell within it in "a perpetual present," in a state of erotic plenitude. Island space in Tournier's novel is a source of transcendental truth and is capable of withstanding the ravages of history and modernization. The novel ends on a note of "solar ecstasy," as Speranza and Crusoe are born again in another tropical dawn: "Drawn up to his full height he was confronting the solar ecstasy with a joy that was almost painful, while the bright splendour in which he bathed washed him clean of the grime of the past day and night. . . . He drew a deep breath, filled with the sense of utter contentment, and his chest swelled like a breastplate of brass. His feet were solidly planted on the rock, and his legs sturdy and unshakeable as columns of stone."[1] The rejuvenated sovereign individual, feet firmly planted on the rock, enacting an Adamic rediscovery of the dawn's solar illumination, powerfully conveys the vision of an enduring mythical order against which history cannot prevail.

Speranza is reborn again and again in the literature of the Caribbean. The island space as rock on which you can feel secure and the spectacular vision of dawn as a new beginning are the true subject of Cabrera Infante's short, idiosyncratic history of Cuba, *View of Dawn in the Tropics*. History is recorded in a series of episodes as a predatory process—futile attempts to master what he calls "a Venus land." At the end of this episodic work, the island reemerges in the clear light of dawn, a Caribbean Speranza *oriens ex undis*: "AND IT WILL ALWAYS BE THERE. As someone once said, that long, sad, unfortunate island will be there after the last Spaniard and after the last African and after the last American and after the last Russian and after the last Cubans, surviving all disasters, eternally washed over by the Gulf Stream: beautiful and green, undying, eternal."[2] Cabrera Infante's island remains primitive, foundational space despite the ravages of greed, ideology, imperialism. Dawn lights up the telluric beauty of this "undying, eternal" rock. "Venus land" is the Caribbean equivalent of Arcadio Buendia's Macondo before the ironic, subversive intrusion of history comes to destroy the dream.

This cluster of images echoes through the Caribbean writing and is particularly evident as a master trope in the classics of Caribbean literature, Roumain's *Masters of the Dew* and Césaire's *Notebook of a Return to the Native Land*. Roumain's novel is set in a closed-off space, a Haitian Macondo, whose images of bedrock and heartland are reinforced by its name, Fonds Rouge (Red Ground). Césairean poetics privileges the island space as an omphalos, the navel of the world. Césaire's rewriting of Shakespeare's play *The Tempest* is similar to the relationship between Defoe's canonical novel and Tournier's work. At the end of Césaire's play, the island has withstood the attempts at mastery from both Prospero and Caliban. In Césaire's text, it is the spirit of Ariel that is privileged, because of its closeness to the land. Island space survives in terms of the transcendental, rupestral truth of the rock, ever renewing itself in the eternal dawn of *verrition*. It is no coincidence that in Césaire's dramatic treatment of Henri Christophe's life, the protagonist achieves apotheosis, petrified in the mortar of his Citadelle, which has the shape of a ship and is an extension of the image of the island in the earlier epic poem *Notebook of a Return to the Native Land*. Through his oeuvre, Césaire's moods swing from the island as Promethean rock to the island as laminarian rock, the ground of heroic sacrifice to the ground of obstinate survival.

If island space is privileged in a foundational discourse, it is also favored in terms of a transversal creole space. This is particularly true of the Caribbean, where all culture is postcolonial; that is, created after the destruction of the autochthonous peoples and within the context of a plantation economy. Michel-Rolph Trouillot puts it clearly when he notes that the Caribbean is marked by history and heterogeneity and concludes that "the Caribbean is nothing but contact."[3] One is tempted to argue that there is as strong an inclination to see the island in terms of a monolithic rock as there is a recognition of the island location in the sea of historical and discursory possibilities. The strength of writers such as Alejo Carpentier, like the writing of García Márquez, is their profound skepticism regarding the immutable rock and the eternal dawn, as we have seen in Carpentier's paradigmatic novel *The Lost Steps*. The erosion of the image of the island rock as transcendental truth is central to the imaginative daring of Walcott's verse. He, too, is tempted to cling to the reassuring solidity of the island rock:

> Inured. Inward. As rock
> I wish, as the real
> rock I make real.[4]

But the poet cannot escape the contingencies of New World history. Walcott's poetry is at its most audacious when it recognizes that there will be no new dawn of new beginnings, but that the truth of the New World is that of twilight. Walcott therefore sets out to explore in his poetry the magical transformations of the Mediterranean in the New World, to subvert a foundational Old World classicism in terms of the magical transformations of the tropical twilight. In his Nobel lecture, he refers specifically to the misreading of the Caribbean dusk by those who have misconstrued the tropics:

> By writers even as refreshing as Graham Greene, the Caribbean is looked at with elegiac pathos, a prolonged sadness to which Lévi-Strauss has supplied an epigraph: *Tristes Tropiques*. Their *tristesse*

derives from an attitude to the Caribbean dusk. . . . The mood is understandable, the melancholy as contagious as the fever of a sunset,
like the gold fronds of diseased coconut palms, but there is something alien and ultimately wrong in the way such a sadness, even a
morbidity, is described by English, French, or even some of our ex-
iled writers. It relates to a misunderstanding of the light and the
people on whom the light falls.[5]

It is this refusal of a paradisal wilderness, of the transcendent rock,
that unleashes in Caribbean writing from the outset a skepticism
about grounded truths and the possibility of an imaginative investigation of the synchronic space of an island. The island is no longer in
limbo but linked to its immediate context, the diverse, nonuniver-
salizing world of the archipelago and the Americas. If a heroic,
modernist practice insisted on the island as imperishable rock, a
postmodern poetics sees the island as threshold—as liminal space, the
confluence of innumerable conjunctions and disjunctions. Wilson
Harris, profoundly aware of the liminality of his native Guyana, in
a lecture delivered in 1964 makes the case for the Caribbean's
American context: "The native and phenomenal environment of the
West indies, as I see it, is broken into many stages in the way in which
one surveys an existing river in its present bed while plotting at the
same time ancient and abandoned, indeterminate courses the river
once followed. When I speak of the West Indies I am thinking of
overlapping contexts of Central and South America as well."[6] Inevitably, Harris gets to the subject of Haiti and speculates that the
Caribbean's first experiment in modernity was not, in the mind of
Toussaint-Louverture, about "the assumption of sovereign status and
power" but "a groping towards an alternative to conventional state-
hood, a conception of wider possibilities and relationships which still
remains unfulfilled today in the Caribbean."[7]

The island crossroads, the mangrove island, the grotesque
aesthetic are all characteristics of the openness and synchronicity that
Harris identifies with the "overlapping contexts" of Caribbean island
space. The shattering force of what Glissant calls the Caribbean's
"irruption into modernity" allows for the possibility of a relational
poetics to emerge. A cross-cultural ideal that privileges neither ossi-
fied sovereignty nor the uniformity of universalizing sameness. To
use Glissant's image from *Caribbean Discourse*, if the island is a
point of submarine, transversal confluence, then the ideal of diversity

and heterogeneity can release the island imaginary from the temptation of a mineralized opacity.

The strength of Glissant's theorizing has always been his skepticism of a grounded truth. From his early essays, the island is exemplary as a point of errancy, as he places island space within its maritime context. As he declares in *L'intention poétique*, "We islanders do not feel the dizzying sweep of the land. This urge is twisted within us in a tight knot; we must contract our space in order to inhabit it. Our field is the sea, which contains and releases."[8] It is the "dizzying sweep" of the sea and not the land that Glissant associates with island space. Indeed, as I have shown elsewhere, rocks are not about an isolating plenitude in Glissant's imagery; rather, they mark the traces and the detours that allow for errancy and the displacement of fixed and absolute meaning.[9]

Ultimately, Glissant reminds us that insularity is not a kind of reductive polarity but the recognition of a field of relations. As he says about his own island space, "One is not Martinican because of wanting to be Caribbean. Rather, one is really Caribbean because of wanting to become Martiniquan."[10] By extension, the Caribbean needs to be understood not in terms of the romantic fantasy of the other island but rather in terms of that larger, relational context of the other America.

Notes

Introduction

1. Steiner, *Extraterritorial*, 21.
2. Rushdie, *Imaginary Homelands*, 68.
3. Paz, *Labyrinth of Solitude*, 192–93.
4. Lang, "No hay centro," 123.
5. King, *New Literatures in English*, King argues that nationalism in itself can be a severe limitation and that "usually the best writing occurs where there is a tension within local culture between nationalists and those with a more international outlook" (215).
6. Walmsley, *Caribbean Artists Movement (CAM)*, 315.
7. González Echevarría, *Alejo Carpentier*, 25.
8. Introduction, Pérez Firmat, ed. *Do the Americas Have a Common Literature?*
9. Ashcroft, Griffiths, and Tiffin, *Empire Writes Back*, 145.
10. Ibid.
11. Clifford, *Predicament of Culture*, 173.
12. Appiah, *In My Father's House*, 68–72.
13. Michel-Rolph Trouillot, "The Caribbean Region," 19–42.
14. Benítez-Rojo, *Repeating Island*, 151.
15. Ashcroft, Griffiths, and Tiffin, *Empire Writes Back*, 173.
16. Kutzinski, *Against the American Grain*, 12.

17. Zavala, *Colonialism and Culture*, 48.

18. Lewis, *Main Currents*, 264.

19. Chamoiseau, *Solibo Magnifique*, 44.

20. Glissant, *Caribbean Discourse*, 141.

21. Glissant, *Poétique de la Relation*, 46.

22. Glissant, *Soleil de la conscience*, 11.

23. James, *Black Jacobins*, 391.

24. Todorov, *Conquest of America*, 5.

25. Gikandi, *Writing in Limbo*, 2.

26. The nonanglophone Caribbean has attracted interesting studies of modernism, such as Arnold, *Modernism and Negritude*, Zavala, *Colonialism and Culture*, Webb, *Myth and History in Caribbean Literature*, and Anderson's recent application of Glissant's ideas to the literature of the other America, *Decolonizing the Text*. The ideas of Glissant, Bakhtin, and the carnivalesque are also dominant in Maximin's recent *Littératures caribéennes comparées*.

1 Tropes and Tropicality

1. O'Gorman, *Invention of America*, 40.

2. Ibid., 41.

3. González Echevarría, *Alejo Carpentier*, 28.

4. White, *Tropics of Discourse*, 88.

5. Geertz, *Works and Lives*, 130–31.

6. Ibid., 137.

7. Said, *Orientalism*.

8. See Miller, *Theories of Africans*, and Mudimbe, *Invention of Africa*.

9. Todorov, *Conquest of America*, 28.

10. Brotherston, *Image of the New World*, 13.

11. González Echevarría, *Alejo Carpentier*, 28.

12. Lewis, *Main Currents in Caribbean Thought*, 3.

13. See Glissant, *Caribbean Discourse*, 115.

14. Lewis, *Main Currents in Caribbean Thought*, 31–32.

15. Franklin, *Discoverers, Explorers, Settlers*, xi.

16. Diamond, *In Search of the Primitive*, 211.

17. Torgovnick, *Gone Primitive*, 8.

18. White, *Tropics of Discourse*, 2.

19. Ibid., 153.

20. Kristeva, *Etrangers à nous-mêmes*, 268.

21. White, *Tropics of Discourse*, 186.

22. Ibid., 191.

23. Ibid., 192.

24. Ibid., 194.

25. Affergan, *Exotisme et altérité*, 27–28.

26. Lewis, *Main Currents in Caribbean Thought*, 86.

27. Chateaubriand, "Génie du Christianisme," *Oeuvres choisis*, 12. The timeless serenity of the American landscape is sometimes disrupted by history in Chateaubriand's works. Jean-Pierre Richard notes that, although Chateaubriand was sensitive to the importance of *metissage*, in his work cultural contact invariably leads to tragic results. See *Paysage de Chateaubriand*, 141–44.

28. Hulme, *Colonial Encounters*, 2.

29. Ibid., 186.

30. Macherey, *Theory of Literary Production*, 242.

31. Ibid., 202–3.

32. This dimension of *Robinson Crusoe* is given greater emphasis in Michel Tournier's rewriting of Defoe's tale. Tournier's Crusoe laments, "My vision of the island is reduced to itself. What I do not see is an *absolute unknown*. Wherever I am not at this point there reigns an impenetrable darkness." Tournier, *Friday or the Other Island*, 47.

33. Hulme, *Colonial Encounters*, 222.

34. These developments are more fully discussed in Leclerc, *Anthropologie et colonialisme*.

35. Segalen, *Essai sur l'exotisme*, 13.

36. Ibid., 18.

37. Segalen, *Equipée*, 11.

38. Glissant, *L'intention poétique*, 96.

39. Bongie, *Exotic Memories*, 15.

40. Ibid., 22.

41. Glissant, *L'intention poétique*, 98.

42. Segalen, *Essai sur l'exotisme*, 24.

43. Bongie, *Exotic Memories*, 38.

44. Hulme, *Colonial Encounters*, 124. In perhaps, one of the most fascinating yet overlooked rewritings of *The Tempest*, Ernest Renan's *Caliban* (1878) imagines Caliban taken back to Milan with Prospero. There, in anticipation of the new age of revolution, Caliban leads the people of Milan in a revolt against their leader. Renan's play already suggests the disruptive force of "elsewhere."

45. Mailer, *Advertisements for Myself*, 272–73. The extent to which the negro in the 1920s becomes, in the emergence of New York's cultural preeminence, the embodiment of the "savage id" of Freud's psychoanalytic discourse is meticulously documented in Douglas, *Terrible Honesty*.

46. Davis, *Passage of Darkness*. Davis sees the Bizango secret societies as the single most powerful political force in Haiti, thereby condemning that country once more to the realm of the occult and the irrational.

47. Breton, *Martinique, charmeuse de serpents*, 37.

48. The tendency to feminize the French colonies in the Caribbean has been noted by Regis Antoine in *Les écrivains francçais et les Antilles,* 380.

49. *Conjonction,* no. 1 (1946): 12. Pierre Mabille published the text of Breton's speech in *Conjonction,* the journal he founded.

50. Mabille, *Messages de l'étranger,* 8. In his introduction to Alfred Metraux, *Voodoo in Haiti* (6), Sidney Mintz regrets the way the West has replaced "difference with sameness" in both Haiti, and "the world outside."

51. Lévi-Strauss, *Tristes Tropiques,* 27.

52. Torgovnick, *Gone Primitive,* 220–23.

53. Lévi-Strauss, *Tristes Tropiques,* 376.

54. Bonjie, *Exotic Memories,* 204.

55. René Ménil, a contemporary of Césaire's but a fierce critic of negritude, claims, in *Tracées,* that negritude as an ideology was shaped by the images of Sartre's influential *Black Orpheus.*

56. Sartre, *Black Orpheus,* 45. It is not an overstatement to suggest that Sartre's essay is a well-intentioned denial of the specificity of a Césairean poetics. Sartre insists on the functionality and transparency of black poetry and, as Frantz Fanon lamented, its eventual disappearance into the ahistorical ideal of "the universal."

57. In chapter 6 of Michael Richardson's unpublished Ph.D. thesis for the University of London, "Surrealism and the Voice of the Other," 130–31. In his introduction to *Refusal of the Shadow,* Richardson has also written perceptively on "the unique series of encounters . . . between Francophone Caribbean writers and French Surrealists" between 1932 and 1946 and the extent to which a potentially liberating ideology congeals into an inversion of European stereotypes and simply serves to further racial mystification. Richardson is perhaps the only critic to pinpoint Césaire's revealing defence of Lévi-Strauss's anthropological project. This defence appears in Césaire's scathing attack on Roger Caillois in *Discourse on Colonialism,* 50–56.

58. Clifford, *Predicament of Culture,* 179.

59. Ashcroft, Griffiths, and Tiffin, *Empire Writes Back,* 156.

60. Todorov, "Race, Writing and Culture," 377. Edward Said expresses a similar dissatisfaction with the negative polemic of orientalism and the need to recognize the rethinking of identitarian thought by intellectuals from "Elsewhere" in his "Representing the Colonized: Anthropology's Interlocutors," 205–25.

61. Gilroy, *Black Atlantic,* 48–49.

62. Ibid., 17.

2 Modernism, Modernity, and Otherness

1. Honour, *New Golden Land,* 161.

2. Césaire, *Cahier d'un retour au pays natal,* 44.

3. Genovese, *From Rebellion to Revolution*, 88.

4. Ibid., 92.

5. Nicholls, *From Dessalines to Duvalier*, 42–3.

6. Vastey, *Reflections*, 14.

7. Fleischmann, "Maroons, Writers and History," 574. Fleischmann also has some interesting ideas on the "invented" maroon and the emergence of a maroonist discourse among Caribbean intellectuals.

8. Glissant discusses this absence of founding myths in "Cross Cultural Poetics," in *Caribbean Discourse*, 134–42.

9. *Le Républicain*, 1 Oct. 1836.

10. Unsigned article in *L'Union*, 24 Jan. 1839.

11. Firmin, *De l'égalité des races humaines*, 662.

12. Firmin, preface to Lochard's *Feuilles de chêne*.

13. Glissant, *Caribbean Discourse*, 148–49.

14. In *Culture and Imperialism*, Said recognizes the crucial relationship between anticolonial resistance and modernism when he argues that "a huge and remarkable adjustment in perspective and understanding is required to take account of the contribution to modernism of decolonization, resistance, culture and the literature of opposition to imperialism," 243.

15. Alexis, "Du réalisme merveilleux des Haïtiens," 261.

16. Fleischmann, "El ambiguo amor por Choucoune," 240–45.

17. Henock Trouillot, *Les origines sociales*, 343–76.

18. Plummer, *Haiti and the Great Powers*, xii.

19. Zavala, *Colonialism and Culture*, 38.

20. Vilaire, *Poèmes de la mort*, xxxiii.

21. *Haïti littéraire et scientifique*, 326.

22. In a series of articles begun in 1896, entitled "Les deux tendances," the literary critic Seymour Pradel categorized Haiti's novelists as "purely Haitian," as opposed to the poets of *La Ronde* who were "humano-Haitian."

23. Marcelin, *Autour de deux romans*, 25.

24. Laforest, *Cendres et flammes*, 201.

25. Sylvain, *Cric? Crac!*, 8.

26. Lewis, *Main Currents in Caribbean Thought*, 300.

27. Zavala, *Colonialism and Culture*, 55.

28. Vilaire, *Poèmes de la mort*, 40.

29. Ibid., 40.

30. Ramire, "Idéologie et subversion," 147.

31. "Haïti Littéraire se présente," *Rond Point*.

32. Glissant, "St. John Perse and the Caribbean," *Caribbean Discourse*, 227. The sense of decay amid tropical luxuriance in Perse's poetry is also noted by Regis Antoine in *Les écrivains français et les Antilles*, 331.

33. Glissant, *L'intention poétique*, 121.

34. Walcott, "The Muse of History," 120.

35. Zavala, *Colonialism and Culture,* 26.

36. Ibid., 91.

37. Lewis, *Main Currents in Caribbean Thought,* 307.

38. Zavala, *Colonialism and Culture,* 48.

39. Fredric Jameson usefully discusses the ideal of European modernism as apolitical in relation to the Third World. Using the example of Ireland and James Joyce, he shows how modernism can be deployed against centers of imperialism—"Modernism and Imperialism," *Nationalism, Colonialism, and Literature,* 43–66. The intention behind *Nationalism, Colonialism, and Literature* is very instructive in the context of Caribbean writing. As is stated in the introduction, at 11, the aim is to retrieve Irish writers from an international modernism and "to restore them to the culture where they were still alive as presences . . . to repossess their revolutionary and authoritative force for the here and now of the present of Ireland." Similarly with the present work: *The Other America* attempts to repossess Caribbean writing.

3 Orphic Explanations

1. Arnold, introduction to Césaire's essay in his *Lyric and Dramatic Poetry 1946–82,* xviii–xix.

2. In this essay, Césaire pointedly criticizes the barbarism of modern technology in western Europe, which is "far surpassed, it is true—by the barbarism of the United States." (*Discourse,* 26). He ends the essay by bluntly declaring U.S. domination to be "the only domination from which one never recovers, I mean from which one never recovers unscarred." *Discourse on Colonialism,* 61.

3. In an interview with Lilyan Kesteloot, Césaire declares: "I absolutely refuse any kind of confused, idyllic pan-Africanism . . . as a result I don't reject negritude, but I look on it with an extremely critical eye." Kesteloot, *Aimé Césaire,* 236.

4. James Clifford, while seeming to sense the importance of this neologism, is prepared to brush aside Césaire's explanation and advance his own hypothesis of veered meanings: "Césaire does not restore the 'meanings' of language, culture, and identity; he gives them a turn" (*Predicament of Culture,* 177).

5. Césaire, *Lettre à Maurice Thorez,* 21.

6. Césaire, *Collected Poetry,* 26. Eshelman and Smith persist, despite Césaire's telling advice, in rendering *verrition* as *veerition* in order to preserve a turning motion. One wonders what is the rationale for this. Their spelling not only distorts the original meaning of scouring or scraping clean but undermines the association of *vers* (verse), *verité* (truth), and *vert* (green), which are likely connotations in Césaire's poetic imagination.

7. Aime Césaire, "Poetry and Knowledge," xliii.

8. Césaire, *Collected Poetry,* 49.

9. Ibid., 357.

10. "Poetry and Knowledge," xlvii.

11. *Présence africaine,* no. 126 (1983), 10.

12. "Poetry and Knowledge," xlix.

13. Ibid. xlviii. This ideal of the demiurgic poet is closely connected to Frantz Fanon's view of the leader as authentic mouthpiece of the masses. Fanon's praise for Keita Fodeba in *Wretched of the Earth* (179–87) as an exemplary practitioner of the art of "awakening the people" illustrates this view of the artist.

14. Walker, *La cohésion poétique de l'oeuvre césairienne,* 43–56.

15. *Collected Poetry,* 103. Joan Dayan explores the images of apocalypse and a poetics of negation in Césaire in "Figure of Negation."

16. Dayan, "Figure of Negation," 67.

17. Ibid., 77.

18. Ibid., 67.

19. From a 1959 letter to Kesteloot quoted in her *Les écrivains noirs de langue francais,* 238.

20. There has been some discussion of the lack of a Caribbean specificity in Césaire's poetry. For instance, Jack Corzani in "Césaire et la Caraibe oubliée," laments Césaire's silence on the Caribbean, and more recently the créolité movement has harshly criticized the absence of creole in Césaire's writing. Césairean poetics, arguably, do not allow for specific social, historical, and linguistic grounding. After all, Césaire describes the Caribbean as a "Polynesia" in his *Cahier.* To this extent, the monist, universalizing poetics of Césaire can be contrasted with Alejo Carpentier's pluralistic view, even though both were influenced by surrealism's sense of the relativity of all cultures. It is perhaps in reaction to this that Glissant begins *Caribbean Discourse* with the declaration that "Martinique is not a Polynesian island."

21. "Poetry and Knowledge," lii.

22. Bachelard, *La psychanalyse du feu,* 35.

23. Césaire, *Lyric and Dramatic Poetry,* 82.

24. Césaire describes himself as having both confidence in and affection for Fanon in an interview with Daniel Maximin in *Présence Africaine* (n. 11), 23.

25. Fanon, *Wretched of the Earth,* 40.

26. Ibid., 40.

27. Said, *Culture and Imperialism,* 275.

28. Fanon, *Wretched of the Earth,* 73, 74.

29. Cited in Herdeck, ed., *Caribbean Writers,* 37.

30. Brathwaite, *Arrivants,* 184.

31. Ibid., 164.

32. Ibid., 266.

33. Brathwaite, "Timehri," 43.

34. The influence of Eliot on Brathwaite's early verse is noted in my essay on Brathwaite in *West Indian Literature*, 211.

35. Aschraft, Griffiths, and Tiffin, *Empire Writes Back*, 147.

36. Lewis, *Main Currents in Caribbean Thought*, 322.

37. Fernández Retamar, *Calaban and Other Essays*, 16. González Echevarría notes in the *Voice of the Masters*, that Retamar has begun to revise "the opinions expressed in his well known essay *Caliban* and, in effect, opens the possibility for a critical rereading of both this essay and the tradition from which it arises," 37.

38. Depestre, *Gerbe de sang*, 77.

39. Brouard, *Pages retrouvées*, 82.

40. Ibid, 23.

41. Price-Mars, *Ainsi parla l'oncle*, 194.

42. See chapter "The Provincial Heritage" in Hymans, *Leopold Sedar Senghor*, 25–29.

43. Michel-Rolph Trouillot, in a wonderfully insightful and detailed analysis of the main figures of Haitian indigenism, argues that the movement was made up of diverse voices and ultimately was undefined ideologically ("Jeux de mots," 35). Others have described *La revue indigène,* the organ of the indigenist movement, as "La revue indigeste," suggesting the undigestable mix of conflicting ideas it tried to swallow. These approaches do not address the relationship between a poetics of origination and an absolutist politics in the 1930s.

44. Piquion, "Force ou dictature," 91.

45. Nicholls, *From Dessalines to Duvalier,* 91.

46. Brouard, *Pages retrouvées,* 91.

47. Ibid., 84.

48. Roumain, *Masters of the Dew,* 89. The page numbers cited are taken from the 1978 edition of the English translation.

49. González Echevarría, *Myth and Archive,* 13–14.

50. Cited by Fowler in *Knot in the Thread,* 183.

51. González Echevarría, *Myth and Archive,* 158.

52. González Echevarría, *Voice of the Masters,* 10.

53. Gikandi, *Writing in Limbo,* 20.

54. Clifford, *Predicament of Culture,* 179.

4 A New World Mediterranean

1. Harris, *History, Fable and Myth,* 21.

2. Ormerod, *Introduction.*

3. Fuentes, prologue, 18.

4. Ibid., 19.

5. González Echevarría, *Voice of the Masters*, 4.

6. Carpentier, *Lost Steps*, 177. Cited page numbers are taken from the 1968 edition.

7. Glissant, *L'intention poétique*, 138.

8. Ibid.

9. In his *Isla a su vuelo fugitiva*, González Echevarría has pointed out the two major influences on Carpentier's ideas—Asturias and Borges—in terms of a movement from ethnology to the postmodern.

10. González Echevarría, *Alejo Carpentier*, 167.

11. Carpentier, *Harp and the Shadow*, 126.

12. Foucault, "Man and His Doubles," *Order of Things*, 323.

13. González Echevarría, *Alejo Carpentier*, 19.

14. Ibid., 102.

15. Ibid., 123.

16. Carpentier, "Prologue," 28.

17. Ibid., 31.

18. Ibid.

19. Coulthard, *Race and Colour*, 54.

20. Lewis, *Main Currents in Caribbean Thought*, 16–20.

21. See Chamady, "Haiti and Marvelous Latin American Reality," and Kutzinski, *Sugar's Secrets*.

22. Kutzinski, *Sugar's Secrets*, 166.

23. Carpentier, *Explosion in a Cathedral*, 190–91.

24. Deleuze, "The Fold," 227.

25. Carpentier, *Explosion in a Cathedral*, 185.

26. González Echevarría, *Alejo Carpentier*, 224.

27. In this regard, the case of the Guyanese novelist Wilson Harris is worthy of note. Harris mentions "marvelous realism" approvingly in his 1970 lecture *History, Fable and Myth*. Later, as we learn from Michel Fabre's "Recovering Precious Words, on Wilson Harris and the Language of Imagination" in Maes-Jelinek, *Wilson Harris*, 43, Harris becomes very interested in the ideas of Jacques Stephen Alexis.

28. Depestre, *Bonjour et Adieu à la Negritude*, 241.

29. Webb, in *Myth and History in Caribbean Fiction*, senses the importance of Carpentier's ideas in Alexis's theories but does not fully develop these links.

30. Alexis, "Où va le roman?" 69.

31. Alexis, "Du réalisme merveilleux," 245–71.

32. Ibid., 258.

33. Ashcroft, Griffittis, and Tiffin, *Empire Writes Back*, 149.

34. Alexis, "Du réalisme mervelleux," 250–51.

35. Alexis, *Les arbres musiciens*, 42.

36. Ibid., 385.

37. Alexis, *L'espace d'un cillement.*

38. Alexis, "Du réalisme merveilleux," 249.

39. Walcott, *Antilles,* 16.

40. Fanon, *Black Skin, White Masks,* 24.

41. Walcott, *Antilles,* 9.

42. Ibid., 24.

43. Ibid., 13.

44. Terada, *Derek Walcott's Poetry,* 16.

45. Pérez Firmat, *Cuban Condition,* 12.

46. Walcott, "Muse of History," 120.

47. Brathwaite, "Caribbean Man," 202.

48. James, *Beyond a Boundary,* 13.

49. Ibid., 149.

50. Ibid., 152.

51. See Bakhtin, "From the Prehistory of Novelistic Discourse," in *Dialogic Imagination,* 51–61.

52. Derrida, "Des Tours de Babel."

53. Walcott, *Antilles,* 11.

54. Bakhtin, "Novelistic Discourse," in *Dialogic Imagination,* 64.

55. Walcott, "Muse of History," 54–55.

56. Bakhtin, "Novelistic Discourse," in *Dialogic Imagination,* 54–55.

57. Walcott, *Fortunate Traveller,* 55.

58. Bakhtin, "Novelistic Discourse," in *Dialogic Imagination,* 60.

59. Terada, *Derek Walcott's Poetry,* 118.

60. Walcott, *Star Apple Kingdom,* 19–20.

61. Walcott, *Arkansas Testament,* 51.

62. García Márquez, *Strange Pilgrims,* 61.

63. Walcott, "Meanings," 49.

64. Raban, *Soft City,* 93.

5　Fields of Play

1. Paz, *Bow and Lyre,* 218. There are remarkable similarities between this work and Césaire's "Poetry and Knowledge." The very first lines of Paz's celebration of the poetic word reads, "Poetry is knowledge, salvation, power, abandonment."

2. Bakhtin, *Dialogic Imagination,* 60.

3. This is, of course, attempted by Benítez-Rojo in his examination of play and the plantation in *The Repeating Island.*

4. Hutcheon, *Poetics of Postmodernism,* 16.

5. Bakhtin, *Dialogic Imagination,* 367.

6. Dayan, "Erzulie," 24.

7. Ibid., 23.

8. Dayan, "Reading Women in the Caribbean," 228–53.

9. Chauvet, *Amour, colère et folie,* 370. The cited page numbers are taken from the 1968 edition.

10. Hurbon, *Comprendre Haiti,* 57.

11. A discussion of the crisis for Haitian intellectuals—in particular those of the generation of 1946—can be found in my essay "Blazing Mirrors."

12. Bakhtin, *Rabelais and His World,* 11.

13. Laferrière, *Comment faire l'amour,* 56. Laferrière's admiration for Chauvet is evident in his essay "Marie Chauvet."

14. Condé, *La parole des femmes,* 106. One is tempted to see "Folie" as a kind of roman à clef, referencing Jacques Alexis (*noir*), René Depestre (*mulâtre*), and Pierre Mabille, the French surrealist who profoundly influenced the generation of 1946.

15. Bridget Jones, "Theatre in the French West Indies," *Carib,* no. 4 (1986): 51.

16. Bakhtin, *Rabelais and His World,* 322.

17. Certainly one of the strengths of Condé's fiction is the dismantling of Césairean negritude, like that of Chauvet with regard to Duvalierist negritude. James Arnold notes the "fictional interrogation" of Césaire in Condé's first novel *Heremakhonon* in "The Novelist as Critic," 711.

18. Condé, *Traversée de la mangrove,* 202.

19. Ibid., 217. In her recent novel *La colonie du nouveau monde* (1993), Condé returns to the issue of the danger of ideological dogma, this time in the context of millenarian thought in the Americas.

20. Published on Césaire's eightieth birthday and accusing him of being blindly Afrocentric, this work has had a *succès de scandale* that has enhanced the créolité movement's reputation for outrageousness.

21. Reed's reference in *Mumbo Jumbo* to "Jes Grew"—a notion still waiting to be defined by a text—bears a close relation to the idea, or figure, who mysteriously appears in Confiant's novel *Eau de cafe.*

22. Confiant, *Bassin des ouragans,* 85–89.

23. Confiant, *Le nègre et l'amiral,* 85.

24. Ibid., 107.

25. Confiant, *L'allée des soupirs,* 87. The cited page numbers are taken from the 1944 edition. The intertextual references become even more comical as one politically militant character in *L'allée des soupirs* criticizes writers who use expressions like "les flamboyants pleurent en flocons de sang" (the flame trees weep flakes of blood) for being too exotic, the same expression occurring in Confiant's own novel *Commandeur du sucre.*

26. Confiant also uses the work of his contemporary, Patrick Chamoiseau, as a pretext in *L'allée des soupirs.* Not only does Solibo, the storyteller, make an appearance, but the comic misunderstanding of de Gaulle's statement on

arriving in Martinique in 1964—"Mon Dieu, que vous êtes français" (My God, how French you are), easily confused for the creole speaker with "Mon Dieu, que vous êtes foncés" (My God, how dark you are)—features in Chamoiseau's novel *Texaco*.

27. Naipaul, *Mimic Men*, 116.

28. Naipaul's later work may represent some attempt to come to terms with disorder. As he observed in *The Enigma of Arrival*, (1987), 130, "I was at the beginning of that great movement of peoples that was to take place in the second half of the twentieth century—a movement and a cultural mixing greater than the peopling of the United States." The street's chaos and anonymity had become globalized. Pastoral retreat was both undesirable and increasingly impossible.

29. Benjamin refers to the "attraction and allure" of the crowd for Baudelaire in *Illuminations*, 167. In the same chapter on Baudelaire, the erotic possibilities of the big city are examined.

30. Brouard, *Pages retrouvées*, 83.

31. Ibid., 23–24.

32. Sontag, *Styles of Radical Will*, 46.

33. Depestre, *Alleluia pour une femme jardin*, 133.

34. Jones, "Comrade Eros," 28.

35. Depestre, "Adieu à la Revolution," 53.

36. Kundera, "Umbrella," 47.

37. Depestre, *Alleluia*, 133–34.

38. Naipaul, *Overcrowded Baracoon*, 16.

39. Geertz, *Interpretation of Cultures*, 447.

40. Ibid., 444.

41. James, *Beyond a Boundary*, 193.

42. Ibid., 103–4.

43. Burton, "Cricket, carnival and street culture in the Caribbean," first published in the *British Journal of Sport* (1985), has been reprinted in *Liberation Cricket*. Quote from 96.

44. In Brathwaite's *Islands*, 43.

45. Scott, *Witchbroom*, 12. Robert Antoni's *Divina Trace* (1991), another novel that belongs to to mode of marvelous realism, is even more self-consciously postmodern in its treatment of the carnivalesque in Trinidad.

46. Scott, *Witchbroom*, 264.

47. Barthes, *Mythologies*, 23.

48. Scott, *Ballad of the New World*, 16.

49. Chen, *King of the Carnival and Other Stories*, 149–54.

50. Harney, *Nationalism and Identity*, 76.

51. Ibid., 75.

52. Lovelace, *The Dragon Can't Dance*, 204. The politics of the novel are interestingly discussed by David Williams in "The Artist as Revolutionary:

Political Commitment in *The Dragon Can't Dance*," in *West Indian Literature and its Social Context,* 141–47. Williams concludes with a comparison between Aldrick and Naipaul's Jimmy Ahmed in *Guerrillas* that is rich with possibilities; Williams, however, reduces the comparison to the usual cliché of pessimistic Naipaul as opposed to optimistic Lovelace.

53. Berman, *All That Is Solid Melts into Air,* 159.

6 A Poetics of Liminality

1. There is a tendency to treat the case of Martinique as *sui generis,* but it would be useful to compare this overseas French department with other dependent states like Puerto Rico. Perhaps the only example of such a comparison is "Quelques dilemmes de la vie politique insulaire: Puerto Rico et La Martinique," in Burac, *Guadeloupe, Martinique et Guyane,* 227–43.

2. Burton, "Towards 1992," 73.

3. Césaire, *Lyric and Dramatic Poetry,* liv.

4. Lucrèce, *Société et modernité.*

5. Aldrich and Connell, *France's Overseas Frontier,* 253.

6. Benjamin, *Illuminations,* 154.

7. Berman, *All That Is Solid Melts into Air,* 147.

8. Eagleton, Jameson, and Said, *Nationalism, Colonialism, and Literature,* 59–60.

9. See Bell, *Gabriel García Márquez.*

10. Jameson, "Modernism and Imperialism," 60.

11. Chamoiseau, *Manman Dlo,* 6.

12. Ibid., 139.

13. Burton, "Patterns of Opposition in the Fiction of Patrick Chamoiseau," 474.

14. Chamoiseau, *Chronique des sept misères,* 15. Cited page numbers are taken from the 1986 edition.

15. The creation of the wheelbarrow from the debris and junk of urban life is a vital fature of the spirit of independence and self-assertion of the community of *djobeurs.* Chamoiseau's interest in the relationship between the tool, productivity, self-expression, and a sense of responsibility may well go back to Glissant's observations in *Caribbean Discourse,* on the importance of the tool to a rehabilitation of the group's unconscious. Glissant notes that in the folktale "the tool is the other's property; technology remains alien," and that in order to save the creole language it will be necessary to transform the conditions of production, releasing, thereby, the potential for total, technical control by the Martiniquan of his country, in that way, the language may truly develop (132–33).

16. Paz, *Labyrinth of Solitude,* 5–9.

17. Chamoiseau, *Antan d'enfance,* 109–10.

18. Chamoiseau, "Les nègres marrons de l'en-ville," 33.

19. Chamoiseau, *Texaco*, 222. Cited page numbers are from the 1992 edition. In some ways, *Texaco* is linked to the preceding novel *Solibo Magnifique*, in which the protagonist dies, strangled by the word, and the author is left to use the written as a relay of the spoken.

20. Kundera, "Czech Wager," 22.

21. The fascination in Césaire's poetic theory for a transcendent state of consciousness and his praise for Breton's ideal of "a point in the mind from which life and death . . . cease to be perceived as opposites," is arguably a product of the American preoccupation with establishing a New World beginning, with founding a new origin. We have already discussed the temptation to political absolutism and authoritarianism associated with this poetic practice.

22. Chamoiseau, *Texaco*, 107.

23. Rushdie, *Imaginary Homelands*, 394.

24. Derby, "Haitians, Magic and Money. Derby analyzes this region as a challenge to conventional ideas of nation and community. "The notion of community implies a self-referentiality and stability inappropriate to the Haitian-Dominican border culture, which existed in a region that was inherently hybrid and pluralistic between nations and cultural loci. This culture represents a challenge to models that presuppose a stable univocal order." (494). It is perhaps no coincidence that Alexis, in almost all his fiction, is fascinated by this border.

25. Glissant, "Le romancier noir," 31.

26. Glissant's interest in Mallarmé is touched on in my study *Edouard Glissant*, 28–29.

27. Richard, *L'univers imaginaire de Mallarmé*.

28. Glissant, *Les Indes*, 9. Glissant uses *voilures*, which can be translated as either "wings" or "sails."

29. Glissant confesses that he is tempted by Mallarmé's faith in the explanatory power of the book. As he says in *Soleil de la conscience*, "Who has not dreamt of the poem that explains everything . . . of the novel that organises all truths." He shows an affinity with Mallarmé as well as an acute sense of the limitations of such an enterprise. In a recent interview, he admits to "the extraordinary influence" of Mallarméan poetics on his early work. "L'imaginaire des langues," 15–16.

30. Glissant, *Ripening*, 180.

31. Ibid., 104.

32. Interview in *CARE*, no. 10 (April 1983): 17.

33. Glissant, *Poétique de la Relation*, 23.

34. Deleuze, "A Theory of the Other," in Boundas, ed., *Deleuze Reader*, 65.

35. Todorov, *On Human Diversity*, 353.

36. Burton, "Ki Moun Nou Ye? The Idea of Difference in Contemporary French West Indian Thought," *New West Indian Guide* (1993), 253.

37. Glissant, *Caribbean Discourse*, 100.

38. Todorov, *On Human Diversity*, 71.

39. Ibid., 72.

40. Glissant *Caribbean Discourse*, 146.

41. Ibid., 140.

42. Glissant, "L'imaginaire des langues," 18.

43. Glissant, *Poétique de la Relation*, 28.

44. Ibid., 203.

45. Glissant, *Caribbean Discourse*, 25.

46. Glissant, *Poétique de la Relation*, 74–75.

47. Ibid., 108.

48. Ibid., 154.

49. Ibid., 152.

50. Ibid., 45.

51. Ibid., 125.

52. Glissant, *Tout-monde*, 223–24.

53. Ibid., 224.

54. *Poétique de la Relation*, 140.

55. Ibid., 135.

56. Glissant, *Tout-monde*, 412–13.

57. Orlando Patterson develops the idea of "Ecumenical America" as a concept that goes beyond the idea of the melting pot in "Cultural Transmission and the American Cosmos," 103.

Conclusion

1. Tournier, *Friday or the Other Island*, 200.

2. Cabrera Infante, *View of Dawn in the Tropics*, 159.

3. Michel-Rolph Trouillot, "The Caribbean Region," 22.

4. Walcott, *Another Life*, 148.

5. Walcott, *Antilles*, 19.

6. Harris, *Tradition, the Writer and Society*, 30.

7. Ibid., 44–45.

8. Glissant, *L'intention poétique*, 158.

9. See my *Edouard Glissant*, 136–37.

10. Glissant, *Caribbean Discourse*, 224.

Bibliography

Affergan, Francis. *Exotisme et altérité: essai sur les fondements d'une critique de l'anthropologie.* Paris: Presses Universitaires de France, 1987.

Aldrich, Robert, and John Connell. *France's Overseas Frontier: Départements et territoires d'outre-mer.* Cambridge: Cambridge Univ. Press, 1992.

Alexis, Jacques Stéphen. "Du réalisme merveilleux des Haïtiens." *Présence africaine,* nos. 8–10 (1956): 245–71.

———. "Où va le roman?" *Présence africaine,* no. 13 (1957): 81–101.

———. *Les arbres musiciens.* Paris: Gallimard, 1957.

———. *L'espace d'un cillement.* Paris: Gallimard, 1959.

Anderson, Debra. *Decolonizing the Text: Glissantian Readings in Caribbean and Afro-American Literatures.* New York: Peter Lang, 1995.

Antoine, Régis. *Les écrivains français et les Antilles: des premiers Pères blancs aux surréalistes noirs.* Paris: Maisonneuve et Larose, 1978.

Antoni, Robert. *Divina Trace.* Woodstock NY: Overlook Press, 1992.

Appiah, Kwame Anthony. *In My Father's House: Africa in the Philosophy of Culture.* New York: Oxford Univ. Press, 1992.

Arnold, A. James. *Modernism and Negritude: The Poetry and Poetics of Aimé Césaire.* Cambridge: Harvard Univ. Press, 1981.

———. "The Novelist as Critic." *World Literature Today* (autumn 1993): 711–16.

Ashcroft, Bill, Gareth Griffiths, and Helen Tiffin. *The Empire Writes Back: Theory and Practice in Post-Colonial Literature.* London: Routledge, 1989.

Bachelard, Gaston. *La psychanalyse du feu.* Paris: Gallimard, 1949.

Bakhtin, Mikhail. *The Dialogic Imagination: Four Essays.* Ed. Michael Holquist, trans. Caryl Emerson and Michael Holquist. Austin: Univ. of Texas Press, 1981.

———. *Rabelais and His World.* Trans. Hélène Iswolsky. Bloomington: Indiana Univ. Press, 1984.

Barnes, Trevor, and James Duncan, eds. *Writing Worlds: Discourse, Text and Metaphor in the Representation of Landscape.* London: Routledge, 1992.

Barthes, Roland. *Mythologies.* Trans. Annette Lavers. New York: Hill & Wang, 1981.

Bell, Michael. *Gabriel García Márquez: Solitude and Solidarity.* New York: St. Martin's, 1993.

Benítez-Rojo, Antonio. *The Repeating Island: The Caribbean and the Postmodern Perspective.* Trans. James Maraniss. Durham: Duke Univ. Press, 1992.

Benjamin, Walter. *Illuminations.* Ed. Hannah Arendt, trans. Harry Zohn. New York: Schocken Books, 1968.

Berman, Marshall. *All That Is Solid Melts into Air: The Experience of Modernity.* New York: Simon & Schuster, 1982.

Bernabé, Jean, Patrick Chamoiseau, and Raphaël Confiant. *Eloge de la Créolité.* Paris: Gallimard, 1989.

Bongie, Chris. *Exotic Memories: Literature, Colonialism, and the Fin de Siècle.* Stanford: Stanford Univ. Press, 1991.

Boundas, Constantin V., ed. *The Deleuze Reader.* New York: Columbia Univ. Press, 1993.

Brathwaite, Edward. "Timehri." *Savacou: A Journal of the Caribbean Artists Movement,* no. 2 (Sept. 1970): 35–44.

———. *Islands.* London: Oxford Univ. Press, 1969.

———. *The Arrivants: A New World Trilogy.* London: Oxford Univ. Press, 1973.

———. "Caribbean Man in Space and Time." In *Carifesta Forum: An Anthology of 20 Caribbean Voices.* Ed. John Hearne. Kingston: Institute of Jamaica, 1976, 199–208.

———. *History of the Voice: The Development of Nation Language in Anglophone Caribbean Poetry.* London: New Beacon, 1984.

Breton, André. *Martinique, charmeuse de serpents.* Paris: J.-J. Pauvert, 1972.

———. "Le Surréalisme." *Conjonction,* no. 1 (1946): 10–26.

Brotherston, Gordon. *Image of the New World: The American Continent Portrayed in Native Texts.* London: Thames & Hudson, 1979.

Brouard, Carl. *Pages retrouvées: Oeuvres en prose et en vers.* Port-au-Prince: Éditions Panorama, 1963.

Burac, Maurice. *Guadeloupe, Martinique et Guyane dans le monde améri-cain: Réalités d'hier, mutations d'aujourd'hui, perspectives 2000.* Paris: Katharla, 1994.

Burton, Richard D. E. "Cricket, Carnival and Street Culture in the Caribbean." In *Liberation Cricket,* ed. Hilary Beckles and B. Stoddart, 89–106 Kingston: Ian Randle, 1995.

———. "Towards 1992: Political-Cultural Assimilation and Opposition in Contemporary Martinique." *French Cultural Studies* 3, no. 1 (Feb. 1992): 61–86.

———. "Patterns of Opposition in the Fiction of Patrick Chamoiseau," *Callaloo* 16, no. 2 (1993): 466–81.

Cabrera Infante, G. *Three Trapped Tigers.* Trans. Donald Gardner and Suzanne Jill Levine. New York: Harper & Row, 1971.

———. *View of Dawn in the Tropics.* Trans. Suzanne Jill Levine. London: Faber & Faber, 1988.

———. *Mea Cuba.* Trans. Kenneth Hall. New York: Farrar, Straus & Giroux, 1994.

Carpentier, Alejo. *The Lost Steps.* New York: Penguin, 1968.

———. *Explosion in a Cathedral.* Harmondsworth UK: Penguin, 1971.

———. *The Harp and the Shadow.* San Francisco: Mercury House, 1990.

———. "Prologue to *The Kingdom of This World.*" *Review: Latin Ameri-can Literature and Arts,* no. 47 (fall 1993): 28–31.

Césaire, Aimé. *Cahier d'un retour au pays natal.* Paris: Présence africaine, 1956.

———. *Discourse on Colonialism.* Trans. Joan Pinkham. New York: Monthly Review Press, 1972.

———. *Lettre à Maurice Thorez.* Fort-de-France: Parti Progressiste Martini-quais, n.d.

———. *The Collected Poetry.* Trans. Clayton Eshelman and Annette Smith. Berkeley: Univ. of California Press, 1983.

———. *Lyric and Dramatic Poetry, 1946–82.* Trans. Clayton Eshelman and Annette Smith. Charlottesville: Univ. Press of Virginia, 1990.

———. *Une tempête: D'apres* La tempête *de Shakespeare: adoption pour un théâtre nègre.* Paris: Éditions du Seuil, 1969.

———. "Poetry and Knowledge." trans. A. James Arnold. In *Lyric and Dra-matic Poetry, 1946–82,* xlii–lvi.

Césaire, Ina. *Mémoires d'isles: Maman N. et Maman F.* Paris: Éditions Caribéennes, 1985.

Chamady, Amaryll. "Haiti and Marvellous Latin American Reality." In *Forging Identities and Patterns of Development in Latin America and the Caribbean,* ed. Patrick Taylor, 350–51. Toronto: Canadian Scholars Press, 1991.

Chamoiseau, Patrick. *Manman Dlo contre la fée Carabosse.* Paris: Éditions Caribéennes, 1982.

——. *Chronique des sept misères*. Paris: Gallimard, 1986.

——. *Solibo Magnifique*. Paris: Gallimard, 1988.

——. *Antan d'enfance*. Paris: Hatier, 1990.

——. *Texaco*. Paris: Gallimard, 1992.

——. "Les nègres marrons de l'en-ville." *Antilla*, no. 473 (1992): 29–33.

Chateaubriand, François-René. *Oeuvres choisies*. Paris: Bibliothèque Larousse, 1930.

Chauvet, Marie. *Amour, colère et folie*. Paris: Gallimard, 1968.

Chen, Willi. *King of the Carnival and Other Stories*. London: Hansib, 1988.

Clifford, James. *The Predicament of Culture: Twentieth-Century Ethnography, Literature, and Art*. Cambridge: Harvard Univ. Press, 1988.

Condé, Maryse. *Hérémakhonon*. Paris: Union Générale d'Editions, 1976.

——. *La parole des femmes: Essai sur des romancières des Antilles de langue française*. Paris: L'Harmattan, 1979.

——. *Ségou*. Paris: R. Laffont, 1984–85.

——. *Traversée de la mangrove*. Paris: Mercure de France, 1989.

——. *La colonie du nouveau monde*. Paris: R. Laffont, 1993.

Confiant, Raphaël. *Le nègre et l'amiral*. Paris: Bernard Grasset, 1988.

——. *Eau de café*. Paris: Bernard Grasset, 1991.

——. *Aimé Césaire: Une traversée paradoxale du siècle*. Paris: Stock, 1993.

——. *Bassin des ouragans*. Paris: Mille et une nuits, 1994.

——. *L'allée des soupirs*. Paris: Bernard Grasset, 1994.

——. *Commandeur du sucre*. Paris: Éditions Ecriture, 1994.

Corzani, Jack. "Césaire et la Caraïbe oubliée." In *Soleil Éclaté: Mélanges offerts à Aimé Césaire à l'occasion de son soixante-dixième anniversaire*, ed. Jacqueline Leiner, 89–99. Tübingen: Gunter Narr, 1984.

Coulthard, G. R. *Race and Colour in Caribbean Literature*. London: Oxford Univ. Press, 1962.

Damas, Léon-Gontran. *Pigments: Névralgies*. Paris: Présence africaine, 1966.

Dash, J. Michael. *Literature and Ideology in Haiti, 1915–1961*. Totowa NJ: Barnes & Noble, 1981.

——. *Edouard Glissant*. Cambridge: Cambridge Univ. Press, 1995.

——. "Edward Brathwaite." In *West Indian Literature*, ed. Bruce King, 210–27. London: Macmillan, 1979.

——. "Blazing Mirrors: The Crisis of the Haitian Intellectual." In *Intellectuals in the Twentieth-Century Caribbean*, ed. Alistair Hennessy, 175–85. London: Macmillan, 1992.

Davis, Wade. *Passage of Darkness: The Ethnobiology of the Haitian Zombie*. Chapel Hill: Univ. of North Carolina Press, 1988.

——. *The Serpent and the Rainbow*. London: Collins, 1986.

Dayan, Joan. "The Figure of Negation: Some Thoughts on a landscape by Césaire." *French Review* 56, no. 3 (1983): 411–23.

———. "Reading Women in the Caribbean: Marie Chauvet's *Love, Anger, and Madness.*" In *Displacements: Women, Tradition, Literatures in French,* ed. Joan DeJean and Nancy K. Miller. Baltimore: Johns Hopkins Univ. Press, 1991.

———. "Erzulie: A Woman's History of Haiti." *Research in African Literatures* 25, no. 2 (1994): 5–31.

Deleuze, Gilles. "The Fold." *Yale French Studies,* no. 80 (1991): 227–47.

Dépestre, René. *Gerbe de sang.* Port-au-Prince: Imp. de l'Etat, 1946.

———. *Bonjour et adieu à la Négritude.* Paris: R. Laffont, 1980.

———. *Alléluia pour une femme-jardin: Récits d'amour solaire.* Paris: Gallimard, 1981.

———. "Adieu à la Révolution." In *Ecrire la parole de la nuit: La nouvelle littérature antillaise,* 53–55. Paris: Gallimard, 1994.

Derby, Lauren. "Haitians, Magic and Money: Raza and Society in the Haitian-Dominican Borderlands 1900–1937." *Comparative Studies in Society and History* 36, no. 1 (1994): 488–526.

Derrida, Jacques. "Des Tours de Babel." In Joseph F. Graham, ed. *Difference and Translation.* Ithaca: Cornell Univ. Press, 1985.

Diamond, Stanley. *In Search of the Primitive: A Critique of Civilization.* New Brunswick: Transaction Books, 1974.

Douglas, Ann. *Terrible Honesty: Mongrel Manhattan in the 1920s.* New York: Farrar, Straus & Giroux, 1995.

Durand, Oswald. *Rires et pleurs 1869–1896.* Port-au-Prince: Éditions Panorama. n.d.

Eagleton, Terry, Fredric Jameson, and Edward W. Said. *Nationalism, Colonialism, and Literature.* Minneapolis: Univ. of Minnesota Press, 1990.

Fanon, Frantz. *The Wretched of the Earth.* Harmondsworth UK: Penguin, 1969.

———. *Black Skin, White Masks.* Trans. Charles Lam Markmann. New York: Grove Press, 1967.

Fernández Retamar, Roberto. *Caliban and Other Essays.* Trans. Edward Baker. Minneapolis: Univ. of Minnesota Press, 1989.

Firmin, Anténor. *De l'égalité des races humaines.* Paris: F. Pichon, 1885.

———. Preface to P. Lochard, *Feuilles de chêne.* Paris: Ateliers Haïtiens, 1901.

Fitz, Earl. *Rediscovering the New World: Inter-American Literature in a Comparative Context.* Iowa City: Univ. of Iowa Press, 1991.

Fleischmann, Ulrich. "Maroons, Writers and History." In *Slavery in the Americas,* ed. Wolfgang Binder. Würzburg: Königshausen & Neumann, 1993.

———. "El ambiguo amor por Choucoune," *Anales del Caribe,* nos. 7–8 (1987–88): 240–56.

Foucault, Michel. *The Order of Things: An Archaeology of the Human Sciences.* New York: Vintage, 1973.

————. *Language, Counter-Memory, Practice: Selected Essays and Interviews.* Ithaca: Cornell Univ. Press, 1977.

Fowler, Carolyn. *A Knot in the Thread: The Life and Work of Jacques Roumain.* Washington DC: Howard Univ. Press, 1980.

Franklin, Wayne. *Discoverers, Explorers, Settlers: The Diligent Writers of Early America.* Chicago: Univ. of Chicago Press, 1979.

Fuentes, Carlos. Prologue to José Enrique Rodó, *Ariel,* 13–28. Trans. Margaret Sayers Peden. Austin: Univ. of Texas Press, 1988.

García Márquez, Gabriel. *One Hundred Years of Solitude.* Trans. Gregory Rabassa. Harmondsworth UK: Penguin, 1972.

————. *Strange Pilgrims: Twelve Stories.* Trans. Edith Grossman. New York: Penguin, 1994.

Geertz, Clifford. *The Interpretation of Cultures: Selected Essays.* New York: Basic Books, 1973.

————. *Works and Lives: The Anthropologist as Author.* Stanford: Stanford Univ. Press, 1988.

Genovese, Eugene D. *From Rebellion to Revolution: Afro-American Slave Revolts in the Making of the Modern World.* Baton Rouge: Louisiana State Univ. Press, 1979.

Gikandi, Simon. *Writing in Limbo: Modernism and Caribbean Literature.* Ithaca: Cornell Univ. Press, 1992.

Gilroy, Paul. *The Black Atlantic: Modernity and Double Consciousness.* Cambridge: Harvard Univ. Press, 1993.

Glissant, Edouard. *Les Indes: Un champ d'îles, La terre inquiète,* Paris: Éditions du Seuil, 1985.

————. *Soleil de la conscience.* Paris: Éditions du Seuil, 1965.

————. "Le romancier noir et son peuple." *Présence africaine,* no. 16 (Oct.–Nov. 1957): 27–31.

————. *L'intention poétique.* Paris: Éditions du Seuil, 1969.

————. *The Ripening.* Trans. [J.] Michael Dash. London: Heinemann, 1985. Originally published as *Le Lézarde* (Paris: Éditions du Seuil, 1958).

————. *Caribbean Discourse: Selected Essays.* Trans. J. Michael Dash. Charlottesville: Univ. Press of Virginia, 1989.

————. *Poétique de la Relation.* Paris: Gallimard, 1990.

————. "L'imaginaire des langues." *Études Françaises,* 28, nos. 2/3, 1992–93: 11–22.

————. *Tout-monde,* Paris: Gallimard, 1993.

————. *Introduction à une poétique du divers.* Paris: Gallimard, 1996.

González Echevarría, Roberto. *Alejo Carpentier, the Pilgrim at Home.* Ithaca: Cornell Univ. Press, 1977.

————. *The Voice of the Masters: Writing and Authority in Modern Latin American Literature.* Austin: Univ. of Texas Press, 1985.

————. *Myth and Archive: A Theory of Latin American Narrative.* Cambridge: Cambridge Univ. Press, 1990.

Graham, Joseph F. ed. *Difference in Translation.* Ithaca: Cornell Univ. Press. 1985.

Harney, Stefano. *Nationalism and Identity: Culture and the Imagination in a Caribbean Diaspora.* Kingston: Univ. Press of the West Indies, 1996.

Harris, Wilson. *History, Fable and Myth in the Caribbean and Guianas.* Georgetown: Ministry of Information and Culture, 1970.

————. *Tradition, the Writer and Society: Critical Essays.* London: New Beacon, 1967.

————. *Carnival.* London: Faber & Faber, 1985.

Herdeck, Donald E., ed. *Caribbean Writers: A Bio-Bibliographical-Critical Encyclopedia.* Washington DC: Three Continents, 1979.

Hill, Jonathan D., ed. *History, Power and Identity: Ethnogenesis in the Americas, 1492–1992.* Iowa City: Univ. of Iowa Press, 1996.

Honour, Hugh. *The New Golden Land: European Images of America from the Discoveries to the Present Time.* New York: Pantheon, 1979.

Hulme, Peter. *Colonial Encounters: Europe and the Native Caribbean, 1492–1797.* London: Methuen, 1986.

Hurbon, Laënnec. *Comprendre Haïti: Essai sur l'État, la nation, la culture.* Paris: Éditions Katharla, 1987.

Hutcheon, Linda. *A Poetics of Postmodernism: History, Theory, Fiction.* New York: Routledge, 1988.

Hymans, Jacques Louis. *Léopold Sédar Senghor: An Intellectual Biography.* Edinburgh: Edinburgh Univ. Press, 1971.

James, C. L. R. *The Black Jacobins: Toussaint L'Ouverture and the San Domingo Revolution.* New York: Vintage, 1963.

————. *Beyond a Boundary.* London: Stanley Paul, 1963.

Jameson, Fredric. "Modernism and Imperialism." In Eagleton, Jameson, and Said, *Nationalism, Colonialism and Literature,* 43–66.

Jones, H. Bridget. "Comrade Eros: The Erotic Vein in the Writing of René Dépestre." *Caribbean Quarterly* 27, no. 4 (1981): 21–30.

————. "Theatre in the French West Indies." *Carib,* no. 4 (1986): 35–54.

Kesteloot, Lilyan. *Aimé Césaire, l'homme et l'oeuvre.* Paris: Présence africaine, 1973.

————. *Les écrivains noirs de langue française: Naissance d'une littérature.* Brussels: Université Libre de Bruxelles, 1965.

King, Bruce. *The New Literatures in English: Cultural Nationalism in a Changing World.* London: Macmillan, 1980.

Kristeva, Julia. *Etrangers à nous-mêmes,* Paris: Fayard, 1988.

Kundera, Milan. "The Czech Wager." *New York Review,* no. 22 (1981): 21–22.

————. "The Umbrella, the Night World, and the Lonely Moon." *New York Review* 38, no. 21 (1991): 46–50.

Kutzinski, Vera M. *Against the American Grain: Myth and History in William Carlos Williams, Jay Wright, and Nicholás Guillén.* Baltimore: Johns Hopkins Univ. Press, 1987.

————. *Sugar's Secrets: Race and the Erotics of Cuban Nationalism.* Charlottesville: Univ. Press of Virginia, 1993.

Laferrière, Dany. *Comment faire l'amour avec un nègre sans se fatiguer.* Paris: J'ai Lu, 1990.

————. "Marie Chauvet: Amour, Colère, Folie." *Littérature haïtienne* no. 11 (July 1983), ed. Jean Jonassaint; special issue, *Mot pour Mot:* 7–10.

Laforest, Edmond. *Cendres et flammes.* Paris: Albert Massein, 1914.

Lang, George. "No hay centro: Postmodernism and Comparative New World Criticism." *Canadian Review of Comparative Literature* (March–June 1993): 105–25.

Leclerc, Gérard. *Anthropologie et colonialisme: Essai sur l'histoire de l'africanisme.* Paris: Fayard, 1972.

Legagneur, S., A. Phelps, and R. Philoctète. "Haïti Littéraire se présente." *Rond Point,* no. 12 (Dec. 1963): 24–27.

Lévi-Strauss, Claude. *Tristes Tropiques.* New York: Pocket Books, 1977.

Lewis, Gordon K. *Main Currents in Caribbean Thought: The Historical Evolution of Caribbean Society in Its Ideological Aspects, 1492–1900.* London: Heinemann, 1983.

Lovelace, Earl. *The Dragon Can't Dance.* Harlow UK: Longman, 1979.

Lucrèce, André. *Société et modernité: essai d'interprétation de la société martiniquaise.* Case Pilote: Édition de l'autre mer, 1994.

Mabille, Pierre. *Messages de l'étranger.* Paris: Plasma, 1981.

Macherey, Pierre. *A Theory of Literary Production.* Trans. Geoffrey Wall. London: Routledge & Keegan Paul, 1989.

Maes-Jelinek, Hena, ed. *Wilson Harris: The Uncompromising Imagination.* Sydney: Dangaroo, 1991.

Mailer, Norman. *Advertisements for Myself.* London: Panther, 1968.

Marcelin, Frédéric. *Autour de deux romans.* Paris: Imp. Kugelmann, 1903.

Márquez, Roberto. "Soul of a Continent." *American Quarterly* 41, no. 4 (1989): 695–704.

————. "Nation, Nationalism and Ideology." In *The Modern Caribbean,* 293–340. Chapel Hill: Univ. of North Carolina Press.

Martí, José. *Our America: Writings on Latin America and the Struggle for Cuban Independence.* Trans. Elinor Randall. New York: Monthly Review Press, 1982.

Maximin, Colette. *Littératures caribéennes comparées.* Pointe-à-Pitre: Jasor, 1996.

Ménil, René. *Tracées: Identité, négritude, esthétique aux Antilles.* Paris: R. Laffont, 1981.

Miller, Christopher. *Theories of Africans: Francophone Literature and Anthropology in Africa.* Chicago: Univ. of Chicago Press, 1990.

Mintz, Sidney. Introduction to Alfred Métraux, *Voodoo in Haiti.* London: Andre Deutsch, 1972.

Morse, Richard M. *New World Soundings: Culture and Ideology in the Americas.* Baltimore: Johns Hopkins Univ. Press, 1989.

Mudimbe, V. Y. *The Invention of Africa: Gnosis, Philosophy, and the Order of Knowledge.* Bloomington: Indiana Univ. Press, 1988.

Naipaul, V. S. *The Mimic Men.* London: Penguin, 1969.

———. *The Loss of El Dorado.* Harmondsworth UK: Penguin, 1973.

———. *The Overcrowded Baracoon.* Harmondsworth UK: Penguin, 1976.

———. *The Enigma of Arrival.* Harmondsworth UK: Penguin, 1987.

Nau, Emile. *Histoire des Caciques d'Haïti.* Port-au-Prince: Éditions Panorama, 1963.

———. "Haïti et les Etats-Unis." *Le Républicain* (Oct. 1836).

Nicholls, David. *From Dessalines to Duvalier: Race, Colour, and National Independence in Haiti.* Cambridge: Cambridge Univ. Press, 1979.

O'Gorman, Edmundo. *The Invention of America: An Inquiry into the Historical Nature of the New World and the Meaning of Its History.* Bloomington: Indiana Univ. Press, 1961.

Ormerod, Beverley. *Introduction to the French Caribbean Novel.* London: Heinemann, 1985.

Patterson, Orlando. "Cultural Transmission and the American Cosmos." *A New Moment in the Americas,* 89–106. Ed. Robert S. Leiken. New Brunswick: Transaction, 1994.

Paz, Octavio. *The Labyrinth of Solitude.* Trans. Lysander Kemp. Harmondsworth UK: Penguin, 1985.

———. *The Bow and the Lyre.* Trans. Ruth L. C. Simms. Austin: Univ. of Texas Press, 1987.

———. Prologue to José Enrique Rodó, *Ariel.* Austin: Univ. of Texas Press, 1989.

Pérez Firmat, Gustavo. *The Cuban Condition: Translation and Identity in Modern Cuban Literature.* Cambridge: Cambridge Univ. Press, 1989.

———, ed. *Do the Americas Have a Common Literature?* Durham: Duke Univ. Press, 1990.

Piquion, René. "Force ou dictature." *La Relève* (April 1934): 13–14.

Plummer, Brenda Gayle. *Haiti and the Great Powers, 1902–1915.* Baton Rouge: Louisiana State Univ. Press, 1988.

Price-Mars, Jean. *Ainsi parla l'oncle.* Paris, Compiegne: Bibliothèque Haïtienne, 1928.

Raban, Jonathan. *Soft City.* London: Harper Collins, 1988.

Ramire, Alain. "Idéologie et subversion chez les poètes de *La Ronde.*" *Nouvelle Optique,* no. 5 (Jan. 1972): 143–61.

Reed, Ishmael. *Mumbo Jumbo.* New York: Avon, 1978.

Renan, Ernest. *Caliban.* Trans. E. Vickery. New York: Shakespeare, 1896.

Richard, Jean-Pierre. *L'univers imaginaire de Mallarmé.* Paris: Éditions du Seuil, 1961.

———. *Paysage de Chateaubriand.* Paris: Éditions du Seuil, 1967.

Richardson, Michael, ed. *Refusal of the Shadow: Surrealism and the Caribbean.* Trans. Krzysztof Fijalkowski and Michael Richardson. London: Verso, 1996.

Roumain, Jacques. *Masters of the Dew.* Trans. Mercer Cook. London: Heinemann, 1978.

Rushdie, Salman. *Imaginary Homelands: Essays and Criticism, 1981–1991.* Harmondsworth UK: Penguin, 1991.

Said, Edward W. *Orientalism.* New York: Vintage, 1979.

———. "Representing the Colonized: Anthropology's Interlocutors." *Critical Inquiry* 15, no. 2 (1989): 205–25.

———. *Culture and Imperialism.* New York: Vintage, 1994.

Saldívar, José David. *The Dialectics of Our America: Genealogy, Cultural Critique, and Literary History.* Durham: Duke Univ. Press, 1991.

Sartre, Jean-Paul. *Black Orpheus.* Trans. S. W. Allen. Paris: Présence africaine, 1963.

Scott, Lawrence. *Witchbroom.* London: Heinemann, 1992.

———. *Ballad for the New World: And Other Stories.* Oxford: Heinemann, 1994.

Segalen, Victor. *Equipée.* Paris: Gallimard, 1983.

———. *Essai sur l'exotisme: Une esthétique du divers.* Montpellier: Fata Morgana, 1978.

Sontag, Susan. *Styles of Radical Will.* New York: Dell, 1978.

Steiner, George. *Extraterritorial: Papers on Literature and the Language Revolution.* Harmondsworth UK: Penguin, 1975.

Sylvain, Georges. *Cric? Crac!: Fables de La Fontaine,* Paris: Ateliers Haïtiens, 1901.

Taylor, Patrick. *Forging Identities and Patterns of Development in Latin America and the Caribbean.* Toronto: Canadian Scholars, 1991.

Terada, Rei. *Derek Walcott's Poetry: American Mimicry.* Boston: Northeastern Univ. Press, 1992.

Todorov, Tzvetan. "Race, Writing and Culture." In *"Race," Writing and Difference,* ed. Henry Louis Gates, 370–80. Chicago: Univ. of Chicago Press, 1986.

———. *The Conquest of America: The Question of the Other.* Trans. Richard Howard. New York: Harper & Row, 1984.

————. *On Human Diversity: Nationalism, Racism, and Exoticism in French Thought.* Trans. Catherine Porter. Cambridge: Harvard Univ. Press, 1993.

Torgovnick, Mariana. *Gone Primitive: Savage Intellects, Modern Lives.* Chicago: Univ. of Chicago Press, 1990.

Tournier, Michel. *Friday or the Other Island.* Harmondsworth UK: Penguin, 1974.

Trouillot, Hénock. *Les origines sociales de la littérature haïtienne.* Port-au-Prince: Imp. Théodore, 1962.

Trouillot, Michel-Rolph. "The Caribbean Region: An Open Frontier in Anthropological Theory." *American Review of Anthropology,* no. 21 (1992): 19–42.

————. "Jeux de mots, jeux de classe: la mouvance de l'indigénisme," *Conjonction,* no. 197 (1993): 29–44.

Vastey, Baron de. *Réflexions sur une lettre de Mazères.* Cap Henry: P. Roux, 1816.

Vilaire, Etzer. *Poèmes de la mort.* Paris: Librairie Fischbacher, 1907.

Walcott, Derek. "Meanings." *Savacou: Journal of the Caribbean Artists Movement,* no. 2 (Sept. 1970): 45–51.

————. *Another Life.* London: Jonathan Cape, 1973.

————. "The Muse of History." *Carifesta Forum: An Anthology of 20 Caribbean Voices,* 111–28. Ed. John Hearne. Kingston: Institute of Jamaica, 1976.

————. *The Star-Apple Kingdom.* New York: Farrar, Strauss & Giroux, 1979.

————. *The Fortunate Traveller.* London: Faber & Faber, 1982.

————. *The Arkansas Testament.* London: Faber & Faber, 1988.

————. *The Antilles, Fragments of Epic Memory.* London: Faber & Faber, 1993.

Walker, Keith Louis. *La cohésion poétique de l'oeuvre césairienne.* Tübingen: Gunter Narr, 1979.

Walmsley, Anne. *The Caribbean Artists Movement, 1966–1972: A Literary and Cultural History.* London: New Beacon, 1992.

Webb, Barbara J. *Myth and History in Caribbean Fiction: Alejo Carpentier, Wilson Harris, and Edouard Glissant.* Amherst: Univ. of Massachusetts Press, 1992.

White, Hayden. *Tropics of Discourse: Essays in Cultural Criticism.* Baltimore: Johns Hopkins Univ. Press, 1978.

Zavala, Iris M. *Colonialism and Culture: Hispanic Modernisms and the Social Imaginary.* Bloomington: Indiana Univ. Press, 1992.

Index

New World Studies

New World Studies publishes interdisciplinary research that seeks to redefine the cultural map of the Americas and to propose particularly stimulating points of departure for an emerging field. Encompassing the Caribbean as well as continental North, Central, and South America, the series books examine cultural processes within the hemisphere, taking into account the economic, demographic, and historical phenomena that shape them. Given the increasing diversity and richness of the linguistic and cultural traditions in the Americas, the need for research that privileges neither the English-speaking United States nor Spanish-speaking Latin America has never been greater. The series is designed to bring the best of this new research into an identifiable forum and to channel its results to the rapidly evolving audience for cultural studies.

New World Studies

Vera M. Kutzinski
*Sugar's Secrets: Race and the Erotics of Cuban
Nationalism*

Richard D. E. Burton and Fred Reno, editors
*French and West Indian: Martinique, Guadeloupe,
and French Guiana Today*

A. James Arnold, editor
Monsters, Tricksters, and Sacred Cows

J. Michael Dash
*The Other America: Caribbean Literature
in a New World Context*